Anita Gets Bail

What Are Our Courts Doing?
What Should We Do About Them?

ARUN SHOURIE

HarperCollins *Publishers* India

First published in hardback in India by
HarperCollins *Publishers* in 2018

This edition published in paperback in India by
HarperCollins *Publishers* in 2019

HarperCollins Publishers India, Cyber City, Building 10-A, Gurugram,
Haryana-122002, India
www.harpercollins.co.in

2 4 6 8 10 9 7 5 3 1

P-ISBN: 978-93-5357-027-9
E-ISBN: 978-93-5277-778-5

Typeset in 11/14 Sabon Roman at
Manipal Digital Systems, Manipal

Printed and bound at
MicroPrints India, New Delhi

HarperCollins Publishers, Macken House, 39/40 Mayor Street
Upper, Dublin 1, D01 C9W8, Ireland

Anita Gets Bail

Scholar, author, former editor and minister, **Arun Shourie** is one of the most prominent voices in our country's public life and discourse. He has written over twenty-five bestselling books.

Praise for *Anita Gets Bail*

'Arun Shourie's latest book demonstrates why, for all its admiration for the judicial institutions, Indian society remains sceptical about the efficacy of the judicial system.'—The Hindu

'*Anita gets Bail* is a book that every Indian who is concerned about the nation must read… The book is so compelling that the reader, even a lay person, would keep turning the pages. At no stage does it lose rhythm or pace, nor does it become dull at any point. It engages the reader all through.'—The Indian Express

'This book can be the starting point to formulate a plan to prevent further erosion in the credibility of our courts.'—India Today

'The narration of his personal experience is gripping and relatable. But, the author goes on to address larger issues ailing the judiciary. Arun Shourie … has always been meticulous in compiling relevant facts, and precise yet deep in his analysis of them.'—The Week

'Arun Shourie's book, *Anita Gets Bail*, illustrates how this concept [of justice] is sometimes a myth, and the process of the courts is itself the punishment.'—The New Indian Express

'Arun Shourie's latest book is a close reading of the past, present and future of the Indian judicial system, offering critical insights for a better democratic future.'—The Hindu BusinessLine

'On the one hand, *Anita Gets Bail* tracks the brilliance of our judiciary, while on the other it lays bare its clay feet.'—The Asian Age

'Shourie tackles serious and profound matters, offers critiques that are unafraid, and goes where not all would be ready to tread.'—Open Magazine

'[Arun Shourie] has put pen to paper, and in his own distinctive style, and with remarkable flair, "called out" the judiciary and those who staff the system.'—The Quint

'A damning indictment of the opaque and often inefficient manner in which our higher courts function.'—The Print

'A bold assessment of the Indian judiciary'—Free Press Journal

By the same author

Two Saints

Does He Know a Mother's Heart?

Self Deception—India's China Policies

We Must Have No Price

Where Will All This Take Us?

The Parliamentary System

Falling Over Backwards

Will the Iron Fence Save a Tree Hollowed by Termites?

Governance, and the Sclerosis That Has Set In

Courts and Their Judgments

Harvesting Our Souls

Eminent Historians

Worshipping False Gods

The World of Fatwas

Missionaries in India

A Secular Agenda

'The Only Fatherland'

The State as Charade

These Lethal, Inexorable Laws

Individuals, Institutions, Processes

Indian Controversies

Religion in Politics

Mrs Gandhi's Second Reign

Institutions in the Janata Phase

Symptoms of Fascism

Hinduism: Essence and Consequence

In the memory of
H.M. Seervai, N.A. Palkhivala, V.M. Tarkunde, K.G. Kannabiran

And for
Fali S. Nariman, Soli J. Sorabjee, Ram Jethmalani, Ashok Desai,
Arvind Datar, Prashant Bhushan

Having known whom, having been able to seek counsel from whom
have been among the privileges of my life

Contents

Introduction

This book elaborates a few of the points that I urged in two lectures: one at the National Judicial Academy, Bhopal, and the other at the National Academy of Legal Studies and Research, Hyderabad. I am grateful to the institutions for inviting me to deliver the lectures.

To illustrate the points with examples from recent judgments, I had to turn to lawyer friends. I am particularly grateful to Ashok Desai, Arvind Datar, Prashant Bhushan and Geeta Oberoi for drawing my attention to the relevant judgments. Saurabh Malik of *The Tribune* and Varinder Bhatia of *The Indian Express* brought me up to speed on the 'cash-at-the-judge's-doorstep' case. My grateful thanks to them. I owe an even greater debt to Rahul Unnikrishnan: at the cost of his own work he helped me get judgments and orders within moments of my requests. I owe as much to my good friend, Shantanu Ray Chaudhuri of HarperCollins, for seeing the book through to press in the face of heavy responsibilities and pressing circumstances. A word of thanks also to Amrita Mukerji of HarperCollins for her work on the book in the final stages.

Some of the episodes, and some of the things that the judges have said, are so exceptional that I feared readers would scarcely believe me if I just quoted a sentence or two. To reassure them that I have not just picked the odd sentence, that what I am alluding to is the pattern, I have quoted passages at length. In one case, I have reproduced an entire judgment—so riveting and so delicious it is. I felt doubly justified in doing so as readers of this book are unlikely to be regular readers of the judgments of the Himachal Pradesh High Court.

At two places I have used examples that I had mentioned in *Falling Over Backwards: An Essay against Reservations and against Judicial Populism*. But as the reader will discover, in quoting myself, I follow very high authority.

That book, and *Courts and Their Judgments,* which is being republished by HarperCollins along with this book, contain a fuller treatment of the points that are mentioned in passing here. I sincerely hope that the three books will be read as complementary volumes.

1

For a house we never built on a plot we did not own

'Sir, police waalaa ayaa hai, Madam ko bulaaney ko keh rahaa hai'—it was the watchman, he had come rushing up: 'A policeman has come, and is asking for Madam.'

'Police waalaa? Anita ko bulaa rahaa hai?' I said in astonishment. And rushed down the stairs.

'Anita Shourie yahaan rehti hai?'

'Ji haan. Meri wife hai. Upar beemaari ke kaaran leti hui hai'—Anita's Parkinson's had continued its relentless march; she had fallen a few times, by now she needed help in standing and walking, even in eating.

'Uskey liye arrest warrant hai.'

'Arrest warrant? Anita ke liye? Par usney kiyaa kyaa hai?'

'Paanch baar summons dodge kiye hain. BW[1] *dodge kiyaa hai. NBW*[2] *dodge kiyaa hai. Ab usey bhagodaa*[3] *ghoshit kiyaa gayaa hai.'*

'Koi summons nahin aaye. Aur summons bhejey kyun gaye?' I asked, totally bewildered.

---

1 Bailable warrants for arrest.

2 Non-bailable warrants for arrest.

3 Absconder.

'Yeh mujhe pataa nahin. Meraa kaam sirf warrant serve karnaa hai. Agar kal subhey nau baje voh court mein pesh naa hui to paanch saal ki qaid.'

I couldn't believe my ears. I didn't even know where the court was in which she had to appear. Frantic, I phoned my friend, Shekhar Gupta, then chief editor of *The Indian Express*. Did he have a correspondent in Faridabad who could help me get to the court? Shekhar deputed a colleague from the administrative side of the paper who handled the paper's legal work.

I left the house early next morning—Faridabad is 40 kilometres from our place; we did not know the way; and there would be the morning traffic jams to get through. On the way, I read the warrant for arrest: I reproduce it—both for the outrage it triggered in me, as well as for its literary elegance:

* * *

Ms 4124 *[Illegible]*

In the court of YASHIKA, HCS, Judicial Magistrate 1st Class-cum-Presiding Officer Speicial [sic] Environment Court, Faridabad

PROCLAMATION U/S 82 CR. P.C.

State *Versus* *Anita Shourie*[4]
FIR Case No.: 363/09
U/s: EP Act
P.S.: [Illegible]
Peshi: 26-8-13 Time: 9 AM

Whereas the complaint has made before that Mrs. Anita Shourie w/o Arun Shourie, R/o A-31 West End, N. Delhi, 11-0021 has committed the offence punishable under section EP Act and it has been returned to a warrant of arrest there upon [sic] issued that the

4 Words that have been underlined were entered by hand. The rest of the document was a printed one. Unless otherwise indicated, words which have been italicized within quotations from judgments have been italicized by me.

said accused cannot be found and therefore it has been shown in my satisfaction that the said absconded or is concealing himself [sic] to avoid the service of the said warrant.

Proclamation is hereby made that the said accused Mrs. Anita Shourie w/o Arun Shourie is required to appear at Faridabad before this court to answer the said complaint on 26-8-13.

Given under my hand and seal of this court on 2-8-13.

Note: Executing Constable is directed to Appear in court for recording his statement On the date fixed 26-8-13

[Initialed]

Presiding Officer
Special Environment Court
Faridabad

934/8/8/13

* * *

For the life of me I couldn't figure out what poor Anita could have done to injure the environment.

Shekhar's colleague met me. He steered me to the court. A lady with a somewhat stern visage was seated on a raised platform. Several persons were simultaneously directing their pleas to her. Many more were sitting on benches. Many, many more were standing and shuffling around. Outside: noise, loud shouting to persons at the other end of the verandah, and over cellphones, names being shouted out. Shekhar's colleague asked me to have a seat, and wait for Anita's name to be called out.

At last it was. I went up to the bar that separated the raised platform from us. 'Who are you?' I explained that I was the husband of Anita Shourie for whom arrest warrants had been issued. 'Why is she not here?' I explained her condition, I explained the effects of Parkinson's.

'But Madam, why have you thought it necessary to issue warrants for her arrest?'

'Because you have evaded summons of this court five times.'

'But we received no summons. If they had come, why would we not obey them forthwith?'

'Yes, sometimes it happens. Our people don't actually take the trouble of going to serve the summons and just write that the summons could not be served.'

I again assured her that we would never have evaded summons that no one had ever come to serve them.

By now, she was slightly softer. So, I made bold to ask, 'But Madam, why did you deem it necessary to summon us in the first place?'

'Because you have built an illegal farmhouse in Aravali.'

'But we have not built any farmhouse at all.'

'Haven't you built a house on'—she looked down at the file in front of her—'plot F-35 in Aravali Retreat?'

'Madam, we had bought a plot there. But we needed money for building a house near Pune, and so we sold it. We had not so much as put down a loose brick on the plot.'

'Yes, Madam, *inhonney plot toh bech diyaa thaa. Isi liye buyer bhi accused hai—accused no. 2. Voh present hai'*—a gentleman standing to my right pointed out. He was the public prosecutor, one who was to be the most helpful of guides in the months to come.

'Madam, the public prosecutor is himself acknowledging that we had sold the plot. And I assure you that we had not put a single brick down. I had myself pointed that out in several letters to the Haryana State Pollution Control Board—in response to routine circular notices that they kept sending us.'

'But now the process has begun,' she said. 'You can record all this in your defence. In any case, Anita Shourie has to be produced before this court.'

Someone prodded me to ask for bail. I did.

'But for me to grant bail, she has to be present.'

I again explained her condition, that we would literally have to carry her.

'But that is the law. The person seeking bail has to be physically present,' she said and closed the matter.

She gave me fifteen days to produce Anita before her.

I got a call: if you can, it will be better to bring your wife earlier as the judge may be transferred, and we don't know what the attitude of the next judge will be.

So, on 2 September 2013, with two of us holding her up, Anita was 'produced' before the judge. As we hauled her before the judge, she must have seen what she—or, in her view, the law—had inflicted on Anita, what with her inability to stand by herself, what with the unsteady, shuffling, short steps typical of a Parkinson's patient. The judge recorded:

> File taken up today as accused no.1 has appeared before the court and moved an application for bail. Since the present is a complaint case, no custodial is required as nothing is there to recover from accused or otherwise also, remaining accused have also been granted bail, hence accused no. 1 is also granted bail on furnishing bail and surety bonds in the sum of Rs. 25,000/- each...

But hadn't that much been evident from the beginning—that there was nothing that had to be recovered from the accused, etc.? I requested that Anita be given exemption from appearing in person, that I was responsible for everything that was done or not done, and that I would be present whenever the court wanted me to be present. The judge said that she would grant bail and exemption only till the next hearing, as it was possible that she would be transferred, and it would be up to the next judge as to what he thought appropriate. ('She is being promoted,' someone said.) In any event, a formal application for permanent exemption would have to be filed. The advocate representing Anita had the application ready. (A venerable, elderly man, he had been the guru of the public prosecutor, and had been recommended by the public prosecutor himself when I had sought his advice on whom I should engage. He seldom said a word, was in court on occasion, but whenever he was, his very presence carried weight; he never charged me a paisa.) The judge took the application on record, and dictated, 'Copy given to opposite counsel. To come up on 04.10.2013 for filing reply and consideration on application.'

And so Anita became the first one in our family

- To be out on bail
- For having evaded summons that were never served

- Summons which had been issued because of a house that we had never built
- On a plot that we did not own

In the event, as directed, we took Anita back to court on the specified date, 4 October 2013. But there was no hearing. The court record is in the form of the faint impression of a rubber stamp:

> Present: None
> Case taken up today as I shall
> be on CL/EL/SL/ML[5] on 4-10-2013
> Case [illegible] 15-11-13
> for the [illegible] already fixed
> Parties/Counsels be informed accordingly

And while the date scribbled below the stamp seems to be '4.10.2013', the judge must have taken up the case on an earlier date. In any case, Anita was now to be produced in court on 15 November 2013. But before the appointed day could come, we were dealt a mighty blow.

A CATASTROPHE

'Sahib, neechey aao, ek dam neechay aao, ek dam'—I was working in the study upstairs; it was the lady who used to help Anita, she was as good as screaming. Anita's Parkinson's had been making its relentless advance, as I noted earlier. She had fallen a few times. I thought she had fallen again. I rushed down. But the scene was entirely different. Anita was panting, she was having the greatest difficulty taking a breath and exhaling it. She seemed exhausted by the struggle.

I called the doctor nearest our home: 'Could you please come to look at her? If you can't, may I bring her to you?'

'I am not coming to your place. Nor are you going to bring her here,' the doctor said. 'There is something serious going on. *Rush her to the hospital immediately.*'

We piled into our car. On the way to Sir Ganga Ram Hospital, I phoned Samiran Nundy, our friend, and a leading surgeon, that we

5 Casual leave/Earned leave/Special leave/Medical leave.

were rushing Anita to the hospital. 'Take her to Emergency. I will meet you there.'

By the time we reached, a team was waiting for her. They swiftly diagnosed that she had suffered a pulmonary embolism—that clots must have formed and travelled to her lungs. They immediately shifted her to the ICU, and commenced treatment.

The emphatic advice of the doctor that we rush her to the hospital, this prompt diagnosis, the care and expertise of the doctors literally saved her. Ten days in the hospital, ten harrowing days equalled in our lives only by the days that had followed the massive convulsions that our son, Adit, had suffered three years earlier, in 2010.

'Twice I felt I was going to die,' Anita told me much later.

At last we were able to bring her back home. In addition to her Parkinson's medicines, she was now to have blood-thinning medicines, and have her INR[6] checked every few days.

Slowly, ever so slowly, we settled into the new routine. With one enormous difference: from now on we were always on edge. For instance, a fall now would not just mean that Anita could fracture some bone, it could trigger internal bleeding which, because of the blood-thinning medicines she was now taking, would be that much more difficult to arrest.

Further proceedings in the court

There was just no way I could risk taking Anita to the court on the date that had been set—15 November. Leaving her in the care of her sisters and helpers, I made my way back through dense traffic over those 40 kilometres. A new judge had taken charge. The court record states:

> Present: Parties in person
> Both the parties requested adjournment on the ground that the Advocates are busy in Bar Election. Heard. Case is adjourned to 28.02.2014 [changed by hand to '07/1/14'] for the purpose already fixed.

6 'International Normalized Ratio'—a measure of the coagulability of the individual's blood. A higher INR means less coagulability—which is why it has to be kept high when the person is at risk of thrombosis, as Anita was following her bout of pulmonary embolism.

Not possible, not all of it in any case: as I am opposed to adjournments being granted, I am unlikely to have requested for an adjournment. But the moving finger had writ, and moved on.

In a separate note, the judge also recorded that this was the first time he was seeing the file after his transfer, and that he had now seen the order of the Punjab and Haryana High Court that the case be disposed of 'as expeditiously as possible, including day-to-day trial'. And so, he directed that the case would come up for 'pre-charge evidence' on the date that had already been fixed, namely 7 January 2014.

I went to the court that day with a full list of evidence I would urge our advocate to present, and the questions I would urge him to ask witnesses that the prosecutor would furnish. To no avail. It turned out that the case had been taken up the previous day, 6 January 2014! The record of proceedings on 6 January 2014 is again the same, only a partially legible rubber-stamp impression:

> Present: None
> Case taken up today as I shall
> be on Haliday [sic] on 7-1-2014
> Case is adjourned to 28-2-14
> for the same purpose as already fixed
> Parties/Counsel to be informed
> accordingly

Mysteriously, the case was again 'taken up'—not on 28 February, the date that had been fixed, but a week earlier. The record of proceedings of 21 February 2014 is again the same rubber stamp—this time almost entirely illegible:

> Present: None
> Case taken up today as I shall
> be on C [illegible, but for a 'tick' over the 'C'] on 28-2-2014
> C [illegible] 15-4-14
> Pa [illegible] ed
> accor [illegible]

On 15 February, at long last our application for granting Anita exemption from personal appearance was taken up. You will recall that the first judge had said that she would give bail and exemption from personal appearance only up to the next hearing, as she could be transferred by then. She had taken on record our application for exempting Anita from being personally present, and directed that 'Copy be given to opposite counsel. To come up on 04.10.2013 for filing reply and consideration on application.' As we have seen, hearings had come and gone but for one reason or another—the Bar election, the 'CL/EL/SL/ML', etc.—the matter could not be taken up.

By now yet another judge was in the chair. He was the third as far as my attendance went. In fact, he was the fourth on our case: for, as we shall see, much had been happening before the policeman's visit had awakened us to the fact that a case was afoot against us.

We had to take Anita again to the court—the bail could not be given, you will recall, nor appearance in person be waived unless the person was physically present.

By now I had run out of forbearance. It wrenched my heart to subject Anita to the journey, up to the court, and then have her waiting in the courtroom when she should have been lying in bed. 'But that is the law,' you will remember our being told. So, when her name was called, I insisted on taking her—leaning to one side, with short, stumbling steps—right up to the bar of the judge's platform. He was a considerate man. When he saw her condition, he said, 'No, no. Let her keep sitting where she is.' But I would have none of it. Holding her firmly, I pulled and shoved her right up to the bar. The judge granted exemption from personal appearance. Taking her back to the chair, in fury, raising my voice so that all could hear me, I blurted out, 'I hope the majesty of the law has now been upheld.'

Recording the proceedings the judge dictated, 'Reply to application for permanent exemption of accused no. 1 not filed. However, learned counsel for the complainant made no objection on the application ... In view of the no objection as well as medical grounds, personal appearance of accused no. 1 before this court is exempted till further orders...'

You will recall that, in view of the High Court's order that the case be dealt with expeditiously 'including day-to-day trial', the previous judge had fixed 7 January 2014 for 'pre-charge evidence'. The current hearing was being held on 15 April 2014. Apart from the judge accepting Anita's application for being exempted, what transpired will be evident from the concluding sentence of the judge's noting: 'No CW[7] is present. Adjournment sought. Heard. Allowed. Now to come up on 12.5.2014 for pre-charge evidence of the complainant.'

This was to be a frequent pattern: the conscientious Public Prosecutor would be present; we, the accused, and some of our counsel would be present. But the official witnesses would be 'on their way', or not even 'on their way'. And that is not counting what they said when they turned up.

The record for 12 May 2014:

> One PW[8] in pre-charge evidence is present and examined. No other PW is present. Adjournment sought. Heard. Now to come up on 26.5.2014 for remaining pre-charge evidence of complainant.

The record for 26 May 2014:

> ...No pre-charge evidence is present. Adjournment sought. Heard. Now to come up on 11.7.2014 for pre-charge evidence of complainant.

On 11 July 2014:

> ...Two PWs are present and examined. No other PW is present. Adjournment sought. Heard. Allowed. Now to come up on 25.8.2014 for remaining pre-charge evidence of complainant.

In each of these hearings, these CWs/PWs would be asked three/four formulaic questions and would give formulaic replies.

---

7 Witness for the complainant, in this case the Haryana State Pollution Control Board.

8 Prosecution witness.

On 25 August 2014:

> One CW is present and recorded. No other CW is present. Learned counsel for the complainant has closed pre-charge evidence, vide his separate statement. Now to come up on 05.09.2014 for consideration on charge.

Before proceeding to the subsequent rounds, I should step back a little.

The cyclostyled notices

Late in the 1980s or early 1990–91, a developer began laying the infrastructure for a residential colony in the Aravali Hills. Like a few hundred others, we had purchased a plot. The plot had an entrance gate, and something that was someone's idea of a barbed wire demarcating it from the adjacent plots.

In August 2005, we received a 'Show Cause Notice' from the Haryana State Pollution Control Board. It was a sort-of printed standardized notice. It stated that on 7 May 1992 the Ministry of Environment and Forests had issued a notification which had prohibited a series of activities except with its permission. Among these were 'locating/expanding/modernizing any new industry'; all new mining, including renewal of mining leases; cutting trees; construction of 'any cluster of dwelling units, farmhouses, sheds, community centres, information centres and any other activity connected with such construction (including roads of [sic] part of any infrastructure relating thereto)'; electrification. For any activity of this kind, the concerned person must get prior permission of the ministry.

No problem with that: that the hills must be protected. Who would quarrel with the intent of the notification? The problem was the facts on ground: notification or no notification, mining was going on there for all to see—newspapers used to regularly publish articles and photographs of trucks carrying mined stuff in broad daylight.

There was no problem with the notification. Nor, as far as we were concerned, with the 'Show Cause Notice'—a printed form, it was manifestly a routine one that had been sent to all and sundry. Yet it disturbed me and angered me a bit, for it began by declaring, 'It is intimated that you have constructed your Farm House/Residence/Establishment on a Ghair Mumkin Pahar[9] in gross violation of Aravali Notification dated...' when, in fact, we had constructed nothing *at all*. The notice concluded in an ominous tone:

> As you have carried out construction activities in Ghair Mumkin Pahar[8] and violated the Aravali Notification why the action as per Environment Protection Act 1986 should not be initiated against you [sic]. You are hereby directed to reply this [sic] show cause notice within 15 days otherwise it will be presumed that you have nothing to say in this regard & action will be taken without further notice and prosecution will be launched against you.

Anita and I replied: we have built nothing at all on the plot ... should you want us to furnish any further information, we will come over...

We heard nothing further.

Two years later, in August 2007, we received another sort-of printed communication. It seemed to have been prepared for every buyer: all that had been done was that three blank spaces—each having a printed underline—had been filled in by hand. It acknowledged that our reply 'to Show Cause Notice No. NIL dated 18-08-05 on the above subject has been received. In order to enable office to appreciate the points raised by you, the following information may also be furnished': dates on which [i] 'plot was allotted to you' [ii] 'on which sale/transfer deed of the same was got registered [sic] before sub registrar'; [iii] 'on which you obtained electricity connection from Electricity Board'; [iv] 'on which tube well was installed'; [v] 'details of approval of building plan, if any, obtained from the Competent Authority'; [vi] details 'of change of

9 Natural hill.

land use/permission obtained from Town and Country Planning Department/Local Administration, if any'.

Again: reply within fifteen days, or else...

We replied at once:

1. Date on which plot was allotted: 31.12.90
2. Date of sale/transfer deed registered before sub-registrar: 31.10.07
3. No electricity connection has been obtained
4. No tube well has been installed
5. No building plan has been submitted for approval
6. Change of land use has not been sought or obtained

Again we offered to personally come over to provide any further information that might be required.

That was in November 2007. By now, Anita was having increasing difficulties in bearing the cold of Delhi's winter. A friend told us about a new 'city' that was being planned beyond Pune. That would be so much better for her and our son, we thought. But to gather money to build that house, we needed to sell the plot in Aravali Retreat.

We sold it on 27 March 2008.

But no one seemed to be paying any attention to what the position was on the ground. We got yet another Show Cause Notice. I rang up the head of the Haryana State Pollution Control Board, and explained the sequence of events to him: in particular that we had built nothing, and that in fact the plot had been sold to someone else. He said that, by chance, the officer dealing with the matter happened to be sitting with him, that he would hand the phone over to him, and I should explain everything to him. I went over the dates and facts for this officer. He seemed satisfied. He asked me to send the sale deed that had been executed when we had sold the plot.

I did so. That was in January 2009.

Manifestly to no avail. For in July 2014 we received yet another printed Show Cause Notice:

> To
> Smt. Anita Shouria [sic]
> ...
> or
> To Whom so ever it may concern
>
> Whereas, it has been reported to me that you have erected unauthorized construction for residential farmhouse purpose (Plot No. F-35)...
>
> You are hereby ordered to stop further contravention and to appear in my office ... within a period of seven days [in bold] and to show cause why you should not be ordered to restore the land of the aforesaid contravention has been committed [sic], to its original state or to bring it in conformity with the provisions of the Act ibid [sic] and Rules framed there under...

I replied the very next day, restating all the facts. I also pointed out that we had been sending replies to the same set of questions and allegations since 2005, and that no one seemed to have paid any attention; that instead a case had been registered in the Special Environment Court, Faridabad, and that this was nothing but vexatious litigation.

No reply.

The court records which I obtained much later showed that, in fact, while we had been under the impression that we had done what needed to be done by sending the facts in response to those Show Cause Notices, unknown to us, matters had been proceeding in the court for quite some time.

The plot had been registered in Anita's name on 31 October 2007. We had sold the plot on 27 March 2008.

A complaint had been filed on 28 October 2009 that we had illegally constructed a farmhouse. The court record had entries of summons having been issued to Anita in February 2010. And then in November that year: 'Notices issued to accused not received back,' hence bailable warrants. And then an order by the then judge containing all the allegations in the complaint. Then in February 2011: 'BWs of remaining accused not received back. Fresh BWs of remaining accused ... be issued for 25.5.11.'

For that day, the same rubbed-out rubber stamp dated 24 May 2011:

> Present: None
> Case taken up today as I shall
> be on CL/EL/SL/ML on 25/5/11...

A new judge.

Waiting for order from the High Court.

Proceedings on 4 May 2012 ... Proceedings on 28 May 2012: accused no. 2 (the gentleman who had purchased the plot from us) present ... So, the court must have got to know that we did not even own the plot.

Next proceeding: Bailable warrant to secure appearance of Anita.

Proceedings of 3 October 2012: '...Inadvertently, the case is fixed for complainant's pre-charge evidence, however, accused no. 1 has not put appearance before the court till date. Now, her presence be secured through warrants of arrest for 30.10.2012 through SHO concerned.'

The same sort of entry for 28 February 2013—that Anita has not appeared, hence, non-bailable warrants be issued again. And again for 23 March 2013, and on 13 May 2013, and on 30 May 2013...

All this while, we were living in our house—the address of which the complainant, the Haryana State Pollution Control Board, as well as the court had, as is manifest from the communications from the Board and the summons and warrants from the court. We were going on with our normal lives—completely oblivious of the avalanche that was building up 30 kilometres away.

Finally, on 8 July 2013:

> Warrants of arrest of accused no.1 not received back executed or unexecuted. On going through the file. [sic] It is seen that warrants of arrest of accused no. 1 is being issued for last several dates and on each, either warrants [sic] is received back un-served or not received back. It is clear that accused is avoiding service and his

> [sic] presence cannot be secured through ordinary process, hence proclamation of accused U/s 82 Cr. P.C. be issued for 26.08.2013. Executing police officer shall also appear on same date for his statement regarding publication of proclamation.

And so Anita became a proclaimed absconder.

'If the case against you were to be dismissed...'

I would go to the court on each date. In all, through those interminable hearings and adjournments, four government functionaries were 'examined'. That is, they were asked a few formula questions: 'Is this the notification...?' 'Is this the entry in the village record...?' 'Did you carry out an inspection...?' And they gave formula answers.

From my point of view, five important points came on record from the exchanges, perfunctory and formulaic though the exchanges were:

- The village record clearly established that the plot had been registered in our name on 31 October 2007, and that we had sold it on 27 March 2008 to accused no. 2.
- What was always being referred to as a 'farmhouse' turned out to be one measly room—the sort that someone might construct for a watchman.
- Departmental rules required that the site be inspected regularly. In fact, only one 'inspection' seemed to have been carried out. The person who was said to have carried out the 'inspection' testified that he had done so on 17 April 2009: that is, well after we had sold the plot.
- In answer to questions, he said that he could not state whether the gate and 'boundary wall' had been constructed, and the road laid before 1992—when the notification had been issued by the environment ministry—or after.
- He could not say whether that one room had been constructed before we got the plot, during the time the plot belonged to us, or after we had sold it.

I was told, 'Of course, the record is clear. You people did not build any structure. The plot belongs to accused no. 2. But if at this stage the case against you is dismissed, it will be alleged that this has been done under political pressure or that money has changed hands.' The person who said this had been, and was to continue to be most considerate and helpful: I couldn't muster anger at him. And it was futile to get angry at 'the system'. The only course was to resign to the circumstances.

Even so, I was incensed when in the hearing on 5 September 2014, the judge ruled, 'Heard. Prima-facie a case punishable u/s 15 of the Environment Protection Act, 1986 is made out against the accused.' And charges that had been framed were handed to us.

'No after-charge evidence is present,' the judge recorded at the next hearing, on 13 October 2014. 'Adjournment sought. Heard. Now to come up on 17.11.2014 for after charge evidence of complainant.'

And on 17 November? 'No after charge evidence is present. Adjournment sought. Heard. Now to come up on 25.11.2014 for after charge evidence of complainant.'

And on 25 November? 'Two PWs are present and examined. No other PW is present.' As the same persons who had been 'examined' and 'cross-examined' in the pre-charge stage were repeating the same litany, the counsel for us stated that 'they do not want to re-cross the remaining witnesses in after charge evidence already recorded in pre-charge evidence.' The prosecutor closed his presentation and arguments. The date for the next hearing was set for 16 December 2014.

And that day the hearing was again adjourned: the record states that this was done 'On the request of the ld. Counsel for the accused'—that must refer to some accused other than us, for I was present and was eager that the case be concluded at the earliest. The judge set 16 January 2015 for recording the statement of the accused.

On that day, as Anita could not be present in person, the judge decided that her answers would be obtained through a questionnaire. I was handed the questionnaire on 16 January before lunch. As the questionnaire was presumably the sort that had been handed to several of the accused, the answers too were ready. And so the answers were handed to the court after lunch.

The other accused were not present at the next hearing. And at the one after that, the counsel for the developers handed a judgment by which the developers had already been discharged in a similar case. He argued that, having been acquitted in that case, they could not be further prosecuted and punished. Our counsel presented his arguments at the next hearing, on 2 March 2015.

That day's record states, 'No defence evidence is present. Learned counsel for the accused no.1 has closed defence evidence ... Vide my separate judgment of even date, all the accused have been acquitted of the charges leveled against them. Bail bonds and surety bonds of the accused stand discharged. File be consigned to record room after due compliance.'

The judgment runs into twelve-and-a-half pages. The Haryana State Pollution Board had alleged that the developers had got wind of the notification before it was issued, and 'colluded with the officers of the revenue department and succeeded in making/ preparing wrong, frivolous and illegal entries in the revenue record of village Raisina'. Together, they had fabricated the status of the land into being one in which a residential colony could be set up. In turn, we were accused of having purchased the plot and 'constructed a farmhouse by way of illegal construction in form of boundary wall, main [gate?] and one room constructed etc. in collusion with other accused...'

The judgment recalled the various submissions. The judge's conclusions were emphatic. As far as the particulars of our case were concerned, the judge recorded, 'In his cross-examination he [the patwari] admitted that from 1991 till the date [of the transfer of land to us] the nature of land was shown as ghair mumkin farm house in the jamabandi.'[10] Second, that on the basis of the village record and the sale deeds, the prosecution witness acknowledged that the land had been registered in Anita's name on 31 October 2007, and that we had sold it on 27 March 2008. Third, that the site had been inspected more than a year after we had sold

10 Record of rights.

the plot. Fourth, 'he [the regional officer] could not tell when the construction was started and for how much time it continued.' Fifth, 'In his cross-examination he [the official who was said to have carried out the inspection, and who had reported that 'a boundary wall and one room' had been constructed] deposed that he could not tell about first construction upon the farm house.'

But the main reason on account of which the case fell through had little to do with us. What was called 'the mother case' by the lawyers was against the developers. You will recall that the Haryana State Pollution Board had maintained that the developer had falsified the records in collusion with village officials to alter the status of the land. It was on this charge that everything that followed had become illegal. After reviewing the evidence, the judge held:

> It is admitted fact that the present land in question has been shown as Ghair Mumkin Farm House etc. in the khasra girdawari[11] of Haadi[12] 1991 and in the jamabandi of 1990-91, i.e. in the land/revenue records maintained by the State Government. Now it was incumbent upon the complainant to prove that this record has been wrongly/falsely prepared in collusion with revenue officials. But surprisingly no any [sic] evidence regarding collusion between accused and revenue officials has been brought upon file...
>
> Further it was incumbent upon the prosecution to prove that these entries were falsely made but as already discussed above there is no any [sic] document upon file which could establish that the present change in khasra girdawari and subsequently in jamabandi was not as per law ... As already discussed above, the complainant has been unable to prove any collusion or forgery in preparation of jamabandi for year 1990-91 and thus has been unable to rebut the presumption.

He adverted to the charges against us and concluded:

> Even if the applicability of Aravali Notification be presumed upon the land in dispute then too there is no any [sic] evidence

11 Record of cultivation.
12 The crop sown in winter.

> that when construction was started [sic] by accused no. 1 and accused no. 2 and when it was completed. There is no any [sic] building inspection report which could show that the construction was completed after 1992. Further it is also not certain that who constructed the room available on the farm house No F-35, hence the benefit of this doubt should definitely be given to the accused.

Hence the judge's conclusion:

> Thus the complainant/prosecution has miserably failed to prove upon file that Aravali Notification was applicable upon the land of the accused situated in Aravali Retreat and he has further failed to prove that the construction in any shape made by accused after the issuance of Aravali Notification has made the present accused liable. Hence accused are liable to be acquitted of the charge framed under Section 15 of the Environment Protection Act for violation of Aravali Notification dated 7.5.1992.
>
> In view of my above discussion all the accused are acquitted from the charge framed under...

A few facts

We had sold the plot on 7 March 2008.

The Haryana State Pollution Control Board filed its complaint on 28 October 2009—and we were implicated in it even though we had sold the plot a year and a half earlier.

We were all acquitted on 2 March 2015, that is, six years after the proceedings began.

For almost this entire period, the racket, as lucrative as it is destructive—illegal mining—continued. In broad daylight.

During the six years, four judges handled the case.

It was taken up in one form or another by the judges forty times.

On these forty occasions, in all, only four witnesses were 'examined' and 'cross-examined'.

As the 'examination' and 'cross-examination' were more or less formulaic, the maximum time for which a witness was questioned was just about fifteen to twenty minutes: a total of one hour for the four witnesses, or, being generous, let us say two hours.

In addition to us, there were 706 accused. Actually, I should have typed '*are* 706 accused', not '*were*'. Because several of the cases are still going on as I type this.

And please remember, for each of the accused, each step involved many, many others. You are going to stand surety so that your wife may get bail? You must get proof of address, a statement from your bank of your current balance, a statement of your assets ... What did you say your wife has? Not enough that you have the medical history of her Parkinson's from 1992; you must have a current certificate. What did you say she was struck by, what 'embo'? Not enough that you have the discharge summary from Ganga Ram Hospital for the pulmonary embolism that nearly took her life. You must have a certificate from a doctor in a government hospital.

A lesson for the media

I alluded to this sequence in passing during a lecture at the National Judicial Academy in Bhopal. I had been invited to address a gathering of judges from four states, including High Court judges.

In the tea break that followed the lecture, I chanced to drift towards a group of senior judges. Two of them happened to be judges of the Punjab and Haryana High Court. 'But why didn't you come to us?' one of them remarked. 'We would have given immediate relief.'

But how was I to find lawyers in Chandigarh? How was I to travel to Chandigarh every time the case came up? How was I to know that the case would come up before judges who would be as understanding as these two?

The other reaction was equally telling: 'If *this* can happen to *you*, can you imagine what the common man has to go through?'

Actually, I could. For in the hours that I spent in the court, I saw first-hand what others were going through. Hundreds milling around for hours, only to learn that yet another date had been fixed. '*Idhar lagaao, idhar,*' someone would take the thumb of an elderly man, of a lady, her face covered by a ghunghat, and press it down on some paper. Did the old man or lady know what they were affixing their thumb impression to? Dumb driven cattle…

A lesson in that for us in the media: if, instead of, or in addition to focusing so much on lofty constitutional issues being debated in the Supreme Court, we were to depute our correspondents once a month on a randomly selected day to a randomly selected local court, and report what happened in that court during that day—that would give readers and viewers a so much truer picture of the state of justice in our country. And may even spur some improvements.

And lessons for us

- If possible, don't buy a plot of land or build a house.
- If you do, do not leave it to the developers to keep track of circulars, notifications, changes in law; train someone in your family in this art, and condition him to devote himself only to it.
- When you build that house, build a separate room to store every scrap of paper, every notice you receive and every reply you send.
- Be sure that no one in that government department will read any of your replies.
- So, if lightning is to fall on your head, it will.
- The only way to retain your sanity through such stretches is to look upon them as yet another service that our systems provide: free lessons in patience.

But why not move to a reason for hope—a sequence that demonstrates, as the phrase goes, 'The wheels of justice grind slow but they grind exceedingly fine'?

2

Justice done, undone, redone

Jayalalithaa was the chief minister of Tamil Nadu for fourteen years, in six separate terms. In her first term from 1991 to 1996, officially she drew a salary of only Re 1 a month. Tamil Nadu politics became a sort of seesaw between her and her arch rival, M. Karunanidhi. In one of the bouts when Karunanidhi was in office, a case was filed against her for having acquired assets disproportionate to her known sources of income.

In a judgment that is a model of meticulous examination of the facts, the trial judge, John Michael D'Cunha,[1] held her guilty of having acquired assets that could not be accounted for by her known sources of income. He also held that Jayalalithaa, her close associate Sasikala Natarajan and other relatives of the latter had acted in concert. He, therefore, found them guilty of conspiracy also. He sentenced the accused to six years' imprisonment and a fine of Rs 100 crore.

An appeal was filed in the Karnataka High Court. In a judgment that is as much a model of misrepresentation and distortion as D'Cunha's judgment had been of meticulousness and rectitude, Justice C.R. Kumaraswamy acquitted Jayalalithaa and her accomplices. By calculations so patently false and absurd as to strain one's credulity that a High Court judge could have advanced

1 At the time of writing, he is a judge of the Karnataka High Court.

them, Kumaraswamy held that while Jayalalithaa and her associates did have assets that exceeded the resources they could explain, the disproportionate assets amounted to a mere 8.1 per cent of her income and, therefore, in accordance with a rule laid down in an earlier case by the Supreme Court, she and her companions were entitled to be acquitted.[2] He also held that the evidence did not establish them to be guilty of conspiracy.[3]

The matter was taken in appeal to the Supreme Court. In a judgment which is also a model of meticulous examination of evidence and close reasoning, Justice Pinaki Chandra Ghose, on his behalf and that of Justice Amitava Roy, threw out Kumaraswamy's judgment and restored the findings of and the sentences that D'Cunha had awarded.[4]

It will pay us to spend a little time on the three successive judgments. We will get to see what upright judges can do, and what the creative lot, so to say, do. And they will point us once again to the one, sovereign remedy.

There were four accused: Accused 1—Selvi J. Jayalalithaa; Accused 2—her close friend and associate, Sasikala Natarajan; Accused 3—V.N. Sudhakaran, the son of Sasikala's elder sister; Accused 4—J. Elavarasi, the wife of the elder brother again of Sasikala.

The resources that the four had at their disposal and the assets that they had acquired between 1 July 1991 and 30 April 1996—the 'check period'—were taken up for examination. No one objected that the period which had been chosen was unfair in any way.

D'Cunha found that during the 'check period', the known sources of monies available to them totalled Rs 9.9 crore—from income as individuals (for instance, as interest from deposits or returns from investments), from loans, from gifts; in addition, there

---

2 In *Krishnanand Agnihotri v. State of MP,* (1977) 1 SCC 816, the Supreme Court had held that if the assets that could not be accounted for by the person's known sources of income amounted to 10 per cent or less than the income, the person could be acquitted.

3 Justice Kumaraswamy retired three months after delivering his justly notorious judgment.

4 *State of Karnataka v. Selvi J. Jayalalithaa,* (2017) 6 SCC 263.

was the income that they claimed their companies had earned from business operations. The expenditures during the period amounted to Rs 8.5 crore. Against these, Rs 53.6 crore worth of assets were acquired, which could not be accounted for by the accused as having come from the resources that they had at their disposal.

The judge also found that the accused had acted in concert. They had set up thirty-four companies and fifty-two bank accounts to cycle and recycle funds. The inflow of cash came only to Jayalalithaa. The assets were shown to be in the names of Accused 2 to 4 and the companies. The accounts were operated by Sasikala. Both of these arrangements were made only to camouflage the fact that the monies were being received by Jayalalithaa alone; and to distance her from the operations—of accounts, of acquiring real estate and the rest—so that it could be claimed that she did not know what was being done.

Twenty-two of the thirty-four companies did not engage in any business activity during the check period. Second, there were huge exchanges of funds between the accounts—the transfers ranged from Rs 12,000 to Rs 25 lakh in single transactions. Indeed, all the numbers boggle our imagination: that a public servant would have to account for *ninety-one* watches; that the expenditure on a single wedding would be Rs *6 crore*; that a public servant would, on her own claim, have received gifts worth Rs *3 crore* on a single birthday; that properties would have been acquired via 146 sale-purchase deeds.

By calculations so patently crafted to an end, Kumaraswamy found that they had a much larger amount of resources available for acquiring assets than D'Cunha had calculated. With equal creativity, he found that the value of assets that Jayalalithaa and associates had acquired was only Rs 2.8 crore.

The moment his judgment was delivered, it was pointed out that even if all his suppositions, concepts and estimates were accepted, the assets that could not be explained by the resources available to the accused came to Rs 14.4 crore. This meant that they were 41.3 per cent of the claimed sources of income, and, therefore, even in terms of the Supreme Court's 10 per cent rule of grace, Jayalalithaa and others stood guilty. Moreover, the income came to Rs 13.5 crore less than what Kumaraswamy had used as his denominator.

This latter exaggeration had come about because Kumaraswamy had taken the loans that he had listed to be Rs 24.2 crore, but in fact they were, by his own listing, Rs 10.7 crore. This is what caught the headlines, and it came to be believed that Kumaraswamy had let Jayalalithaa off because of an 'arithmetical error'.

Innumeracy of that order would not be excused even in a schoolboy. But what was at display was not that Kumaraswamy could not add. What was at display was *a pattern*.

By one bizarre device after another, Kumaraswamy inflated the income of Jayalalithaa and associates; he deflated the expenses they had incurred (so as to leave a larger surplus that was supposedly available to them to acquire assets); and he drastically reduced the value of the assets they had acquired.

Let us start with income. D'Cunha had examined sixty-four heads, and arrived at a total of Rs 9.9 crore. The High Court added seven heads, and got to a total of Rs 34.7 crore. And even where the heads tallied, the High Court arrived at a much higher figure. For instance, Jayalalithaa and others claimed that they had been growing grapes. Upon generous assumptions, the trial court estimated that they had earned Rs 5.8 lakh from this activity. The High Court as good as multiplied the figure by ten and arrived at an income under this head of Rs 52.5 lakh.

Jayalalithaa and others claimed that their company, Jaya Publications, published a paper/magazine, *Namadhu MGR*, and that from this they earned Rs 14.2 crore over six years. The device by which they earned this much would be the envy of newspaper owners. They claimed that in 1990 they had started a scheme by which subscribers could receive four, five or six copies of the publication free if they made an interest-free deposit of Rs 12,000, Rs 15,000 or Rs 18,000 annually. (The firm was also claimed to have earned Rs 1.1 crore from job-printing and sale of advertisements; and from 'agricultural activity'.) They pointed to the income tax returns that had been filed on behalf of the firm. Courts have held that by themselves, income tax returns are not proof of the veracity of a claim—submissions in the returns have to be tested for their truthfulness. But more than that, these claims had been made well after the events: the returns for 1991–92 onwards had not been filed till 1998 and 1999. First, the account books did not reflect the inflows from the deposit scheme. Thirty-one AIADMK faithfuls were produced as witnesses. They affirmed that they had indeed made the requisite deposits ranging from Rs 12,000 to Rs 18,000. Their averments ran to a pattern. None of them could produce any receipt for the deposit. Moreover, the balance sheets showed the amounts that were said to have been collected as deposits to be liabilities of the firm. The firm was asked to submit applications that potential depositors had made, the counterfoils of receipts that had been issued, etc. It claimed that these had been lost. As the Supreme Court noted:

> The Trial Court was categorical in bringing on record the fact that it was only after the CIT (Appeals) had set-aside the assessment order i.e. 3.3.1988 rejecting the claim of scheme deposit of the assessee on 15.9.1998 that Jaya Publications filed its returns for the assessment years 1991-92, 1992-93, 1993-94 on 6.11.1998 mentioning for the first time such deposits.
>
> ...The Trial Court on an overall assessment of the evidence concluded that the story of scheme deposit had been introduced by the defence only after the charge-sheet had been filed on 4.10.1997 i.e. through the income tax returns filed in the year 1998. That no evidence had been produced before the Court to show that the scheme had been floated in the year 1990, was recorded.

The High Court noted all these facts, the Supreme Court observed, yet confined itself to just one of them, and then disposed of that singular one with a toss of its hand:

> The High Court categorically held that delayed and unexplained submission of income tax returns did give rise to doubt of the genuineness thereof. This notwithstanding, the High Court only in the face of the oral evidence of the 31 witnesses claiming themselves to be the depositors/subscribers for the newsletter, returned a finding that the whole claim of the assessee could not be rejected only on the ground of delay in filing of the income tax returns. Acting solely on this consideration, the High Court

thus allowed addition of a sum of Rs 4 crores as income of Jaya Publications.

Notice, Jayalalithaa and associates had claimed a net profit of only Rs 1.15 crore for Jaya Publications between 1992–93 and 1996–97. As against this, the High Court 'awarded a sum of Rs 4 crore as income earned by Jaya Publications acting solely on the evidence of ardent party workers *de hors* any independent corroboration'.

And so the Supreme Court concluded:

> In other words, though the High Court itself was left unconvinced about the acceptability of the claim of scheme deposit, due to largely delayed income tax returns, it benignly did award an income of Rs. 4 crores to the assessee only on the basis of the oral testimony of 31 witnesses who, as noted by the Trial Court, owed unstinted allegiance to AIADMK party with no legally acceptable documentary evidence to corroborate the same.

Another one of their firms, Super Duper TV, Jayalalithaa and associates claimed, earned Rs 1 crore by providing TV equipment. But, the Supreme Court noted:

> ... there was nothing on record to show how the investments were made for the purchase of equipment claimed to have been supplied by the company to various subscribers and that in any case, this amount could not have been available with the A3 as the stable corpus of income for purchase of immovable properties, as claimed.

Moreover, there was another telling fact:

> ... the Trial Court recorded the huge cash inflow and outflow to and from the account of the company. Noticeably, such deposits and withdrawals had been vis-à-vis several accounts involving A1 to A4 and the firms and companies floated by them during the check period of which they were partners/directors, as the case may be.

These deposits and withdrawals acquired significance in the light of the charge of conspiracy and abetment, the Supreme Court observed. 'The summary treatment of the evidence on this issue by the High Court, in our comprehension, lacks the desired approach and insight and, therefore, cannot be sustained.' The trial court had followed the money trail, it noted. The High Court, by contrast, had confined itself to the oral statements of the 'subscribers'.

In another typical instance, it was claimed that out of the earnings of one of their companies, Sasi Enterprises, Jayalalithaa had received Rs 6.3 lakh as her share. It turned out that the amount consisted of nothing but exchanges of reserves between Jayalalithaa and Sasikala.

Jayalalithaa claimed that she had earned Rs 2.7 crore from Jaya Publications. Upon examining the evidence, as the trial court had done, the Supreme Court concluded that the receipts were fictitious:

> The deposits and withdrawals represented through the different entries in the bank accounts suggest multiplication of transactions stemming from the same corpus. The maze of financial exchanges in fragments involving different combinations hint at the attempt to inflate individual and collective income of the respondents. The banking transactions, though resorted to for proclaiming genuineness thereof, having regard to the overall factual conspectus do not appear to be real. The claim of income of Rs 2,70,82,900/- of A1 by way of receipts from Jaya Publications, therefore, is unconvincing.

In the same way, incomes were shown to have accrued to Sasikala and her two relatives. Kumaraswamy took a generous view of these also: he took them to be Rs 26.5 crore, instead of Rs 6 crore. These included huge foreign remittances—no one could explain the sources from which and why these had come to them. They claimed to have received Rs 2.2 crore as income from the front firms which had been set up. You will recall that so many of these 'firms' had been registered on the same day, each of them having the same address. The conclusive fact was that there was absolutely no evidence that the 'firms' had earned the income that they were then supposed to have passed on to Sasikala and her relatives.

One of the 'firms' was Anjanya Printers. In 1994–95, Anjanya Printers had shown income from business operations to be Rs 747—yes, Rs 747, that's all. Income tax returns were filed only in August 1997. They now declared undisclosed income for 1986–1996 to have been Rs 10 lakh. Besides, they claimed that the firm had received Rs 30 lakh from Jaya Publications as share application fee in 1993 and 1994: of course, Jaya Publications had not filed income tax returns for those years. Furthermore, it was now claimed that between 1 April 1994 and 31 March 1996, Anjanya Printers had received Rs 55 lakh as net income and as advance rent. As you would by now expect, the 'firm' had not maintained any regular books of accounts. On this head also, Kumaraswamy accepted the claims made on behalf of the 'firm' wholesale. Reviewing the evidence on the point, the Supreme Court observed, '...there seems to be no consideration of the oral and documentary evidence in support thereof by the High Court'.

Let's now consider Sasi Enterprises. It was claimed first of all that it had earned Rs 96 lakh from rent and from 'agricultural activities'. Needless to say, income tax returns had not been filed. Moreover, the lease documents on the basis of which rent would have been received turned out to be of questionable veracity. And there was no evidence to substantiate the claim that the firm had undertaken any 'agricultural activities'.

No matter! Kumaraswamy accepted the 'documents' in their entirety, leading the Supreme Court to observe:

> It is however noteworthy that the narration in relation thereto does not reveal any analytical approach to fathom the probative value thereof on the touchstone of acceptability of the proof of the facts proposed thereby. Neither the oral nor the documentary evidence has been tested independent of the income tax returns, profit and loss accounts and the balance sheets to determine the intrinsic worth thereof.

Having accepted the documents wholly, Kumaraswamy opted for moderation: instead of the Rs 96 lakh that had been claimed as income, he allowed Rs 25 lakh. On what grounds did he cut down the claim? Prima facie, none.

Next, it was claimed that Sasi Enterprises had earned income from business operations in 1994 and 1995 amounting to Rs 2.4 lakh. As no one was able to furnish any evidence to support the claim, the trial court rejected the claim. Next, it was claimed that Sasi Enterprises had received a 'capital introduction' of Rs 75 lakh: this was taken as 'income'. Upon reviewing the evidence, the trial court concluded that this was nothing but a diversion of funds into the account of Sasi Enterprises that had found their way to Jayalalithaa. And Kumaraswamy? 'The High Court did not deal with the oral and documentary evidence to this effect in detail,' the Supreme Court noted.

After reviewing several such claims, and the complete absence of evidence to substantiate them, the Supreme Court concluded:

> The High Court generally referred to the evidence adduced by the respondents and without any endeavour to evaluate the same to ascertain its probative worth, readily acted thereon to return a finding that the income of the firm, cumulatively having regard to the various sources claimed by it, was assessable at Rs 25 lakhs.

Next, Sasikala and her two relatives claimed that they had received Rs 62 lakh as dues paid back to Sasi Enterprises by two parties. D'Cunha examined the profit-and-loss statement of the firm and found it to be 'not reliable and authentic'. He also found that the transaction had not been disclosed to the income tax authorities 'at any point of time before the registration of the case'. And the persons who were supposed to have borrowed the amounts and returned them were never examined. And Kumaraswamy? The Supreme Court furnishes the answer:

> The High Court, however, accepted on its face value the relevant balance sheet, the profit and loss account as well as the orders of the income tax authorities to this effect without embarking upon any independent verification of the contents thereof to ascertain

> the correctness or genuineness of the same, in the teeth of the finding of the Trial Court, contrary thereto.

And so on: item after item turned out to be bogus—so patent a concoction that even Kumaraswamy did not take some of them into account.

The next fount of resources that Jayalalithaa, Sasikala and her relatives claimed was available to them were loans that they had taken from their 'firms' and from the banks. First, the so-called loans that they had taken from their own companies were never repaid. More significant, the sources of the income of these companies, as we have seen, were themselves suspect.

Then there were huge loans from banks. As our subject is what the High Court did rather than the malfeasance of Jayalalithaa and associates, how Kumaraswamy dealt with the loans is of even greater interest. To sustain the conclusion that Jayalalithaa and others had enough resources to have purchased thc pile of assets that they had acquired, it was necessary to inflate the amount they had received as loans from the banks. So, what did Kumaraswamy do?

Simple. First, he added ten more heads from which loans were received and thereby added Rs 24.2 crore to the resources that were available to Jayalalithaa and associates. Presumably, as this did not prove sufficient, Kumaraswamy topped the total by his special contribution to our jurisprudence—the 'arithmetical error': even if all the additions that Kumaraswamy had incorporated were taken into account at face value, the additional resources available through loans would have been Rs 10.7 crore: he just took that to read Rs. 24.2 crore.

Second, in a bold act of double-counting, he added to the total loans that D'Cunha had already taken into account: an agricultural loan from the Indian Bank—Rs 3.7 crore; a loan to Sasikala from the Indian Bank—Rs 25 lakh; a loan to Sudhakaran, the nephew of Sasikala, from the Indian Bank—Rs 1.57 crore; a loan to one of their 'firms', Mahalakshmi Mandapam, from the Indian Bank—Rs 17.8 lakh. Each one of these had already been taken into account by the trial court when totalling the resources that Jayalalithaa and associates had for acquiring assets. Incidentally, the Indian Bank was and remains a public sector bank—the felicity with which this lot acquired loans from it proves once again what I have said all along: the only truly 'private sector' in India is the public sector: it is the private property of whoever happens to be in office.

Third, Kumaraswamy took as available loans, amounts that had not even been disbursed: a loan of Rs 25 lakh was sanctioned for Jaya Real Estate, but only Rs 5 lakh had been disbursed; a loan of Rs 12.5 lakh was sanctioned (again by Indian Bank) to JS Holding, but only Rs 7 lakh had been released; a loan of Rs 50 lakh had been sanctioned (again by Indian Bank) but only Rs 28 lakh had been released; a loan of Rs 1.65 crore had been sanctioned for Ramraj Agricultural Mills, but no amount had been released during the check period. A loan of Rs 90 lakh had been taken from the Indian Bank—but this was taken *after* the check period and so could not have been available during that period for acquiring assets. There was yet another loan, but it had been repaid during the check period along with an interest of Rs 51 lakh, and so it too could not have been available for acquiring assets. Kumaraswamy was not deterred by such trivialities—of loans not having been disbursed, of loans having been received after the check period, of loans having been repaid. In each and every instance, he added the nominal value of the loan that was sanctioned to the pool of resources that Jayalalithaa and associates had for acquiring assets.

Just 'errors'?

Finally, Jayalalithaa claimed that she had received gifts of Rs 3 crore on her birthday. These included remittances from abroad. It was claimed that 300 to 500 admirers and party faithfuls had given these gifts. Of course, no receipts had been issued, nor accounts kept. It turned out that they were also not mentioned in the income tax returns for the relevant year. They first surfaced in supplementary returns filed one to five years later. Even that could not settle the matter—receiving gifts of this magnitude was in blatant contravention of the Prevention of Corruption Act.

The next task was to put a value on the assets which Jayalalithaa, Sasikala and her relatives had acquired during the period in question. The substantial differences between the trial court's estimate and the value that the High Court placed were in regard to two main items. The Supreme Court focused on these.

The first was about the value of additional construction that had been undertaken by them. Jayalalithaa and associates claimed that at the beginning of the check period, their assets were worth only Rs 2 crore. The director of vigilance and anti-corruption (DVAC) estimated that at the end of the check period, they had become worth Rs. 68.4 crore. The trial court placed the value at Rs 55 crore. Jayalalithaa and others valued them at Rs 29.8 crore. The High Court went one better: it valued them at Rs 25 crore. On all items except one, in effect the High Court accepted the valuation of the DVAC and the trial court. Only on new and additional construction did it take a different view: while the DVAC and the trial court had estimated additional and new construction to be worth Rs 28 crore, the High Court pulled the estimate down drastically—to Rs 5 crore. This figure was even less than the value estimated by Jayalalithaa and associates.

First of all, even if the estimate was accepted, the total value of the assets came to Rs 43.75 crore rather than the Rs 25 crore that the High Court made them out to be.

Second, how did the High Court alight on a figure of Rs 5 crore for additional and new construction rather than the Rs 28 crore that the DVAC and the trial court had estimated it to be? By three simple devices. First, it excluded four of the twenty-one items that had been identified. Second, it hived off a quarter of the area that had been constructed. The third device was the most delicious: in estimating the cost of constructing the most prominent structure—in which marble and granite had been used liberally, and which was studded with other expensive fixtures—it took, as the basis of calculating, the cost per square foot of constructing the sentry shed outside the building! As a result, in a typical instance, the cost of installing an Otis lift came to be taken as Rs 15,000 only! In the event, Kumaraswamy's estimate of the value of new and additional construction came to be less than the estimate that even the accused had furnished: they had claimed the value to be Rs 8.6 crore; the High Court placed the value at Rs 5.1

crore! *Gavah chust, muddai sust.* The Supreme Court found that there was just no basis for what Kumaraswamy had done—that his estimates were neither realistic nor rational, that they were 'patently erroneous', they were 'visibly wrong', and deserved to be rejected.

Kumaraswamy was equally helpful in regard to the expenditure on that nephew's marriage: the accused had said that Rs 3 crore had been spent; after examining each of the items on which money had been paid, the prosecution had said that double that amount—Rs 6.4 crore—had been spent; Kumaraswamy slashed the expenditure to Rs 28.7 lakh. Having re-examined the evidence, the Supreme Court observed, 'On an overall consideration of the evidence adduced by the parties, we are inclined to hold that the computation of the expenditure incurred by A1 [Jayalalithaa] in the marriage as made by the High Court is unacceptable in the teeth of the materials on record to the contrary.'

Such slashing was not just a random swinging of the sword: it inevitably left a larger pool of resources from which assets could be said to have been acquired by Jayalalithaa and associates.

The next item on which there was a substantial difference was the set of immovable properties that Jayalalithaa and associates had acquired. The trial court had estimated these to be worth Rs 20 crore. Kumaraswamy slashed the value down to Rs 6.2 crore. Even Jayalalithaa and associates had valued them at Rs 16.2 crore.

How did Kumaraswamy accomplish this? Simplicity itself. Properties had been acquired through 146 sale deeds. The High Court looked at only ninety-seven of these, and just shut its eyes to forty-nine sale deeds.

But there was so much more to the acquisition of these properties—features that had a direct bearing on the charge of conspiracy. Evidence had been brought on record during the trial that the purchases of property had been 'uneven bargains'; the properties had been undervalued; officers of the state administration had been tasked to locate properties that could be acquired; often the name of the purchaser was not disclosed—indeed, some of the sale-purchase deeds had been registered without any mention of the name of the purchaser. As we learn from the Supreme Court judgment:

> Evidence on record disclosed that instructions were issued from the higher authorities to the Registrars/Sub-Registrars to respond to the directions issued from the office of A1 [Jayalalithaa] for documentation and registration of the deeds involving such purchases and as a matter of fact, on various occasions, such precepts did come and were readily complied with.

In a typical case, the district registrar admitted that 'he proceeded with the registration solely because the properties were purchased by A1…' The Supreme Court further noted:

> The evidence of PW47, PW 71 and PW 159 taken together attest that officials were used to locate and purchase lands at various places…
>
> …the vendors were kept unaware of the purchasers' identity and in some cases were also put under duress to agree to the transactions. Their statements also divulge that not only was A1 [Jayalalithaa] aware of these transactions but on several occasions, the registrations thereof were performed at her residence.
>
> …The Trial Court rightly remarked as well, referring to the evidence of PW 159 Sub-Registrar, North Beach, Sub-Registrar's Office, and PW71 Radha Krishnan, Horticulture Officer, that they were called to Poes Garden and on the instructions of higher officers, they did oblige A1 even by relaxing the rules in the registration of large number of documents by taking personal interest and even overlooking that the properties were undervalued to hold a deep-seated involvement of A1 in these transactions. That the registering authorities had gone to the extent of permitting registration of six documents even without incorporating the names of the purchasers, was referred to.

To camouflage the purchases, they were registered in the names of the firms that Jayalalithaa, together with Sasikala, had set up. Examination showed that the firms had not had any funds for the purchases, that the funds had—nominally—come from other front companies and their activities—*Namadhu MGR* of Jaya Publications, etc. The companies in whose names the properties were registered had maintained no regular books of account, they had filed no income tax returns from the date of their incorporation to the date on which their properties were attached. No sale-purchase deed had the seal of any of these companies, none had the signatures of either the secretary or a director of the company. Enormous amounts had flown into the accounts of these so-called companies, but they could not explain why such funds had come into their accounts. A single passage from the Supreme Court judgment summarizing the findings of the trial court will give a flavour of what was going on:

> The Trial Court held the view that the respondents in the case in hand had failed to offer any satisfactory explanation with regard to the enormous unexplained credit/accumulations in their bank accounts. It rejected the confirmatory letter offered by the respondents as false and bogus and further held that the identity of the person who disclosed the source, had also not been proved. Further the transactions which generated such cash credits were also not established. It rejected as well the balance sheet and the profit and loss statement claimed to have been filed before the income tax authorities and on which the respondents primarily relied as their defence, as not proved in accordance with law besides being not in conformity with the statutory prescriptions. It discarded as well the evidence of the auditors examined by the respondents who, as the evidence on record testified, were not conversant with the true facts and had not handled their accounts during the check period. The Trial Court returned the finding that the evidence on record cumulatively substantiated that the returns, the balance sheet and the profit and loss accounts were framed and fashioned to offer an explanation to the otherwise titanic unexplained credits in their respective bank accounts. The Trial Court thus held that the respondents had failed to prove their defence, when tested on the evidence adduced even by the standard of preponderance of probability.

All these facts pointed to Jayalalithaa, Sasikala and her relatives having acted in concert in pursuance of a conspiracy. There were other telling details that pointed to the same fact. So many of the 'firms' had been registered on the same day. So many of them had given the same address. Officers used to go to the Poes Garden residence of the chief minister for enabling purchases and registering documents. Banks and persons associated with the 'firms' were given 'a blanket instruction' by the chief minister that they should act in accordance with instructions that Sasikala would give them from time to time. To top it all, there were massive inter-account exchanges—but the only cash that was actually coming in and then being distributed and redistributed into the accounts of the 'firms' was the cash that came via Jayalalithaa. This became so patent during the proceedings that not just the trial court, even Kumaraswamy treated the accounts, income, assets and expenditures as belonging to one entity. No objection was raised on behalf of the accused. And yet Kumaraswamy declared that there was neither abetment nor conspiracy.

No surprise then that the Supreme Court restored D'Cunha's judgment in its entirety and threw out the High Court judgment just as completely:

> After analysing the facts and circumstances of this case and after taking into consideration all the evidence placed before us and the arguments put forward by all the parties, we are of the unhesitant opinion that the impugned judgment and order rendered by the High Court is untenable and is thus set aside. We have considered the facts of this case and in our opinion, the percentage of disproportionate assets as 8.12% as computed by the High Court is based on completely wrong reading of the evidence on record compounded by incorrect arithmetical calculations...

By the time the Supreme Court judgment came, Jayalalithaa had died. Kumaraswamy had retired. The consolations were that the courage and meticulousness of a trial court judge had been upheld, and that at least Sasikala was sent to jail.

As for the judges, three lessons strike one. First and foremost, the ultimate judgment of Justices Ghose and Roy gives one confidence that the Supreme Court is there to see that eventually justice will be done. Yet that reassurance itself underlines an imperative: everyone—from important personages like judges to ordinary citizens like us—must be ever watchful, and fight off any and every attempt, from outside the court or within, to breach this last dyke. Second, as we have seen earlier, mechanical solutions will not do. Both Kumaraswamy and D'Cunha had been elevated step by step from the cadre of district judges. Unlike C.S. Karnan, whom we will encounter later, neither had been picked unknown from the Bar. Third, if a High Court judge could resort to such incredible distortions in such a conspicuous case—the judgment on which, he might have apprehended, would be scrutinized far and wide—what was he not capable of doing in run-of-the-mill cases, judgments on which, he could be confident, would not attract attention other than of the parties directly affected? Or is there reason for such a judge to feel confident that his judgment even in such a prominent case will scarcely be read, that there may be criticism here and there but that the matter will soon be forgotten, and he will have proceeded to greener pastures?

3

Prosecutor hunting, and other devices

The complaint against Jayalalithaa—that she had amassed assets beyond her known sources of income—was filed in June 1996. The first charge sheet was filed a year later, in June 1997.[1] The final verdict was delivered by the Supreme Court in February 2017—that is, *twenty years* after the charge sheet was filed. By that time, as we have seen, Jayalalitha had already died. That speaks of the condition of our courts, of course. But also of several other features.

Intertwined fortunes—political and legal

Consider first the effects of the fortunes of Jayalalithaa herself.[2] She was the chief minister from 1991 to 1996. From 1997, her opponents, the Dravida Munnetra Kazhagam (DMK), were in office. Tasked by the DMK, the Directorate of Vigilance and Anti-Corruption carried out investigations. In 1997, a case was

1 There was one more charge sheet relating to the purchase of a hotel in London. We will come to that in a moment. For now, all we need to note is that in the end it was not pursued.

2 In addition to the chronologies and facts mentioned in judgments of the Supreme Court, I have relied on the account set out by one of the heroes of the case, the distinguished senior advocate, B.V. Acharya, in his memoir, *All From Memory: An Autobiography,* Universal Law Publishing, 2014, in particular Chapter XXV and Appendix V.

registered against Jayalalithaa and three others. A special court was constituted to try the case. In what was to be the pattern for the next twenty years, Jayalalithaa and the other accused promptly approached the Supreme Court and challenged the decision to set up a special court. The Supreme Court rejected the challenge.[3] The trial proceeded before a special judge in Chennai. Two hundred and fifty-nine witnesses were examined for the prosecution. Only ten more needed to be examined. In May 2001, Jayalalithaa became the chief minister again. But soon enough, the Supreme Court held that she could not be chief minister as she had been found guilty of corruption in an earlier case.[4] She had to vacate her office in September 2001. A factotum chosen by her became chief minister. A while later, the conviction was set aside. She won a by-election, and returned as chief minister in February 2002.

Thereupon, as the Supreme Court was to note later, 'The trial ... went through some kind of a legal tumult...'[5] The investigating officer, the senior advocate representing the state, as well as three public prosecutors all resigned. Jayalalithaa's government appointed a new team, including a new public prosecutor. The special judge who had been trying the case also happened to get changed. 'It must be mentioned, even though we are sure that it has nothing to do with the change in government,' the Supreme Court noted in a case to which we shall come in a moment, 'that due to retirements and routine transfers there were changes in the Special Judge also.'

The trial had come to a stop from February 2002. It resumed only in November. Seventy-six witnesses were recalled for re-examination, 'on the ground that counsel appearing for the respondents [Jayalalithaa & Co.] or some of them had earlier been busy in some other case filed against them,' the Supreme Court noted. Out of the seventy-six, sixty-four witnesses now resiled from what they had stated on oath earlier. The new public prosecutor did not object to their being recalled. He did not declare them hostile. He did not seek to question them as he was entitled to do under Section 154 of the Indian Evidence Act—the section that provides,

---

3 *J. Jayalalitha v. Union of India,* (1999) 5 SCC 138.

4 *B.R. Kapur v. State of Tamil Nadu,* (2001) 7 SCC 231.

5 In *K. Anbazhagan v. State of Karnataka,* (2015) 6 SCC 158, para 5.

'The Court may, in its discretion, permit the person who calls a witness to put any questions to him which might be put in cross-examination by the adverse party.' He did not request the court to proceed against them for perjury.

The Supreme Court steps in

The general secretary of the DMK, K. Anbazhagan, brought these and other facts before the Supreme Court. The facts showed that a fair trial was no longer possible in Tamil Nadu, he affirmed, and pleaded that the case may be transferred to a court in any other state. In its judgment,[6] the Supreme Court took serious note of these facts. It observed that the ground that had been given for recalling the witnesses—that some of the counsel had been busy in some other case at the time of their examination and cross-examination—'could hardly have been a ground for recall of witnesses'. It noted the conduct of the new public prosecutor—that he had raised no objection, that he had not taken recourse to Section 154 of the Indian Evidence Act, that he had neither moved to declare them hostile nor to have them prosecuted for perjury. After reviewing the facts and earlier judgments on the matter as well as the relevant provisions of law, the court was emphatic:

> ... As revealed from the aforesaid recital of the facts, great prejudice appears to have been caused to the prosecution which could culminate in grave miscarriage of justice. The witnesses who had been examined and cross-examined earlier should on such flimsy ground never have been recalled for cross-examination. The fact that it is done after the second respondent [in this instance, Jayalalithaa] assumed power as the Chief Minister of the state and the Public Prosecutor appointed by her Government did not oppose and/or give consent to the application for recall of witnesses is indicative of how judicial process is being subverted. The Public Prosecutor neither resorting to Section 154 of the Indian Evidence Act nor making any application to take action

6 *K. Anbazhagan v. Superintendent of Police,* (2004) 3 SCC 767.

> in perjury taken against the witnesses also indicates that trial is not proceeding fairly. It was the duty of the Public Prosecutor to have first strenuously opposed any application for recall and in any event to have confronted the witnesses with their statements recorded under Section 161 of CrPC[7] and their examination-in-chief. No attempt was made to elicit or find out whether witnesses were resiling because they are now under pressure to do so. It does appear that the new Public Prosecutor is hand in glove with the accused thereby creating a reasonable apprehension of likelihood of failure of justice in the minds of the public at large. There is strong indication that the process of justice is being subverted.

The court recalled earlier judgments in which it had been held that even if a witness resiles from what he had deposed earlier, '...his evidence cannot, as a matter of law, be treated as washed off the record altogether. It is for the judge to consider whether as a result of such cross-examination [by the public prosecutor] and contradiction, the witness stands thoroughly discredited or can still be believed in regard to a part of his testimony...' But when the public prosecutor does not even cross-examine such a witness 'the court may find it difficult if not impossible to accept the earlier statement. The Trial Judge may find it difficult not to

7 The relevant Section of the Code of Criminal Procedure provides: '161. Examination of witnesses by police.—(1) Any police officer making an investigation under this Chapter, or any police officer not below such rank as the State Government may, by general or special order, prescribe in this behalf, acting on the requisition of such officer, may examine orally any person supposed to be acquainted with the facts and circumstances of the case.

'(2) Such person shall be bound to answer truly all questions relating to such case put to him by such officer, other than questions the answers to which would have a tendency to expose him to a criminal charge or to a penalty or forfeiture.

'(3) The police officer may reduce into writing any statement made to him in the course of an examination under this section; and if he does so, he shall make a separate and true record of the statement of each such person whose statement he records...'

3 [Provided that statement made under this sub-section may also be recorded by audio-video electronic means...]

accept the subsequent testimony of the witness, which has remained uncontroverted. This causes great prejudice to the prosecution culminating in great miscarriage of justice.'

The judges came to similar conclusions regarding the application of Jayalalithaa not to be examined in person but via a questionnaire through counsel. It had been submitted on behalf of Jayalalithaa that she was exhausted after electioneering in a by-election. Of course, the public prosecutor had not opposed the application. 'In our view,' the judges held, 'the grounds recited in the application ... were not at all mitigating circumstances to have granted dispensation of personal appearance. To say the least, that was a ploy adopted to circumvent the due process of law ... The conduct of the Public Prosecutor in not opposing such a frivolous application has to be deprecated.'

Accordingly, they directed that the case be shifted to the neighbouring state of Karnataka. Henceforth, in consultation with the Chief Justice of the Karnataka High Court, the Government of Karnataka would constitute a special court for the case, it would appoint the public prosecutor, and so on. In a word, all duties for the conduct of the case that would have been the responsibility of the Government of Tamil Nadu would now devolve on the Government of Karnataka. In view of what had happened in regard to those sixty-four witnesses who had resiled, while listing its directions, the court specifically said,

> (f) The Public Prosecutor will be at liberty to apply that the witnesses who have been recalled and cross-examined by the accused and who have resiled from their previous statement, may be again recalled. The Public Prosecutor will be at liberty to apply to the court to have these witnesses declared hostile and to seek permission to cross-examine them. Any such application if made to the Special Court shall be allowed. The Public Prosecutor will also be at liberty to apply that action for perjury to be taken against some or all such witnesses. Any such application(s) will be undoubtedly considered on merits.

The special court was duly constituted. The Karnataka government appointed B.V. Acharya as the special public prosecutor (SPP). Known for his fairness, thoroughness and rectitude, in his distinguished career at the Bar, Acharya was advocate general for five terms, and handled several crucial cases.

A DEVICE

That was in November 2003. The accused now remembered, perhaps in response to a query from the new special judge, that in February the previous year they had filed an application that this case—of Jayalalithaa & Co. having acquired assets disproportionate to their known sources of income—should be clubbed with that other case—that of their having acquired the hotel in London. Acharya filed objections: the accused had themselves waived the claim that was now being advanced, he pointed out; no objection had been filed on their behalf for three years. 'Moreover, while the wealth case has reached the final stage of trial, in the London hotel case even the charges have not been framed,' he pointed out. Clubbing the two cases at this stage would drag out the trial indefinitely. And the Madras High Court had earlier approved the procedure that had been adopted by the trial court judge in Chennai.

The special judge, however, decided that the two cases should be merged, and be tried as one case. Acharya described the consequence:

> The effect of the order was that on merger of records of two cases there was only one new case and proceedings had to commence afresh. Immediately, one after the other accused went on filing applications for discharge, as with the merger of the cases, the case had to commence from the stage of framing charges and before that every accused had a right to seek discharge.

This was in 2005—by this device, two years had been gained since the special court had begun its hearings. The DMK's general secretary filed an appeal in the Supreme Court against the merger of the two cases. The Supreme Court took the appeal on board, and stayed all proceedings of the case. For a year, Acharya notes, neither the accused nor the respondents were served, 'and even after the service, completion of the pleadings, the Supreme Court went on adjourning the case and did not finally decide the appeal till as late as January 2010. Hence, these cases were pending before the Special Judge for about five years without any progress.'

After strenuous efforts, Acharya succeeded in delinking the London hotel case. He could now focus on the disproportionate assets case. He recalled twenty-one witnesses. 'The process of recalling witnesses took a very long time,' Acharya recorded, 'as several interlocutory applications were filed on behalf of the accused seeking several reliefs and there were several criminal petitions before the High Court and SLPs[8] filed before the Supreme Court challenging the orders of the trial court.'

Though at a pace slower than that of a snail, the trial proceeded. In May 2011, Jayalalithaa again became the chief minister. Somersaults commenced again. The Directorate of Vigilance and Anti-Corruption of the Tamil Nadu government now decided that it had to carry out 'further investigations', and that it would henceforth have another counsel to represent it. Acharya strenuously opposed these somersaults. The matter went to the High Court. The High Court upheld Acharya's position on both counts. The directorate challenged these orders in the Supreme Court. That court also upheld Acharya's position.

Two-pronged assault

Attacks now commenced from two directions. First, a petition was filed with the governor that Acharya should not be allowed to hold two posts at the same time—that of advocate general and special public prosecutor. Petitions were simultaneously filed in the High Court seeking the same outcome—one of the petitions was a public interest litigation (PIL)! Furthermore, two petitions were filed before the special judge alleging malpractices in an educational trust of which Acharya was the chairman, and seeking a CBI inquiry. The judge gave a peculiar order. The High Court stayed the order. There were further twists and turns. Eventually the High Court struck down the petition that had sought to embarrass

8 Special leave petitions.

Acharya and besmirch his reputation by alleging malpractices in the educational trust.

And those petitions asserting that two posts should not be held simultaneously? The 'vested interests'—as Acharya refers to them out of politeness—had expected that, pressed into a corner, Acharya would give up his position as the special public prosecutor. He surprised them: he resigned from his post as advocate general!

But his heart was no longer in the case. Even though he realized that were he to give up his position as the special public prosecutor he would be helping those 'vested interests' attain their objective, he resigned. The Government of Karnataka tried to make him change his mind. He stuck to his decision.

The acting Chief Justice's suggestion

The Karnataka government then approached the acting Chief Justice of the High Court for appointing a successor to Acharya. It proposed four possible names. The acting Chief Justice asked them to consider appointing another person, G. Bhavani Singh, even though his name was not in the list submitted by the Karnataka government. Accordingly, in February 2013, the Karnataka government appointed G. Bhavani Singh as the one to argue the case.

He had been special public prosecutor-2 earlier before the High Court. However, in the present case, the trial judge, Michael D'Cunha, was to note that apart from just reading out pages that were already on record, Bhavani Singh made no other contribution. In fact, he did, says a senior: when the request on behalf of the accused for adjournments would be turned down, Bhavani Singh would ask for them! The trial judge was compelled to note that Bhavani Singh was not cooperating to ensure that the case progressed, and instead he had been placing impediments. At one stage—in March 2014—a heavy penalty of Rs 120,000 was levied on him: as the fee he was receiving was Rs 60,000 a day, the fine was fixed at two days' fee. The High Court confirmed the fine. An appeal was filed in the Supreme Court. The Supreme Court upheld the order, though it reduced the fine to Rs 20,000. In its judgment, the trial court was constrained to observe that while the senior counsel for accused no. 1—Jayalalithaa—had argued for about eighty hours, the public prosecutor had only read out the examination-in-chief of the prosecution witnesses and with that concluded his arguments.

The accused get to choose the prosecutor

By now, the continuation of Bhavani Singh had become an embarrassment. On 26 August 2013, the Government of Karnataka issued a notification withdrawing the appointment of Bhavani Singh as SPP. It did not assign any reason, and it did so without having consulted the Chief Justice of Karnataka.

The accused—Jayalalithaa, etc.—approached the Supreme Court against the removal of Bhavani Singh. Those who had not been following what had been happening in the trial court would say 'surprisingly the accused approached the Supreme Court ...' The accused argued that doing so would delay the trial, and the Supreme Court itself had directed that the trial be concluded expeditiously. You have to appreciate the audacity of the argument: here were the very persons who had been dragging the case out by every conceivable device for over *fifteen years* arguing that a step was wrong, as it would prolong the trial!

On 30 August 2013, the Supreme Court issued a notice to the Karnataka government and added, 'In the meanwhile, no fresh appointment to the post of Special Public Prosecutor be made.'

Caught on the wrong foot, on 10 September 2013, the Karnataka government withdrew the notification it had issued on 26 August, so that, it now said, it may, in accordance with the earlier orders of the Supreme Court, consult the Chief Justice of the Karnataka High Court. Simultaneously, it issued a letter to Bhavani Singh not to appear before the special judge.

Jayalalithaa, etc., swiftly—on 13 September—approached the Supreme Court against the new notification, the one that the Karnataka government had issued three days earlier, as well as the letter to Bhavani Singh. The Supreme Court stayed the notification.

The Karnataka government now took another ham-handed step: on 14 September, even as Jayalalithaa's writ was pending before the

Supreme Court, it approached the Chief Justice of the Karnataka High Court in regard to the removal of Bhavani Singh. By a letter, the Chief Justice, Karnataka, concurred with the proposal that Bhavani Singh no longer continue as SPP.

Thus armed, on 16 September, the Karnataka government issued a new notification removing Bhavani Singh as SPP. Jayalalithaa, etc., now approached the Supreme Court challenging this new notification. The challenge was heard by Justice Dr B.S. Chauhan and Justice S.A. Bobde.[9] On behalf of Jayalalithaa and Co., the counsel argued that the Supreme Court had itself directed that the trial proceed expeditiously,[10] that this manoeuvre of removing the SPP was designed to delay the trial—especially as the trial court judge was due to retire within a few days, on the 30th of that very month. They argued that delay in the trial would jeopardize the rights of the accused under Article 21 of the Constitution; this, as I just mentioned, from persons who had been adopting every device under the sun—and the moon—to drag out the trial. The irony aside, the Supreme Court saw merit in one part of their claim—that, with the record of the trial now running into 34,000 pages, a new special judge or, by implication, a new prosecutor would necessarily take time to acquaint himself with the matters on record. 'Accordingly, we have no hesitation in holding that the notification purporting to revoke the appointment of Shri G. Bhavani Singh as SPP is liable to be struck down.' It was further argued on behalf of Jayalalithaa and Co. that Bhavani Singh had been functioning as SPP for six months—the Karnataka government had not objected. The reason they were objecting to his continuance now was different: in May 2013, there had been a change in the government in Karnataka, and this was what lay

9 For the following, *J. Jayalalithaa v. State of Karnataka,* (2014) 2 SCC 401.

10 In its order delivered in November 2003 on *K. Anbazhagan v. Superintendent of Police*, op. cit., the Supreme Court had observed, inter alia, 'As the matter is pending since 1997 the State of Karnataka shall appoint a Special Judge within a month from the date of receipt of this order and the trial before the Special Judge shall commence as soon as possible and will then proceed from day to day till completion.'

behind his removal.[11] This argument also seemed to resonate with the Supreme Court bench for, citing an earlier judgment, it observed:

> The principles of governance have to be tested on the touchstone of justice, equity and fair play. A decision may look legitimate but as a matter of fact, if the reasons are not based on values but to achieve popular accolade, the decision cannot be allowed to operate. Therefore, unless it is found that the act done by the authority earlier in existence is either contrary to the statutory provisions or unreasonable, or is against public interest, the State should not change its stand merely because the other political party has come into power. Political agenda of an individual or a political party should not be subversive of rule of law.

—words so apt for the chief minister of Tamil Nadu, and what she had done in regard to this case after returning to power in February 2002!

But there was another twist to the matter. On behalf of the Karnataka government, the attorney general, G.E. Vahanvati, advanced as his principal argument one that was just asking to be struck down. He argued that the ab initio appointment of Bhavani Singh was not made after due consultation with the Chief Justice of the Karnataka High Court as directed by the Supreme Court. His reasoning was that Bhavani Singh's name had not figured in the list of four whom the government had recommended to the acting Chief Justice. The Supreme Court was compelled to characterize this argument as 'rather unusual'—after all, the government had adopted the name suggested by the acting Chief Justice, and issued the notification appointing Bhavani Singh;

11 B.V. Acharya was appointed as special public prosecutor in 2003; S.M. Krishna of the Congress was the chief minister at the time. The BJP came to office in Karnataka in May 2008. B.V. Acharya resigned in December 2012. The BJP government, with Jagadish Shettar as chief minister, tried to persuade him to continue. He declined. Bhavani Singh was appointed as special public prosecutor in February 2013; Jagadish Shettar of the BJP was still chief minister—his term as CM lasted from 12 July 2012 to 12 May 2013. In May 2013, the Congress returned to power with Siddaramaiah as chief minister.

moreover, it had not raised any objection to his appearing in the case for six months. 'It is not legitimate for the party who has the duty to consult and who has failed in that duty, to make a grievance that there has been no consultation ... There is nothing on record to indicate that the Government of Karnataka has been forced by anyone to make the said appointment. The Government thus voluntarily acquiesced in the process and is now not entitled to raise this grievance. The grievance is thus baseless and does not carry any conviction.'

On such considerations, Justice Chauhan, on behalf of the two judges, declared that 'we are of the considered opinion that the order of removal of Shri G. Bhavani Singh ... is a product of *mala fides* and the impugned order is not sustainable in the eye of the law, as such the same is hereby quashed.'

The net result? The accused got to choose the public prosecutor![12]

The accused fight to retain a prosecutor

In any event, as we have seen, with the help of or in spite of the public prosecutor, Judge D'Cunha roundly indicted Jayalalithaa and her associates—in a judgment that stands as an example of a meticulous examination of the facts.

Jayalalithaa and associates filed appeals in the Karnataka High Court. We have already seen how the High Court saw such great merit in their appeals—sometimes even outdoing the averments of the accused! But at the moment, we have to traverse another proceeding.

Bhavani Singh had been appearing on occasion to handle the case in the trial court. The question now was whether, by virtue of having appeared in the trial court, he was automatically entitled to handle the appeals in the High Court. Or, considering his

---

12 As for the delay that might be caused by the retirement of the special judge, the Supreme Court explained that the extant rules permitted the government to extend his services on a contractual basis. The government requested him to continue. But he declined. Judge Michael D'Cunha was selected by the High Court to hear the case henceforth.

sterling performance, could the appointing authority, the Karnataka government, appoint someone else to do so?

In the appeals that they filed in the Karnataka High Court, Jayalalithaa and Co. did not make the Government of Karnataka a party. The Government of Karnataka had been given sole charge of conducting the case. But, perhaps on the specious reasoning that it had not been made a party in the appeals, it did not move immediately to appoint the SPP who was to handle the appeals in the High Court.

'On the other hand, Tamil Nadu acted with remarkable alacrity,' Justice Madan B. Lokur was to note later, 'and on 29-9-2014 [that is, within *two days* of D'Cunha pronouncing his judgment] the Principal Secretary to the Government of Tamil Nadu passed an Order authorising the Directorate of Vigilance and Anti-Corruption, Chennai, to engage the services of Mr. Bhavani Singh, Special Public Prosecutor to appear before the High Court of Karnataka for and on behalf of the said Directorate in any appeal/bail petition, any other petition that may arise out of the conviction of the accused persons.'

K. Anbazhagan of the DMK now sent a representation to the chief secretary against this step. As he received no reply, he filed a writ in the Karnataka High Court against Bhavani Singh continuing to argue the matter. He maintained that the Supreme Court had given the power to appoint a special public prosecutor for this case only to the Government of Karnataka. After Acharya had resigned, the Karnataka government had appointed Bhavani Singh to handle the case only in the trial court. That government had not issued any notification appointing Bhavani Singh to argue against the appeals in the High Court. Jayalalithaa and Co. argued that he had been appointed to handle the 'case', and 'case' encompasses all stages—including inquiry, trial, appeals, etc.—until it reaches a finality and the accused are either convicted or discharged.

The High Court held that, indeed, the Supreme Court had given all powers in regard to the conduct of the case to the Karnataka government. The Government of Tamil Nadu had no role in the matter. Hence, its order appointing Bhavani Singh to argue the appeals 'is without authority and *non est* in the eye of the law. That order did not confer any right on the fifth respondent [Bhavani Singh] to represent either the state of Karnataka or the state of Tamil Nadu in the pending appeals before this Court.' But on the other hand, the High Court held, the relevant section of the Criminal Procedure Code—Section 301(1)—authorizes the person appointed to handle a case to appear in 'any court' in regard to that case, and that would include arguing in the High Court. Once he is appointed, he is in charge of the case till it reaches a finality, and can appear, without any further written authorization, in any court.[13] Because of this latter fact, Bhavani Singh could continue to appear on behalf of the Government of Karnataka in regard to the appeals against the trial court judgment, even though the government had not authorized him to do so by any fresh communication.[14]

The judges disagree

There was no dispute about the fact that Tamil Nadu did not have the authority to appoint Bhavani Singh. The question was about what the Criminal Procedure Code provided. That brought the dispute to the Supreme Court. Two judges heard arguments, and came to opposite conclusions. Justice Lokur held that Bhavani Singh did not have authority to represent the state of Karnataka. Justice R. Banumathi, on the other hand, held that Bhavani Singh could continue through all stages of the case, till it reached finality in the conviction or discharge of the accused.

Justice Lokur pointed out that the original notification of the Karnataka government by which Bhavani Singh was appointed was specific, and it had appointed him to handle the case only in the trial court—the notification had stated that he was being appointed 'to conduct Special CC No. 208 of 2004 (in the case of Kumari Jayalalithaa and others) pending on the file of XXXVIth Additional

---

13 The relevant sub-section reads, '301. Appearance by Public Prosecutors: (1) The Public Prosecutor or Assistant Public Prosecutor in charge of a case may appear and plead without any written authority before any Court in which that case is under inquiry, trial or appeal.'

14 *K. Anbazhagan v. State of Karnataka,* Writ Appeal No. 260 of 2015, decided on 11 February 2015 (KAR).

Civil and Sessions Court (Special Court) Bangalore'. The Supreme Court's direction too was limited to proceedings in the special court. If Bhavani Singh was automatically entitled to deal with the appeals in the High Court, Justice Lokur pointed out, where was the need for the Government of Tamil Nadu to issue a new order and appoint him to do so?

When appeals were filed, the Karnataka government could have come back to the Supreme Court asking for a clarification of its directions or for fresh directions about the procedure to be followed for appointing a special public prosecutor for proceedings in the High Court, Justice Lokur held. That it had not done so was 'unfortunate', it was 'a shirking of its duty and responsibility'. Perhaps they were confused, Justice Lokur allowed: it may be that as the state of Karnataka had not been made a party to the appeals, the government had not acted on the apprehension that, when it was not a party, by appointing a special public prosecutor it would be held to be interfering in a case with which it had no concern. This 'reason' was unjustified, Justice Lokur pointed out. 'But then, it was equally the duty and responsibility of Tamil Nadu to either take the opinion of Karnataka on the future course of action with regard to representation in the criminal appeals or to have brought the "vacuum" to the notice of the learned judge hearing the criminal appeals rather than rushing in with the ill-advised Order dated 29-9-2014. That Tamil Nadu sought to take advantage of a situation that ought not to have even existed is also unfortunate. However, to give it the benefit of doubt, it is possible that Tamil Nadu was also in a state of confusion.'

Either way, 'the directions given by this Court were limited only to the trial of the case before the Special Court in Bengaluru and even Karnataka understood the directions to be limited to the trial and acted only to that limited extent'. The notification that the Karnataka government had issued and which limited the role of Bhavani Singh to the case in the trial court 'correctly reflected the intent of this Court'.

As for reading Section 301(1) and others in the way that was being suggested, Justice Lokur pointed to several anomalous situations that could arise. The lower court would come to a decision. Those convicted would file appeals. The state would appoint a special public prosecutor to argue against those appeals in the High Court. But the prosecutor who had handled the case in the lower court could turn up in the High Court, assert that, though he had not been authorized by the state, by virtue of his initial appointment, he and not the special public prosecutor had the right to argue the matter, and he could support the appeals. Nor were such situations hypothetical, Justice Lokur pointed out:

> That such an eventuality is not theoretical is clear from the facts of this case itself. As mentioned above, the accused persons applied for suspension of the sentence. However, when the application was heard, the Special Public Prosecutor (Mr. Bhavani Singh) did not oppose the suspension of sentence. The learned Single Judge hearing the application recorded in his order rejecting the application as follows ...
>
> > '4. When the Special Public Prosecutor was asked as to whether he has any submission in this regard to make, he has openly submitted that he has no arguments to make and that the sentence may be suspended and the accused may be released on imposing conditions deemed fit under the circumstances of the case. But he did not make any submission as to whether he does not press the written objections already filed.'
>
> Had the State of Karnataka appointed a Public Prosecutor for the High Court to contest the appeals filed by the accused persons, it is quite possible that the said Public Prosecutor would have supported the written objections and opposed the suspension of sentence. In that event, there would have been a rather piquant situation (if not a spectacle)—the Special Public Prosecutor (Mr. Bhavani Singh) supporting suspension of the sentence of the accused persons and the Public Prosecutor for the High Court opposing suspension of the accused persons on the basis of written objections. Surely, Section 301(1) of the Code is not required to be interpreted in a manner so as to cause confusion.

Indeed, the person appointed to handle the matter in the lower court could appear in the High Court and argue that the public prosecutor be removed as he and he alone had the authority to deal with the 'case' in 'any court' right till the case reached finality. Other anomalies too could arise. Justice Lokur showed, for instance, that on the interpretation which was being pressed, Bhavani Singh as public prosecutor could be subordinate to the deputy director of prosecutions. For such anomalies not to arise, one must see what is plain—that the sections circumscribe jurisdictions for each appointment: a public prosecutor may be appointed to handle a case or a class of cases within a district, for instance. When he is so appointed, by virtue of the sections, the public prosecutor is entitled to attend to matters relating to the case in any court *in that district*. It is in this sense that he does not need a fresh written authorization as he moves from court to court within that jurisdiction.

Jayalalithaa and Co. pressed another argument, 'the doctrine of *de facto*'. The fact, they said, was that Bhavani Singh, the special public prosecutor for whose continuance they, the ones who had been convicted, were arguing, had been appearing in the High Court in regard to the appeals. Justice Lokur turned down this argument neatly: 'If Mr. Bhavani Singh is not authorised to represent the prosecution in the High Court in the appeals filed by the accused persons, he simply cannot do so and if he does so, the accused persons cannot put forward a *fait accompli* or rely upon the *de facto* doctrine and say: so be it.'

For reasons such as these Justice Lokur concluded that the 'overbroad opinion expressed by the High Court' could not be accepted.

Justice Banumathi agreed with Justice Lokur as far as the order of the Tamil Nadu government was concerned, by which it had authorized the Directorate of Vigilance and Anti-Corruption to engage Bhavani Singh to represent it in the appeals: given the directions that the Supreme Court had given while transferring the case to Karnataka, the state of Tamil Nadu had no authority to appoint Bhavani Singh to represent the DVAC for arguing on the appeals in the High Court, she held. But she came to the opposite conclusion as regards the authority of Bhavani Singh to argue the appeals in the Karnataka High Court by virtue of his having been appointed by the Karnataka government to assist in the trial court.

Her reasoning was two-pronged.

First was her reading of the law. She held that public prosecutors can be of three types:

> By a plain reading of Section 24 CrPC, three main types of Public Prosecutors are discernible: *First* are those who are attached to a particular High Court, district or local area; *second* are those who are attached to a particular case or class of cases but in a specified jurisdiction and *lastly,* the one appointed to a particular case or class of cases. The last category belongs to 'Special Public Prosecutor' appointed under sub-section (8) of Section 24 CrPC, in which there is no mention about the jurisdiction/territory in which the Special Public Prosecutor has to conduct the case or class of cases. The limitation of acting in [a] particular court or area is conspicuously absent in the provision of Section 24(8) CrPC, when compared with other provisions.[15]

Hence, once Bhavani Singh was appointed as special public prosecutor to conduct the case, he could appear without any further

---

15 For the contrasting conclusions of the judges, the following sub-sections of Section 24 of the Code of Criminal Procedure are relevant. They read as follows:

> 24. Public Prosecutors.—(1) For every High Court, the Central Government or the State Government shall, after consultation with the High Court, appoint a Public Prosecutor and may also appoint one or more Additional Public Prosecutors, for conducting in such Court, any prosecution, appeal or other proceeding on behalf of the Central Government or State Government, as the case may be.
> (2) The Central Government may appoint one or more Public Prosecutors for the purpose of conducting any case or class of cases in any district or local area.
> (3) For every district, the State Government shall appoint a Public Prosecutor and may also appoint one or more Additional Public Prosecutors for the district:
> Provided that the Public Prosecutor or Additional Public Prosecutor appointed for one district may be appointed also to be a Public Prosecutor or an Additional Public Prosecutor, as the case may be, for another district...
> (8) The Central Government or the State Government may appoint, for the purposes of any case or class of cases, a person who has been in practice as an advocate for not less than ten years as a Special Public Prosecutor...

written authorization in any court where the case was under inquiry, trial or appeal. And, in fact, during the trial proceedings, writs, appeals, etc., had been filed on several occasions, and Bhavani Singh had argued the matter in the High Court. No one had raised an objection. But that did not quite meet the point that had appealed to Justice Lokur. For those appeals, etc., had arisen *during the course of the trial*—and the point at issue was that the appointment of Bhavani Singh, having been for the course of the trial, had ceased with the verdict having been delivered by the trial court.

To reinforce her conclusion, Justice Banumathi placed emphasis on the words used in Section 301: the public prosecutor was 'in charge of a case'; he could appear in 'any court'.

She also opted for the expansive meaning of the word 'case' used in the section—it covers inquiry, trial as well as appeals, she maintained. 'I am conscious that the term "case" in the Code at certain instances has been used to link only with "trial" and has been categorically distinguished with the term "appeal",' she herself noted. She also acknowledged that in several sections—like Sections 209, 406, 407, 409—the words 'case', 'trial', 'appeal' had been used to signify different stages of a case. But she got around that, holding that the legislature had left it to the courts to decide the ambit of the word 'case' with reference to the particular context in which it was being used and the one which they were considering. A slight giveaway there, I would have thought.

The judge soon remedied that. Having dealt at length with the ambit of the word 'case', she said:

> However, I am of the view that such authority of the Special Public Prosecutor to appear and plead a case in respect of which he is in charge in any court or at any stage of proceedings in such court may not emanate from the term 'case' of for that matter 'class of cases' as appearing under sub-section (8) of Section 24 CrPC, but for the reason of the broader context in which the term 'case' has been used in Section 301(1) CrPC to include any court in which that case is under 'inquiry, trial or appeal'. The Special Public Prosecutor, after the trial is over, derives its [sic] authority to continue to appear and plead before appellate forum

> by virtue of language used in sub-section (1) of Section 301 CrPC and the Special Public Prosecutor will continue to have such authority due to wide language of Section 301 CrPC, until the notification appointing him has been cancelled by the appropriate State Government.

Next, was her perception of the facts. Justice Banumathi adverted to the timing of the writ that had been filed objecting to Bhavani Singh appearing for the prosecution in regard to the appeals in the High Court. The trial court had given its verdict on 27 September 2014. Those who had been convicted had filed their appeals in the High Court on 29 September. Bhavani Singh had appeared for the state on the 30th. No objection had been filed. The next day, Bhavani Singh had filed his memo of appearance and filed objections to the accused being given bail. That matter of bail had gone twice up to the Supreme Court. It was only on 24 December 2014 that Anbazhagan had filed a representation before the Tamil Nadu government against their asking the DVAC to engage Bhavani Singh to represent it as special counsel in the High Court. And that date 'is interesting to note', Justice Banumathi remarked. 'The said representation [to the Tamil Nadu government] was made after this Court by its order dated 18-12-2014 had directed hearing of the appeals on a day-to-day basis and also fixed the period of three months for disposal of appeals.' Even then the Karnataka government did not come to the Supreme Court for clarification or consult with the Chief Justice of the Karnataka High Court for initiating the process of appointing a new special public prosecutor. It was only on 6 January 2015 that Anbazhagan filed a writ in the High Court, praying that some other senior counsel be appointed as special public prosecutor to represent the state of Karnataka. That too Justice Banumathi found 'interesting': 'Interestingly, here again the appellant chose to file the writ petition before the High Court instead of directly taking recourse to the jurisdiction of this Court [that is, the Supreme Court].' In fact, as the full bench was to note later, Anbazhagan had written to the Government of Karnataka as well as the Chief Justice of the Karnataka High Court, objecting to the appointment of Bhavani Singh as special public prosecutor. It is only when he had not received any reply that he had filed a writ in the Karnataka High Court.[16]

Even when the single judge rejected the plea, the Government of Karnataka did nothing, Justice Banumathi proceeded to note: it did not appeal against his order; it did not commence consultations with the High Court Chief Justice; it did not come to the Supreme Court for directions or, given its professed doubts about what it was supposed to do, for clarification.

Instead of directly coming to this court, Justice Banumathi observed, Anbazhagan appealed against the decision of the single judge to the division bench of the High Court. The division bench held that Bhavani Singh was entitled to continue especially in view of the direction of the Supreme Court that the appeals must be disposed of within three months. Even after this decision, the Karnataka government did not come to the Supreme Court: 'What the State did is that they took the shelter of the appeals filed by the appellant [Anbazhagan] and kept on rhyming about their inability to appoint a new Prosecutor/counsel to conduct the appeal proceedings. If the State of Karnataka was of the view that Mr. Bhavani Singh cannot continue to appear for the appeals, in consultation with the Chief Justice of the Karnataka High Court, it could have issued the notification appointing another Special Public Prosecutor or it could have sought direction from this Court. But that was not to be so…'[17]

By its 'inactive attitude' the state of Karnataka had failed to discharge its duty 'miserably', and the conduct of the appellant, Anbazhagan, 'lacks *bona fides*', Justice Banumathi concluded.

The quandary of laypeople

The reasons for going through the reasoning of the two judges would have become apparent by now. Both of them were faced with the same facts. They inferred different conclusions from them. Both cited the same provisions of law. They drew different

16 C.f., *K. Anbazhagan v. State of Karnataka,* (2015) 6 SCC 158, para 8.

17 In the relevant period, the government that was in office in Karnataka was the Congress government headed by Siddaramaiah.

deductions from them. Often, upon hearing submissions of lawyers, they reflected upon the same case that the court had decided earlier. One held that the case was 'not quite apposite', and gave cogent grounds for that conclusion. The other affirmed that the issue at hand—whether a special public prosecutor appointed under Section 24(8) appearing in the appeal might lead to an anomalous situation—'has been addressed and answered by a Constitution Bench' in that very case.[18]

From the point of view of judges and courts, that they often differ in what they infer from the facts, in what they glean from earlier judgments, and what they take the meaning of law to be is but natural. That is why we do not have just one judge. Nor are the judges robots. Each must exercise his own mind on facts and precedents and the law.

All true. But equally, from the point of view of the layperson who may get caught in the web of courts, this compounds uncertainty: it does lead to the apprehension that the outcome of his case will too often come to depend on chance—on before whom his case lands.

Another feature would strike him even more: the two empirical facts that would be conclusive for him—the conduct of the special public prosecutor in the trial court and the fact that *the accused who had been convicted* were the ones who were so eager to have him handle on behalf of the state their appeals in the High Court—weighed hardly at all in the conclusions that the judges reached. One judge let them intrude only by allusion. The other abjured looking at them altogether—though she did consider at quite some length the conduct of the appellant, Anbazhagan, and that of the Government of Karnataka. How did this self-denial—the decision not to look at the two most obvious facts—compare with what the Supreme Court had declared when it initially transferred the case to Karnataka? The court had said:

> Free and fair trial is *sine qua non* of Article 21 of the Constitution. It is trite law that justice should not only be done but it should

---

18 See the contrasting treatment of *State of Punjab v. Surjit Singh*, AIR 1967 SC 1214 in paras 86–89 and 158–59 of the judgment we are going through, *K. Anbazhagan v. State of Karnataka*, op. cit.

> be seen to have been done. If the criminal trial is not free and fair and not free from bias, judicial fairness and the criminal justice system would be at stake shaking the confidence of the public in the system and woe would be the rule of law. It is important to note that in such a case the question is not whether the petitioner is actually biased but the question is whether the circumstances are such that there is a reasonable apprehension in the mind of the petitioner.[19] In the present case, the circumstances as recited above are such as to create reasonable apprehension in the minds of the public at large in general and the petitioner in particular that there is every likelihood of failure of justice.[20]

—words that would apply to the T were Bhavani Singh, given his conduct in the trial court, to continue, as the accused/convicted so fervently wanted him to, and argue the appeals in the High Court.

Order of the full bench

In the event, as the two judges had come to different conclusions, they referred the matter to a larger bench. A bench of three judges—Justices Dipak Misra, R.K. Agarwal and Prafulla C. Pant—heard the matter. The judgment was delivered by Justice Dipak Misra.[21]

They observed how vital it was to scotch corruption from our public life. They noted the 'enormous anxiety' which had spurred the Government of Tamil Nadu to issue its order to enable Bhavani Singh to appear in the High Court, 'possibly being worried about the "borrowed troubles of future" and forgetting the age-old sagacious saying that "anxiety is the poison of human life".' On the import of sub-sections and sections of the Criminal Procedure Code, they upheld the conclusions that Justice Lokur had spelled

---

19 The petitioner in the case in which these observations were made was the same K. Anbazhagan who was the petitioner in the present case urging that Bhavani Singh would not assist in obtaining a fair consideration of appeals by the High Court.

20 In *K. Anbazhagan v. Superintendent of Police,* op. cit., para 30.

21 *K. Anbazhagan v. State of Karnataka,* (2015) 6 SCC 158.

out. As Justice Lokur had done, they also drew attention to Rule 30 of the Karnataka Law Officers (Appointments and Conditions of Service) Rules, 1977: it makes a distinction between a case and an appeal, they pointed out—'This Rule clarifies that if any counsel is to be appointed for the purpose of an appeal, the State Government may do so after consulting the authorities mentioned therein,' and that 'There is nothing on record that the fourth respondent [Bhavani Singh] was appointed to defend the prosecution in appeal in the High Court.'

They considered the opposing conclusions that Justice Lokur and Justice Banumathi had reached regarding the expressions 'case', 'any court', 'without any written authority'. They noted that Section 24(1) and 24(8) of the Criminal Procedure Code confer authority on the government to appoint public prosecutors and special public prosecutors. If by putting too wide a construction on the word 'case', one were to proceed on the premise that once a person had been appointed to represent the prosecution in a trial he automatically had the authority to represent the state at the appellate stage, 'it will be denuding the power of appointing authority. The law does not so countenance.' Agreeing with what Justice Lokur had held, they concluded:

> Therefore, much stress cannot be given on the words 'without any written authority' as used in Section 301. It can only mean that the Public Prosecutor once engaged/appointed by the State, he can prosecute the appeal without filing any formal authority for the said purpose. It cannot be construed to the extent that solely because he has been appointed in connection with the trial case, he can appear before the High Court for which he has not been appointed in pursuance of Section 24(1) CrPC. Section 301(1) CrPC cannot be stretched to that extent. In that event, it would really lead to an anomalous situation. A Public Prosecutor has to be specifically appointed for the appeals or revisions or other proceedings in the High Court. The anomalous situations, which have been highlighted by Lokur, J. have our respectful concurrence ... Therefore we ingeminate that a Public Prosecutor

> who is appointed to conduct a case before the Trial Court cannot be deemed to be appointed for the purpose of appeal arising therefrom solely because of the language employed in Section 301(1) CrPC.

Bhavani Singh, therefore, could not represent the prosecution in the High Court.

A LITTLE TWIST

But the judges turned down the further request that, given what had transpired, they should direct the High Court to hear the appeals de novo. They recalled what they had said about the importance of rooting out corruption from our public life, and expressed confidence that the single judge who was hearing the appeals would bear that imperative in mind.

As we have seen, they had underestimated Justice C.R. Kumaraswamy!

And there was a surprising twist to the order. The judges gave Anbazhagan leave to file written submissions in the High Court up to ninety pages, and to the Karnataka government leave to file written submissions up to sixty pages. But here was the strange part. The full bench delivered its order on 27 April 2015. While giving leave to Anbazhagan and the Government of Karnataka to file written submissions, the judges laid down that these must be filed by 28 April 2015—that is, *within one day* of their pronouncing the judgment!

The Karnataka government again approached Acharya and requested him to take over the case. He filed the written submissions by the next day.

Kumaraswamy was unaffected!

It is best to record the end of this sequence in the words of Acharya himself:

> I gave a written opinion strongly recommending that appeals be filed against the judgment of the High Court. The Advocate General also fully agreed with me. So did the Law Department. In

> spite of a lot of political pressure, the Government decided to file appeals and I was appointed as Special Counsel to argue before the Supreme Court. Accordingly, appeals were filed by me before the Supreme Court and the Supreme Court heard arguments from February 2016 to June 2016. In December 2016 Accused 1 [Jayalalithaa] expired.
>
> On 14.02.2017 the Supreme Court pronounced the judgment restoring the judgment of the Trial Court in toto, except for recording that the appeal as against A1 has abated. On behalf of the State of Karnataka a review petition was filed challenging the order that the appeal as against A1 had abated. This was dismissed.
>
> Since then, a curative petition has been filed in this regard. According to settled law there can be no abatement of appeal once arguments have been concluded and the judgment is reserved.

These developments were one part of the story—they give us a glimpse of how the fortunes of an accused, the political fortunes in this instance, as well as differences among judges over the most elementary points of law and procedure come to affect the journey of a case. But there was also another dimension, and that is what was being done by the lawyers for the accused in the different courts. That has lessons of its own.

Lawyerly devices

In theory, lawyers are, first and foremost, officers of the court. Ashok Desai, the former attorney general, recounts a conversation with Lord Bingham, later the Lord Chief Justice of England.

Ashok asked him, 'What would you do if a lawyer arguing in your court lied?'

Bingham didn't seem to understand the question. 'What do you mean, "if he lied"?' Bingham said. 'You mean if he did not know the law, and misrepresented it?'

'No, no. I mean that he *lied*—if he sought to advance his case with a falsehood?'

Bingham still couldn't get the point. Ashok explained yet again.

'But how could he lie?' Bingham asked, and added, 'Soon after the hearing, we would be assembling in the dining room of the Inns of Court having lunch together. If he had lied to me how would he look me in the eye? And it would get known that he had lied in court and that would be end of him.'

Bingham added that as an officer of the court, a lawyer has the further duty to be candid. He gave an illustration. A QC[22] had applied for an ex parte injunction against the imminent publication of a defamatory statement. The matter came up before a recently appointed judge who asked the counsel, 'Mr Smith, I am new to this jurisdiction. You are the expert in the field. Tell me if you have made such applications in the absence of the other side even on the ground of urgency.' The lawyer replied, 'Yes, my lord, on more than one occasion.' He paused, and added, 'But my lord, none of them were granted.' And that was the end of his application.

How different the world in which we live and move!

One of the reasons that the case took over twenty years was that at every turn, indeed at virtually every hearing, the lawyers appearing for Jayalalithaa and Co.—those 'officers of the Court'—moved one petition after another. They raised one objection after another. On occasion, when the objection or petition filed on behalf of one accused was rejected, lawyers representing the other three accused would take up the baton and file the same, or slightly altered objection or petition. And when these too were rejected, they would file appeals in the High Court.[23]

A special court cannot be set up for a case of this kind ... Taken right up to the Supreme Court ... The entire record of depositions and documents be made available in English ... The two cases be clubbed ... The order of the trial judge taking cognizance be struck down ... The schedule for the trial be refixed ... (This matter was taken all the way to the Supreme Court) ...

22 Senior advocate.

23 The list in the following paragraph reproduces some of the items in Appendix V of B.V. Acharya's *All From Memory*, op. cit., pp. 314–331.

The proceedings be dropped entirely as the investigation that was conducted was illegal ... The proceedings be adjourned as the special leave petition is coming up ... Three sets of copies of papers be supplied: each set numbered around 70,000 pages ... The English translations that have been supplied be scrapped, and new translations be supplied ... An interpreter be appointed ... Lawyers for accused be allowed to cross-examine the interpreter ... The attachment order be lifted ... Petition has been filed in the High Court, and that court has observed that the trial should not proceed ... Case should be adjourned to enable accused to approach the Supreme Court ... Translations of evidence tendered by some witnesses be corrected ... An expert be appointed for translation ... Mistakes be corrected in the new set of translations ... The case be adjourned for three weeks as the father of one of the counsel representing another accused has died ... Case be adjourned for six months to enable legal teams of the accused to locate mistakes in translations ... Corrections in translations be carried out at the place where the defect has occurred and not at the end of the translated version ... Again: mistakes in translation ... Yet again: mistakes in translation of evidence of some more witnesses ... One witness be recalled ... Lawyers for Sasikala challenge the rejection of that petition ... They make DVAC as the sole respondent ... The DVAC does not apprise the special public prosecutor, instead engages some other law firm to represent it ... DVAC informs court directly that it has decided to conduct further investigation ... Special public prosecutor has not been informed of this ... Court objects to DVAC writing directly to it rather than through the prosecutor ... Prosecutor is compelled to point to collusion between accused and DVAC and prays that the contents of the letter be ignored ... Court admonishes DVAC for approaching it directly, decides to ignore contents of letter, accepts apology of DVAC ... Jayalalithaa files an application that the case be adjourned for four weeks as a new counsel will be appearing on her behalf ... Sasikala files an application in the High Court ... High Court dismisses the application with strictures that DVAC is subverting the course of justice and that Sasikala has filed the application only to drag out the proceedings ... Accused 1 [Jayalalithaa] be examined by video conference and be exempted from personal appearance ...[24] A judge in the High Court recuses himself from hearing a petition ... Even so the petition comes up before him ... Hearings be adjourned as an application against a rejection by trial court has been filed in the Supreme Court ... Court directs DVAC to stop further investigation, and directs the trial court to bear in mind the direction of the Supreme Court that the case be heard day-to-day till completion ... Statement of Jayalalithaa is being recorded, at 5 p.m.; her counsel seeks adjournment for three weeks to seek order from the Supreme Court whether the rest of her statement can be recorded by video conference ... Sasikala files an application seeking eight weeks as she is not well-versed in English and would like to record her statement in Tamil ... Trial court dismisses the application, she now seeks three weeks to challenge the order ... Writ is filed challenging continuance of Acharya on the ground that he is holding two posts ... Writ is withdrawn ... A PIL is filed to the same effect ... Series of applications filed by lawyers of Jayalalithaa and Sasikala are rejected by the High Court and the Supreme Court ... Their lawyers now file applications to be allowed to examine 'all unfiled documents in the case' ... Sasikala files an application seeking adjournment on medical grounds ... When the case comes up, she files yet another application for further adjournment on medical grounds ... Two of the accused file applications that the case be held in abeyance 'since there is no notification appointing the Special Judge to conduct the case'—this in 2012, even though the case has been going on since 2009 and they and their counsel have been participating in the proceedings ... An application that

24 Again, this in spite of what the Supreme Court had prescribed in its 2004 order:

> The Special Judge shall, after completion of evidence, put to all the accused all relevant evidence and documents appearing against them whilst recording their statement under Section 313. All the accused shall personally appear in court, on the day they are called upon to do so, for answering questions under section 313 of the Criminal Procedure Code.

the 'question of law' that they have raised be referred to the High Court ... An application that the court exercise its power under Section 309 of the Code of Criminal Procedure and adjourn the case ...[25] [By now, moves have been set afoot to get Acharya to resign as special public prosecutor and to besmirch his reputation. Eventually, he resigns—first from the post of advocate general, and then, after he has been vindicated in regard to the working of the educational trust, as special public prosecutor] ... Accused be allowed time to produce certified copies of an order of the Supreme Court ... Dispute is now raised about the number of days that the Supreme Court has allowed for inspection—21 days or 21 *working* days ... Matter is taken back to Supreme Court...

And this was only till 17 January 2013 when the government accepted the resignation of B.V. Acharya as special public prosecutor.

Reflecting on these devices, Acharya wrote:

> My appearance in the above case has taught me such variety of novel grounds on which adjournments could be successfully sought that I could write a book on the subject 'Law of Adjournments'. However, I desist from doing so, as I do not want any accused intending to prolong trials to take advantage of it.[26]

---

25 In point of fact, the section is only an enabling one, and the emphasis is on proceeding day to day. The section provides:

309. Power to postpone or adjourn proceedings.
(1) In every inquiry or trial, the proceedings shall be held as expeditiously as possible, and in particular, when the examination of witnesses has once begun, the same shall be continued from day to day until all the witnesses in attendance have been examined, unless the Court finds the adjournment of the same beyond the following day to be necessary for reasons to be recorded.
(2) If the Court, after taking cognizance of an offence, or commencement of trial, finds it necessary or advisable to postpone the commencement of, or adjourn, any inquiry or trial, it may, from time to time, for reasons to be recorded, postpone or adjourn the same on such terms as it thinks fit, for such time as it considers reasonable, and may by a warrant remand the accused if in custody...

26 B.V. Acharya, *All From Memory*, op. cit., p. 219.

'But, Sir, the scoundrels and their lawyers already know the tricks,' I tell Mr Acharya, trying to needle a few more examples out of him.

In response, Mr Acharya gives further details about some of the devices, and recounts more examples.

About those applications for translations of documents, Mr Acharya adds, 'Though translation copies of the documents had been furnished in 2005, more than four or five years later objections were frequently raised with regard to correctness of the translation.' And these were raised 'in installments' so that each objection had to be ruled upon in turn. And the documents in question had to be translated all over again.

Next, lawyers were changed. The new set of lawyers would plead that they needed time to study the case. And then they would apply for certified copies of the three sets of all the documents running, as we have seen, into thousands of pages on the ground that the previous lawyer had not handed over all the documents. The office could not furnish the certified copies of such a large number of documents in a hurry.

In almost every instance, the plea would be rejected. That provided occasions to the lawyers to challenge the decision. 'Every interlocutory order was challenged either before the High Court or before the Supreme Court,' Mr Acharya recalls, 'and though there was no order of stay by the superior courts, adjournments were sought on the ground that the matter was coming up before the superior courts very soon and hence the case should be adjourned.'

We have encountered a reference to Sasikala's lawyers asking for adjournment 'on health grounds'. It turns out that several adjournments were sought on the ground that Sasikala was getting treatment for her eyes. The result, Mr Acharya recalls, was that 'the recording of her statement which should have been over in a day or two, took more than eleven months to complete'.

And then, as we have seen, soon after Jayalalithaa once again became chief minister in 2011, the DVAC decided that it needed to further investigate the case. The public prosecutor pointed out how this was totally uncalled for—in his assessment the sole objective of this 'further investigation' was to gather material to support the accused. Even so, 'further investigation' was conducted. The matter had to be taken to the High Court: it quashed the stratagem. And then, as we saw, in regard to that order of its principal secretary, the Tamil Nadu government had gone ahead and appointed as its own counsel the same Bhavani Singh. The High Court held that it could not do so, and only the special public prosecutor should appear in the High Court. The law prevailed. But each of the devices served the purpose: each of them necessitated further adjournments.

Next, applications were repeatedly filed seeking exemption from personal appearance and permitting Jayalalithaa to answer questions in absentia. The matter was taken all the way to the Supreme Court: it turned down this request also and directed her personal appearance. Again, a purpose was served for these proceedings also led to number of adjournments.

And so on.

Lessons

Several lessons leap from the foregoing. It would be enough for us to note three of them. The role of an Acharya is of course exemplary. But what about the other lawyers who participated in the protracted proceedings?

- The purpose of the applications for adjournment would have been clear to the most innocent person. Can our courts not do more to neutralize these devices?
- Is dragging cases in this way the proper role of lawyers? After all, they are supposed to be in the first instance 'officers of the court'.
- Recall also that, seized of just one question—whether the disproportionate assets case and the London hotel case should be clubbed or not—the Supreme Court itself was responsible for the case remaining at a standstill for *five years* in the trial court. Had the Supreme Court not directed that the case be concluded as expeditiously as possible?

WHY DO THINGS NOT GET DONE?

That the case was being dragged out was for all to see. And most certainly, this is not the only instance in which lawyers representing the rich and powerful have used devices to stretch out the proceedings in court. The question, therefore, arises: Is it that nothing *can* be done? Or that, for the usual reason, nothing gets done?

That litigants and lawyers *can* be impelled to shun these devices is evident from the experience of other countries. Why is it that those convicted in the US do not go on filing appeals? One part of the answer is simple: because they run the real prospect that, if their appeal is found to be without foundation, the sentence will be severely enhanced. Why is it that lawyers and litigants do not deploy these devices in the UK? Again, one part of the answer is simple: because very high costs are imposed on those who are found to be using the proceedings in court to escape or even delay justice. Moreover, in the US, while deciding the extent to which the sentence shall be enhanced and, in the UK, while deciding the quantum of costs that a party shall have to pay, the judge considers the conduct of the litigant before as well as during the trial. In the UK, each individual application during trial or appeal may invite a separate order as to costs. Recall those applications that were filed on behalf of Jayalalithaa and Co.; recall that almost every order turning down their applications was appealed against, every so often, all the way to the Supreme Court. Would this have been done if the litigants knew that every single application, every single appeal could compound the amounts that they would have to pay in the end? And not just because of the time of the courts that the issue or appeal would entail but also because of the impression that these devices would be fortifying in the minds of the judges regarding the litigants' conduct?

In India, that the problem is extreme has long been recognized; that the existing provisions of law are wholly inadequate to deal with it has also been long recognized. And possible solutions too have been listed for long. What happens in practice? An analogy from civil law will bare the state of affairs.

Taking note of the way cases were being dragged out, in 1973 the Law Commission, in its 54th report, recommended that a new section be introduced in the Civil Procedure Code. The section should provide, 'The Court may, while passing an order for costs, make the party responsible for delay with reference to any step in the litigation, pay the costs proportionate to that delay, whatever may be the ultimate event of the suit.'[27] In 1976, the provision was introduced in the form of Section 35-B. It reads:

> Costs for causing delay.
> (1) If, on any date fixed for the hearing of a suit or for taking any step therein, a party to the suit-
> (a) fails to take the step which he was required by or under this Code to take on that date, or
> (b) obtains an adjournment for taking such step or for producing evidence or on any other ground,
> the Court may, for reasons to be recorded, make an order requiring such party to pay to the other party such costs as would, in the opinion of the Court, be reasonably sufficient to reimburse the other party in respect of the expenses incurred by him in attending the Court on that date, and payment of such costs, on the date next following the date of such order, shall be a condition precedent to the further prosecution of-
> (a) the suit by the plaintiff, where the plaintiff was ordered to pay such costs
> (b) the defence by the defendant, where the defendant was ordered to pay such costs...

The first thing that strikes one is that this provision is woefully inadequate to deal with the sorts of derailments that we have just encountered. For, in the section, the focus is solely on the litigant not doing in time what the Code requires him to do or what the court has asked him to do. The second feature is that even when the courts levy costs on the errant litigant, they require him to pay an

27 'Whatever be the ultimate event of the suit' refers to whatever is the ultimate decision in the case.

inconsequential amount—while courts are allowed and do exercise discretion, the indicated ceiling is a paltry Rs 3,000.

In judgment after judgment, the Supreme Court itself has held that the provision in the Code as well as the amounts that are levied are wholly inadequate to meet the kinds of litigants who need to be brought to heel. 'The present system of levying meagre costs in civil matters (or no costs in some matters), no doubt, is wholly unsatisfactory and does not act as a deterrent to vexatious or luxury litigation born out of ego or greed, or resorted to as a "buying-time" tactic,' the court observed in an oft-cited case. 'More realistic approach relating to costs may be the need of the hour...'[28] That was in 2009—nine years ago. In the following year, the Supreme Court again spoke in the same vein: 'The lack of appropriate provisions relating to costs has resulted in a steady increase in malicious, vexatious, false, frivolous and speculative suits, apart from rendering Section 89 of the Code ineffective.[29] Any attempt to reduce the pendency or encourage alternative dispute resolution processes or to streamline the civil justice system will fail in the absence of appropriate provisions relating to costs. There is therefore an urgent need for the legislature and the Law Commission of India to revisit the provisions relating to costs and compensatory costs contained in Section 35 and 35-A of the Code.'[30] The Supreme Court also pointed out that the limit that had been laid down on the costs that may be imposed on the litigant had reduced the amount that the litigant would have to shell out to as good as nothing: 'The provision relating to compensatory costs[31] in respect of false or vexatious claims or defences has become virtually infructuous and ineffective, on account of inflation. Under the said Section, award of compensatory costs inflation and vexatious litigation, is subject to a ceiling of Rs. 3,000/-. This requires a realistic revision keeping in view the observations in *Salem Advocate Bar Association (II)...'* Not just that. The court noted that while the provision for this

28 *Ashok Kumar Mittal v. Ram Kumar Gupta,* (2009) 2 SCC 656.
29 Section 89 empowers the courts to assign a dispute for settlement to avenues outside the court—such as arbitration, mediation, Lok Adalat, etc.
30 *Vinod Seth v. Devinder Bajaj,* (2010) 8 SCC.
31 In Section 35A of the Code.

meagre amount exists, 'Section 35A providing for costs for causing delay is seldom invoked ... It should be regularly employed, to reduce delay,' it declared—to what effect, we shall just see.

In the following year the question came up again. The Supreme Court requested the Law Commission to assist it in formulating steps that would keep litigants from dragging out cases and which would also keep them from embarking on vexatious, false and frivolous litigation. The Law Commission recommended several steps. The Supreme Court incorporated these in an important judgment, and urged Parliament and the High Courts to make appropriate changes—both in the Code and in the rules that govern the conduct of cases.[32] It also stressed that while directing a litigant to pay costs, the amount ordered must be realistic, given the actual costs that the opposing party would have had to bear; moreover, it specifically observed that the amounts that must be levied against frivolous and vexatious litigation stand on a different footing: in such cases, the mischief-maker must not be asked to pay just 'compensatory costs'; the amount levied must be punitive. It listed five goals that the levies must serve. For our present discussion, the first two alone need be contrasted with the years and years it takes for cases to reach any stage of finality, and, though that was on the criminal side, with the twenty years that it took the Jayalalithaa case to reach a conclusion:

> (a) It should act as a deterrent to vexatious, frivolous and speculative litigations or defences. The spectre of being made liable to pay actual costs should be such, as to make every litigant think twice before putting forth a vexatious, frivolous or speculative claim or defence. (b) Costs should ensure that the provisions of the Code, the Evidence Act and other laws governing procedure are scrupulously and strictly complied with and that parties do not adopt delaying tactics or mislead the court.

As far as the Supreme Court itself is concerned, the court noted, it can impose costs higher than the Rs 3,000 ceiling that has been

32 *Sanjeev Kumar Jain v. Raghuvir Saran Charitable Trust,* (2012) 1 SCC 455.

set. It can do so because of the unique plenary powers that it has been given under Article 142 of the Constitution. This Article, the reader will recall, states:

> *Enforcement of decrees and orders of Supreme Court and orders as to discovery, etc.*—(1) The Supreme Court in the exercise of its jurisdiction may pass such decree or make such order as is necessary for doing complete justice in any cause or matter pending before it, and any decree so passed or order so made shall be enforceable throughout the territory of India in such manner as may be prescribed by or under any law made by Parliament and, until provision in that behalf is so made, in such manner as the President may by order prescribe...[33]

Soon, the court was faced with a case in which, to quote its words, 'The appellants ... have harassed the respondents to the hilt for four decades in a totally frivolous and dishonest litigation in various courts. The appellants have also wasted judicial time of the various courts for the last 40 years.'[34] The court once again adverted to the need to impose adequate costs to stop such malpractices:

> Imposition of actual, realistic or proper costs and/or ordering prosecution would go a long way in controlling the tendency of introducing false pleadings and forged and fabricated documents by the litigants. Imposition of heavy costs would also control unnecessary adjournments by the parties. In appropriate cases the courts may consider ordering prosecution. Otherwise it may not be possible to maintain purity and sanctity of judicial proceedings.

---

33 Fali S. Nariman, one of our foremost jurists, has often drawn attention to this article in diverse contexts. Under it, '...for doing complete justice in any cause or matter pending before it' the court 'may pass such decree or make such order as is necessary...' No other court in India has been given such power, he has emphasized. Indeed, no other Constitution anywhere in the world confers such a decisive and wide-ranging power on any court as this Article does on our Supreme Court, he has reminded us.

34 *Ramrameshwari Devi v. Nirmala Devi,* (2011) 8 SCC 249.

It imposed a cost of Rs 200,000 on the offending litigants. Did this set the trend? We shall see in a moment.

The afflictions—of delays, and of vexatious and frivolous litigation—continued. The Law Commission decided to study the matter in detail.[35] It recalled what the Supreme Court had observed in cases such as the foregoing. It once again listed recommendations for dealing with the problem. Two points that stand out from its narrative explain why things continue the way that we have seen them do.

The Law Commission noted that the Civil Procedure Code provides that the court shall direct what costs should be paid by whom soon after or along with its verdict—'following the event', as the phrase goes. That shall be the norm. And where it decides that costs may not be paid, it shall record its reasons in writing.[36] Citing another well-known case in which the Supreme Court had dealt with the matter of levying costs, the Commission noted that the Supreme Court itself had drawn attention to the model rules that had been drawn up by a committee headed by the chairman of the Law Commission. These rules had provided:

> 8. Costs: So far as awarding of costs at the time of judgment is concerned, awarding of costs must be treated generally as mandatory inasmuch as the liberal attitude of the courts in directing the parties to bear their own costs had led parties to file a number of frivolous cases in the courts or to raise frivolous and unnecessary issues. *Costs should invariably follow the event.*

---

35 Law Commission of India, *Costs in Civil Litigation,* Report Number 240, May 2012.

36 Section 35 of the Code of Civil Procedure provides:
(1) Subject to such conditions and limitations as may be prescribed, and to the provisions of law for the time being in force, the costs of and incident to all suits shall be in the discretion of the Court, and the Court shall have full power to determine by whom or out of what property and to what extent such costs are to be paid, and to give all necessary directions for the purposes aforesaid. The fact that the Court has no jurisdiction to try the suit shall be no bar to the exercise of such powers.
(2) Where the Court directs that any costs shall not follow the event, the Court shall state its reasons in writing.

> Where a party succeeds ultimately on one issue or point but loses on a number of other issues or points which were unnecessarily raised, costs must be appropriately apportioned. *Special reasons must be assigned if costs are not being awarded.*
>
> Costs should be assessed according to rules in force. If any of the parties has unreasonably protracted the proceedings, the Judge should consider exercising discretion to impose exemplary costs after taking into account the expenses incurred for the purpose of attendance on the adjourned dates.

The model rule on this point for an appellate court was along similar lines.[37]

That is what the Code lays down. That is what the model rules that the Supreme Court had noted lay down. That is what the Supreme Court itself has held in case after case. In practice? This is what the Law Commission found:

> Sub-section (2) is indicative of the legislative policy that ordinarily costs shall be awarded to the party who succeeds and if it is otherwise, the Parliament requires the Court to record reasons for disallowing costs. Very often, the rule that costs should follow the event is observed in breach. Many of the cases are disposed of either by saying 'no order as to costs' or 'parties to bear their own costs'. When the Court, especially the superior courts, disallow costs or say 'no order as to costs,' reasons are seldom recorded. Such cryptic directives do not contain anything which indicate the mind of the Court as to why costs are being disallowed.

The Law Commission went on to state two further facts:

> [One] There are also instances where the High Courts and the Supreme Court have been directing costs to be paid to a body other than a party to the proceeding, for e.g., a charitable organization or legal services authority, which practice is disapproved in some judgments while in others it is so done.

---

37 The Supreme Court took note of these rules in *Salem Advocates Bar Association v. Union of India,* (2005) 6 SCC 344.

> [Two] Judgments of the Hon'ble Supreme Court wherein costs are awarded or not allowed, do not give any indication of any underlying principle and no guideline or rationale can be deduced therefrom.

We will see the relevance of both these observations as we come to an exemplary fine that was levied in a recent case involving contempt of court.

In an annexure to its report, the Law Commission listed cases upon cases in which the Supreme Court as well as High Courts concluded their judgments with those words, 'No order as to costs' or 'Parties to bear their own costs' without stating any reason. Indeed, in several of the cases listed by the Law Commission, the Supreme Court observed that the case was a fit one for levying 'exemplary costs', and yet in the very next sentence, sometimes in the same sentence, declared that it was, nonetheless, not going to levy any costs. If the Supreme Court itself does not follow the provision in law; if the Supreme Court itself does not do what it has so often proclaimed must be done, why would others?

The Commission's report also showed that no norms or rules were being followed in fixing the quantum of costs: in the cases it cited where one or the other party was asked to pay costs, the parties were directed to pay anywhere between Rs 500 and Rs 500,000. The range is one aspect. The maximum amount—Rs 500,000—that it imposed too has a lesson: do keep this amount in mind when we come to that case involving contempt of court.

And then there was the other feature. No rules seemed to govern what the court would decree about the party to whom the costs should be paid. Sometimes it was the party that had been subjected to the travail of protracted litigation; in others, the party was directed to pay the amount to the Supreme Court Mediation Centre, or the National Association for the Blind, or the Legal Aid Society of the Supreme Court. For this reason, do keep an eye out for the organizations to which and the causes for which the Supreme Court has recently directed the money to be paid in that contempt case.

Now, it is nobody's case that the quantum of costs and penalties should be determined uniformly and mechanically, and that courts must have no discretion. After all, no one would want the costs and penalties to be put so high that the poor widow and the giant corporation should risk having to pay an identical amount. Judges must be able to determine the amount taking into account the capacity of the litigant to pay, as well as the relevance and intrinsic merit of the issues that are being raised. Even more so, they must have the discretion to discern the pattern of the litigant's conduct. The point is that the levies betray none of these considerations as having determined the outcome.

But why?

We noted above, 'For the usual reason, nothing gets done.' What is 'the usual reason'? It is that in this sphere, as in others, the decision to affect improvements rests in hands of persons who would be the first to be nailed were the improvements to be brought about.

Two small changes—one in the way cases are reported and the other in a provision of law—will help.

Today, it is customary for judgments of the higher courts to record the date on which the case was instituted or the writ was filed, and the date on which the judgment is being delivered. This should be supplemented with recording how many adjournments have been allowed in the case. And while the courts need not be burdened with the task, others—journalists, public-spirited organizations and individuals—should list the kinds of issues that have been raised in at least cases involving public servants. Similarly, currently a judgment reports the date on which, say, *the particular writ which is being disposed of in this instance* was filed and the date on which it is being disposed of. But from this we do not get an idea of the length of time for which the overall case has been knocking about in the courts. We will learn, for instance, when the appeal against a trial court order regarding documents being imperfectly translated was filed and when it is being disposed of. But we will not know the date from which the disproportionate assets case has been going on. The least that court clerks can record, in any case the least that our legal correspondents can do while reporting the higher court's ruling regarding translations is to also remind readers that this writ is part of a case that has been going on since 1997.

That is about reporting. But the basic problems are different. First, as we have seen, the provisions of law are not such as would deter anyone from dragging out cases. Surely, if we really are serious about discouraging litigants from doing this, the law must provide for not just 'compensatory costs'—reasonable costs that the other party would have incurred had, say, the adjournment not been wrested—it must explicitly provide for punitive and exemplary costs. The even greater problem is the reluctance of judges to use such powers as the law has given them. Recall the felicity with which sixty-four of the seventy-six witnesses went back on what they had stated on oath—the moment Jayalalithaa came back to power. Either what they had stated earlier was false, or what they stated subsequently was false. The punishment for false evidence is imprisonment from three to seven years, and fine.[38] Was even one of those making the somersault punished with imprisonment for even one day? Was any of them asked to pay even a single rupee?

The principal remedy lies with civil society. We must, all of us must put pressure on the political class to implement the reforms that have been suggested so often and for so long. We must, all of us must name and shame litigants as well as professionals like ourselves—lawyers in this instance—who use such devices to keep their clients from getting what they deserve. If precedent is what we

---

38 See Sections 191 and 193 of the Indian Penal Code. The latter provides,

> *193. Punishment for false evidence*
> Whoever intentionally gives false evidence in any stage of a judicial proceeding, or fabricates false evidence for the purpose of being used in any stage of a judicial proceeding, shall be punished with imprisonment of either description for a term which may extend to seven years, and shall also be liable to fine, and whoever intentionally gives or fabricates false evidence in any other case, shall be punished with imprisonment of either description for a term which may extend to three years, and shall also be liable to fine.
> ... *Explanation 2-* An investigation directed by law preliminary to a proceeding before a Court of Justice, is a stage of a judicial proceeding, though that investigation may not take place before a Court of Justice.

need—well, the UK officially publishes a 'List of vexatious litigants, banned from starting court cases without permission', and updates it from time to time.[39] We can improve on that and publish a list of litigants and lawyers who specialize in securing adjournments and deploying other devices to keep cases lingering. Cases involving public servants would be a good place to start.

39 https://www.gov.uk/guidance/vexatious-litigants

4

When courts are compelled to step out of their domain

In the 1950s, socialism was much in the air. The 'socialist pattern of society' as distinct from 'socialism'. The 'socialis*tic* pattern of society' as distinct from the 'socialist pattern of society'—these were subjects of heated debates across campuses. The distinguished and taciturn civil servant, Dr Tarlok Singh, the then secretary of the Planning Commission, had come to our college. 'What is the difference between "the socialist pattern of society" and "the socialistic pattern of society"?' we had asked, hoping to get a list of features that we could reproduce in our exams. 'The same as between "four o'clock" and "four o'clockish",' he had explained, and, satisfied that he had explained it all, moved on to the next question.

A team had gone to study 'cooperatives' in China. It produced an effusive report—in retrospect, its value consists in showing us how little they gleaned of what was actually going on in China behind the façade of 'cooperatives'. Dr V.K.R.V. Rao had come to the college to deliver a lecture on the subject. He alluded to the way some major public figures changed their position depending on the issue. We are all against dowry when our daughters are getting married, he said. But when our sons are getting married, we want ancient traditions to be preserved! Much the same goes for our attitudes towards judicial activism. We want judges to be activists when the cause or case is one to which we are committed. And we are against their activism when the cause or case is one we oppose!

Hence, we need criteria that go beyond individual decisions, criteria that go beyond even activism in pursuit of particular causes.[1]

But first two general points:

The *need* for the judiciary to step outside its traditional role has arisen, as we have noticed earlier, because the executive has failed to discharge its functions. The Supreme Court passed its far-reaching orders in *Hussainara Khatoon*[2] and similar cases after we established beyond doubt that the executive had been inhuman in regard to undertrials. Following up an account by Mr K.F. Rustomji, a police officer renowned for his integrity and service to the country—he was one of the major organizers of the Mukti Vahini—my colleagues at *The Indian Express* visited jail after jail and established that some of the inmates had been languishing in jails for up to *fourteen years* awaiting trial; ever so many had been languishing in those jails waiting for the courts to take up their cases for periods far in excess of the maximum periods for which they would be sentenced if they were convicted of the crime for which they had been charged. The same sequence unfolded in regard to consumer protection. And later in regard to the environment.

Sometimes the Supreme Court has had to intervene not because the executive has been inactive but because it has not been doing its job conscientiously. Recall how investigating agencies were being misused—to pursue an investigation or to dilute a case in accordance with the partisan convenience of the rulers of the day. This is what spurred the Supreme Court, from *Vineet Narain*[3] onwards, to take a direct role in monitoring the investigation—even when it was fully conscious that a lower court could be influenced by the fact that the evidence and logic which were being

---

1 For an overall assessment of judicial activism, Ashok Desai, 'Judicial Overreach', (2013) *SCC Journal Section*, J-1.

2 *Hussainara Khatoon v. Home Secretary, State of Bihar,* AIR 1979 SC 1369.

3 *Vineet Narain v. Union of India,* AIR 1998 SC 889.

subsequently placed before it had resulted from an investigation supervised by the Supreme Court itself.

The same thing happened in the case of legislators. Legislators often proclaim that the House alone shall decide on the conduct of legislators during the proceedings of the House. The anti-defection law explicitly provides that the decision of the Speaker shall be final. But some years ago, the decisions of the Speakers were so manifestly partisan that legislators themselves went to courts for redress. The courts heard them and gave verdicts. Legislators did not—in fact, in view of how very partisan the Speakers had been—they *could not* object.

Exactly the same sequence unfolded in regard to misuse of governors. It has long been accepted that when it comes to the grounds on which a governor has recommended President's Rule, the courts shall not examine the validity of the grounds. But so manifestly partisan have the actions of governors been on occasion that the courts have had no difficulty in getting around this rule of self-denial by the make-believe that, while they shall not examine the validity of the grounds on which the governor recommended a course of action, they *shall* examine whether he had any grounds at all. And some of the most far-reaching judgments have been delivered using this toehold.

Second, the *opportunity* to intervene has arisen because the executive and legislatures have become less and less legitimate. For neither of these developments—whether for the need to intervene or for the opportunity to do so—is the judiciary responsible. But as the judiciary is pulled farther and farther afield, it would be well-advised to adhere to some rules of thumb:

1. Lest they acquire the reputation of being knights-errant rushing around hunting for issues on which they can pronounce, courts should intervene only after the fact that the executive is not going to discharge its responsibilities has been unequivocally established.
2. When the judiciary does intervene to goad the executive to do something, its decision must be informed by the highest expertise, and after thinking through the varied situations that

may develop as a consequence of its orders. Unfortunately—as we will have occasion to see when we glance at its orders on admissions, on shutting down liquor vends, on playing the National Anthem—that is not always the case. On occasion, when it has set up panels of 'experts', these have consisted of activists whose advice, as a matter of principle, is not always constrained by facts.

3. One of the elements in this expert analysis must be the effects that alternative directions will have on the ground. This is vital for several reasons:

- These cases are often brought up by activists. Many of them are one-issue fundamentalists. For them, the 'principle' to which they are wedded must prevail, irrespective of collateral consequences.
- Unfortunately, our lawyers do not always think it to be their duty to present the *whole* truth, to present *all* the facts to the courts. They proceed on the assumption that their duty is to present only those facts that will bolster the side of the case that they happen to be representing.
- The judges themselves are not always sufficiently acquainted with the situation on the ground: few journalists would have been inside factories and yet we pronounce on them; in the same way, few judges would have been inside factories and yet their rulings have life-and-death implications for projects and enterprises.
- Among the effects that must be considered are the effects of adjournments, and allowing lawyers to go on with their arguments. The project to develop Lavasa was a leap of the imagination. For reasons that are still not clear, the government of the day called a halt to all construction—and this ostensibly on the basis of a 'report' by officials who paid just a perfunctory visit to the site. All work at the site was brought to a standstill. The matter went to the Bombay High Court. From November 2010, when the first hearing took place, to November 2011, there were fifteen hearings. The benches changed several times. During the first two months, and then again during the last six months, law

officers appearing for the government would say that they needed another few weeks to secure instructions from Delhi. It was only in November 2011, when the judge gave an ultimatum to the law officer appearing for the government to either give substantive reasons for shutting down the project or clear it, that the government cleared the way for work to resume. By that time the Lavasa Corporation had suffered irreversible damage. And the instance—along with those involving POSCO, Vedanta and Cairn—became an example that was cited at investor conferences as an argument against investing in India. In *Courts and Their Judgments*, I have described the case of Narmada. The Supreme Court stayed the raising of the dam height on 5 May 1995. The final hearings concluded, *five years* later, in May 2000. The final judgment came in September 2000. Over Rs 10,000 crore had already been invested before the court's stay order. There was, of course, the loss in terms of interest. But even greater was the loss in regard to production forgone.

- And I have found it truly shocking that in justifying their conclusions, some judges have invoked the worst 'authorities'. In *Indra Sawhney*,[4] the Supreme Court cited with approval the speech of V.P. Singh at his most opportunist moment—the moment when he had panicked, fearing the rally that Devi Lal had threatened. 'You talk of "merit", but what is the merit of a system which…?' he had declaimed. In another judgment, the Supreme Court cited the words of a man who had spent two decades justifying our subjugation by the British; who for two decades had not just spread, but advocated hatred between sections of our society; who had openly advocated violence—all this so that the judges could join him in proclaiming that the notion of merit is an 'Aryan invention' to continue the suppression of the Scheduled Castes and Scheduled Tribes!

Unfortunately, their pronouncements suggested that several judges had themselves been infected by the activists' virus. How

4 *Indra Sawhney v. Union of India*, AIR 2000 SC 498.

could a judge of the Supreme Court—Justice D.A. Desai, in this instance—proclaim that he had joined the bench to overturn this system from within, and still continue to adhere to the oath he had sworn on his appointment?

Nor can one believe that all this flowed from a bleeding heart. Two venerable and acutely observant ladies used to tour India, as they did other Asian countries, to select persons who might be considered for the Magsaysay Award. They used to seek the opinion of previous award winners because they had come to know them well. On one of their visits, they asked me, 'But who is this judge...?' I explained how he was one of the best-known judges, well known for enlarging the ambit of our rights—albeit *after* the Emergency was over—and asked in turn, 'But why do you ask me about him?'

'He keeps sending us his judgments through some friend of his, a judge in Australia, so that he be selected for the award.'

I couldn't have felt smaller: a judge so well-known drawing attention to his judgments for a mere award. In another case, it did seem to an observer like me that the judge had got carried away by his public image of being a saviour of the voiceless. And the tragedy—one for which the country is paying today—was that, because of the nature of discourse in India during the last thirty years, this handful acquired the high moral ground, and their pronouncements determined the direction of so many subsequent judgments. Of course, the progressive judges were not the only ones who were responsible for this outcome: much of what happened subsequently in jurisprudence was due to the diffidence of the liberal judges. They did not have the courage to stand up to the intellectual fashions of the day.

Finally, it is imperative that once a court does give an order, it must ensure that it is obeyed to the dot. In many instances, ringing pronouncements were made, they were sent around. And that was it. In the undertrial cases, the Supreme Court directed that a census of all jail inmates be taken every two years—has it inquired if such a census is indeed being conducted? Several pronouncements on the environment have suffered the same fate. Look at the Supreme Court's pronouncements on cleaning our rivers, and look at the condition of the river that flows within three to four minutes' drive from it, the Yamuna.

The most consequential of such instances, and the one that has a direct bearing on the security of the country and the violence that we have witnessed in Assam periodically, is, of course, the Supreme Court's ringing judgment in the *Sarbananda Sonowal* case.[5] Having concluded that the Illegal Migrants (Determination by Tribunal) (IMDT) Act was enacted precisely to protect illegal infiltrators; having concluded that the scale of such infiltration was by now a grave and imminent threat to the security and integrity of the country, should the court not have set up some mechanism to monitor whether anything was being done to implement its judgment?

A case that the Supreme Court has taken up recently provides a good test case. In 2014, the Supreme Court had taken note of reports that as many as 1,581 criminal cases were pending against legislators. On 10 March 2014, it passed orders that cases in which legislators were implicated must be disposed of within a year. The prime minister appropriated the idea, and declared from the ramparts of the Red Fort that he would bring a law to ensure that cases against lawmakers are finished within a year. More than three years have passed since the Supreme Court gave its order. In a hearing on 1 November 2017, it asked what had happened to those cases: how many had been disposed of? Far from enacting the law that the prime minister had proclaimed his government would have the Parliament pass, the government could not even give information on the status of those cases. The judges said that special courts should be established for cases involving legislators. The government demurred: setting up such courts is the responsibility of the states, it said! When the judges persisted, the government sought six weeks to come up with a scheme.

That three years should have passed without any action having been taken since the order on so important a matter was given speaks volumes. On the other hand, imagine what a beginning the Supreme Court would make if it now persists in this matter, and

5 *Sarbananda Sonowal v. Union of India,* (2007) 1 SCC 174.

ensures that the cases involving legislators are indeed disposed of within a year.

Hence, I would urge Lenin's maxim, 'Fewer but better'—that is, if the issue is of such importance that the court feels compelled to step outside its traditional bounds, it must follow up its decision and institute a mechanism to ensure that its directives are carried out.

Above all, for the decisions to be effective, the people must innately respect them. And they will have this respect for decisions to the extent that they have respect for the court. Hence, nothing is more important than integrity of every single judge. The more activist a court is, the more every judge must be seen to be a paragon of virtue and impartiality. The more every single judgment must be based on the soundest legal principles. The more cogent and immaculate must the reasoning be. And the more it must be comprehensible to even laypeople so that no interested party—in particular the executive and the legislators—is able to sow doubts in the minds of people, 'The judiciary is stepping out of line.'

Of these, let us take up two requirements in turn: one, when the court feels compelled to intervene, it must ensure that its orders are obeyed to the dot; and two, that its reputation must always be spotless.

5

Adherence?

Time and time again courts pass far-reaching, detailed orders, and then just don't look back to see whether they have been obeyed.

Several years ago, I had occasion to examine two such orders that the Supreme Court had given in 1996 and 1998 regarding the disposal of solid waste in Delhi. Apart from giving specific directions, the court had asked that reports be submitted every two months; later this was changed to every four months. In all, thirty-two reports were submitted, twenty-two after the Supreme Court's orders. Each and every report stated that little had been done, that the problem was getting worse. Yet, no one was the worse for them. It seemed that the reports, having been asked for and received, were just filed.[1]

Of course, there are counter-instances: the doggedness with which the Supreme Court has continued to follow Sahara to ensure that the controllers of the company meet their obligations is an excellent example.

But it is distressing that that is not the case in too many instances. The other day, as I was asking a distinguished advocate about the mechanism that the Supreme Court has for examining the extent to which its directions are being followed, he referred me to a case that

---

1 'Demand and file', in Arun Shourie, *Governance: The Sclerosis that Has Set In,* ASA, Rupa, New Delhi, 2004, pp. 161–80.

created some flutter in government circles recently: *Common Cause v. Union of India.*[2] The record indicated that the original writ was filed in 2003. That must have been by my father—before he passed away in 2005, he was the one-man *Common Cause*. The judgment came in 2015, twelve years after the original writ was filed, and ten years after the one who filed it, my father, had passed away. The court was emphatic in its original judgment. However, in deference to the urging of governments, it issued a partial modification in 2016. Even so, important directions survived.

The petition to the court under Article 32 had pointed to the colossal amounts that were being spent on advertisements by ruling parties at the Centre and in the states, amounts out of the taxes we pay. It pointed out that these advertisements gave an unfair advantage in the ensuing elections to whichever happened to be the ruling party. Moreover, the photographs of prime ministers, chief ministers, ministers and others helped build personality cults—sometimes of unworthy persons. It prayed that the court spell out guidelines to regulate government advertisements.

The judgment came ten years after my father had passed away. In many ways, it was a vindication of what he had urged. For our present purpose, we may confine ourselves to just five points.

The Supreme Court said that photographs did indeed foster a personality cult, that in future government advertisements could carry the photographs only of the president, the prime minister and the Chief Justice of India—and, in each case, only after their permission. In the subsequent review which it issued in 2016, the court relaxed this direction somewhat: in the case of advertisements put out by state governments, photographs of the governor and the chief minister could be published. Second, in this regard the court said that the photograph of the minister handling the portfolio or project could be published 'in lieu of' the prime minister or chief minister as the case may be.

Who cannot see the matter that is being projected in government advertisements these days—say, since 2015 and 2016, the years in which the court gave its directions? On certain days, photographs

2 (2015) 7 SCC 1, and the review order (2016) 13 SCC.

of the prime minister appear on multiple pages of a newspaper: it almost seems that ministries and departments are under instructions that they *must* include the photograph of the prime minister. Even in advertisements of states ruled by the Bharatiya Janta Party (BJP)—for instance, those put out by the Government of Madhya Pradesh, the state many senior people of which are implicated in the Vyapam scam, a scam that is in the hands of the CBI—the prime minister's visage appears prominently; in most cases it is larger than that of the poor chief minister. And there can be no doubt that this has been one of the devices by which a personality cult is being sought to be built. Do these advertisements suggest that the order of the Supreme Court is being complied with? And could it be that judges do not see full-page ads appearing day after day in the papers?

Another guideline on which the Supreme Court was emphatic was that multiple advertisements marking the same event (say, the birth or death anniversary of some dignitary) or scheme must not be issued by different departments and ministries. You just have to look at the papers, and see that the guideline is being flouted day in and day out.

Third, the Supreme Court had directed that an ombudsman be appointed to ensure that government advertisements adhere to the guidelines. As governments objected strenuously to this mandate, the court said that, all right, if not an ombudsman, let a three-person committee monitor compliance with the guidelines—a committee of three persons known for their expertise and impartiality. For almost a year no committee was formed. Eventually, the committee was indeed formed: I leave as homework for the reader to find out who the three members are, and whether they fit the description of persons that the Supreme Court had mandated. Nor is it that the committee has not been doing anything. The committee has indeed been taking the Aam Aadmi Party (AAP) government in Delhi to task for its advertisements, but not a word on the ever-more blatant violation of the Supreme Court guidelines by the Central government.

Next, the court stressed that advertisements using government funds must not be used to advance the interests of a ruling party. When full-page advertisements are taken out, and grand functions organized to resurrect, say Pandit Deendayal Upadhyaya, are the interests of a particular party not advanced?

Finally, the court re-emphasized that government advertisements must not become a device of patronage or punishment, that the distribution among media must be according to some objective criteria like circulation. Is it at all possible that the court would not have noticed any instance at all of discrimination? It would have to look no farther than Jaipur: government advertisements to the *Rajasthan Patrika* were stopped when they started publishing facts about the Rajasthan government.

'Wilful and deliberate' disregard

In the functions they perform—for instance, that of investigating crimes, of presenting evidence to courts—the police are as much an arm of the judiciary as they are of the executive. However, over the decades the police have become the private armies of those who are in office. Cases that rulers-of-the-day want pursued are pursued, the ones they want derailed are derailed. 'Evidence' they want produced is fabricated, evidence they want suppressed is suppressed. Lathi charge, false encounters ... such things have become synonymous with the word 'police'.

And yet the primary blame does not lie with the police. That lies with the political rulers—they are the ones who have thought nothing of converting what should be a shield for lawful citizens into a private posse. The fault of the police—and that means, its senior personnel—lies is going along.

It was in November 1977—*forty years ago*—that the National Police Commission was appointed. It consisted of distinguished, experienced persons. The Commission submitted eight reports between its appointment and May 1981 when it gave its final report. In the years that followed, several other committees and commissions were appointed to look into the same sorts of questions that the National Police Commission had examined. They also submitted their reports. The Union home minister did his bit: he wrote a letter! To the chief ministers and state home ministers, urging them to implement the recommendations. In 2002, the National Human

Rights Commission noted that far from steps being taken to reform the police, the situation had deteriorated further.

An officer who had been director general of police of our largest state, Uttar Pradesh (UP), and also of one of our most troubled states, Assam, and then the director general of the Border Security Force, Prakash Singh, watched all this with mounting dismay. Having waited for *fifteen years* for governments to implement measures to save and reform the police, he at last filed a petition in the Supreme Court requesting the court to give directions to governments to take the necessary steps in this regard. The petition set out specific, 'glaring instances' of wrongdoing. It urged specific and eminently practical measures that could be taken.

The Supreme Court gave its verdict *a decade after* the petition was filed, *twenty-five years* after the National Police Commission had given its recommendations.[3] The court directed the formation in each state of a State Security Commission that would insulate the police from undue interference by the government of the day. It directed that the directors general of police, the inspectors general and other officers must be posted for fixed tenures, it specified the minimum time before which the officers must not be shunted out of their assignments. It directed that the investigative functions be separated from policing and prosecution. It directed that each state constitute a Police Establishment Board to determine all postings, transfers and promotions of and below the rank of a deputy superintendent of police. And it directed that a Police Complaints Authority be set up at the district level to which citizens could report police highhandedness.

It specified that its directions must be implemented by 31 December 2006, and that the Cabinet secretary in the case of the Union government and the respective chief secretary in the case of each state government must report compliance by 3 January 2007.

The court heard the matter twice in January 2007 to assess what the states had done. Most of the states had not implemented the directives. Instead of hauling those responsible for contempt, the Supreme Court extended the time to 10 April 2007.

---

3 *Prakash Singh v. Union of India,* Writ Petition (Civil) 310 of 1996; decided on 22 September 2006; (2006) 8 SCC 1.

The deadline over, Prakash Singh filed a petition requesting the Supreme Court to hold six states in contempt for not having implemented its recommendations.

Instead of complying with the directives, one state government after another now found fault with the directions. Some, like Tamil Nadu, maintained that in fact the Supreme Court had no authority to issue directions in this regard. States now asked for review of the judgment. In August 2007, the Supreme Court dismissed the review petitions that had been filed by six states—Gujarat, Karnataka, Maharashtra, Punjab and UP.

Soon, state governments, led by Gujarat, passed laws and issued ordinances to, in effect, circumvent and nullify the Supreme Court's directions.

In November 2007, Prakash Singh again moved the Supreme Court to haul up the concerned states—this time the four that had done the least to implement the Supreme Court's directions—for contempt. He pointed out how a state like UP was 'openly and brazenly defying the directions'. To take one example, it had been transferring senior officers at whim: about 200 officers had been shunted around, some twice in the preceding months.

He requested the Supreme Court to also ask the High Courts to monitor compliance or to itself set up a monitoring committee headed by some former judge of the Supreme Court.

The court set up a monitoring committee under Justice K.T. Thomas. The committee submitted four reports between October 2008 and September 2009. The committee recommended contempt proceedings against six states for not at all implementing the court's directives: Orissa, Madhya Pradesh, West Bengal, UP, Tamil Nadu, and Jammu and Kashmir. It is not just that they had not been implementing the court's directives, the committee reported, they had been 'totally indifferent for months together even to letters from the Chairman of the Monitoring Committee seeking their comments on reasons for non-compliance'.

Several states again directly challenged the authority of the Supreme Court to give directions in regard to the police. The Union government, in its turn, repeated the very arguments which the court had earlier considered and rejected.

Therefore, in September 2010, for the third time Prakash Singh moved the court to proceed against the states for contempt. He provided details of how the court's directives were being flouted. To take one instance, while the court had directed that the directors general of police should be posted for fixed tenures, and that they should not be shunted to other assignments till the minimum period was over, in UP six of the directors general had had tenures respectively of one year, eight-and-a-half months, two months, ten months, one month, and two months.

This contempt petition has been listed quite a few times for hearing, but somehow has never come up for hearing. *Forty years* have gone by since the National Police Commission submitted its reports. *Twenty-five years* have gone by since Prakash Singh brought the facts to the notice of the Supreme Court about those recommendations having remained on paper. *Ten years* have gone by since the court issued its directives. *Seven years* have gone by since Prakash Singh filed his contempt petition once again.

Of course, the primary responsibility for the near-collapse of the police is that of politicians. But is the judiciary so powerless that, even when facts are brought before it about the condition to which the police has been reduced, even when it itself passes specific orders, and then facts are brought before it that establish that its directives are being flouted openly and brazenly, is it so powerless that it cannot do anything? Is it not an accessory to the resulting deterioration?

The judiciary itself

In the early 1990s, The All India Judges' Association approached the Supreme Court. It showed how appalling the conditions were in which the subordinate judiciary had to work. It requested the court to direct the Central and state governments to take remedial steps. The Supreme Court went into the facts in detail, and then issued a series of specific and eminently implementable steps and directed that governments implement them.[4]

---

4 *All India Judges' Association v. Union of India,* (1992) 1 SCC 119.

The governments took some nominal steps, but these were far short of what was needed. The Association went back to the Supreme Court. The Central as well as state governments raised all sorts of objections, they advanced all sorts of arguments against being asked to do more. The tenor of what they insisted upon can be gleaned even twenty-five years later from the decision of the Supreme Court: 'Each of the specific and general objections of the Union of India and the states/UTs was dealt with and rejected,' the court noted.

Far from taking steps to ensure that citizens get justice, governments trotted out the usual argument against the court giving directions—you are stepping on the toes of the executive and the legislature. This is what the court was pushed to observe:

> By giving the directions in question, this Court has only called upon the executive and the legislature to implement their imperative duties. The courts do issue directions to the authorities to perform their obligatory duties whenever there is a failure on their part to discharge them ... The further directions given, therefore, should not be looked upon as an encroachment on the power of the executive and the legislature to determine the service conditions of the judiciary. They are directions to perform the long overdue obligatory duties.

The ultimate justification for not doing anything more was also predictable: financial stringency—and this from the very governments and legislatures which had been squandering public funds with utter irresponsibility. The court nailed this argument good and proper:

> The contention with regard to the financial burden likely to be imposed by the directions in question, is equally misconceived. Firstly, the courts do from time to time hand down decisions which have financial implications and the Government is obligated to loosen its purse recurrently pursuant to such decisions. Secondly, when the duties are obligatory, no grievance can be heard that they cast financial burden. Thirdly, compared to the other plan and non-plan expenditure, we find that the financial burden

> caused on account of the said directions is negligible. We should have thought that such plea was not raised to resist the discharge of the mandatory duties. The contention that the resources of all the States are not uniform has also to be rejected for the same reasons. The directions prescribe the minimum necessary service conditions and facilities for the proper administration of justice. We believe that the quality of justice administered and the calibre of the persons appointed to administer it are not of different grades in different States. Such contentions are ill-suited to the issues involved in the present case.

Infrastructure and emoluments of the lower judiciary were just two facets of the directions that the Supreme Court gave. An equally vital point was that the number of judges—at all levels—was just too small for a country like India. In its 120th report, the Law Commission recommended that the number of judges for every ten lakh Indians, which was 10.5, should be raised to 50. The recommendation was strongly endorsed by the Standing Committee of Parliament.

Nothing substantial was done in this regard or, indeed, in regard to emoluments of the subordinate judiciary or the infrastructure for them to discharge their functions. The All India Judges' Association returned to the Supreme Court a third time.

The court set out the directions that had been given in its earlier decisions and the fate they had met.[5] On the question of the imperative to multiply the number of judges, the court was emphatic. It recalled the recommendation of the Law Commission and its endorsement by the Standing Committee of Parliament. And, given that the requisite enlargement and improvements would have to be made in the infrastructure of courts also, it directed that this process of increasing the number of judges fivefold be taken up in a phased manner—but that it must be completed 'within five years from today'.

That was said on 21 March 2002, the day the judgment was pronounced. Fifteen years later, and how much of that directive has been complied with?

---

5 *All India Judges' Association v. Union of India*, (2002) 4 SCC 247.

Keeping the judiciary in the position of a supplicant

That point about the number of judges, and how successive governments have systematically ignored the Supreme Court's directions in this regard is just one facet of the executive's dogged efforts to keep the judiciary under its heel, to keep it in the position of a supplicant. It is not just the number of judges that has not been increased, the infrastructure that courts need has been kept woefully inadequate, and rules and regulations that ensure that the judiciary will have to keep coming to the executive at every turn for the barest essentials have been kept in place.

In successive judgments, the Supreme Court has emphasized:

- The right to speedy justice is a fundamental right.
- It is, therefore, the constitutional duty of courts to provide that kind of justice.
- By the same reasoning, as a constitutional duty, governments are duty-bound to provide the judiciary with the wherewithal to provide justice to citizens.
- The plea of financial limitations cannot be advanced as an excuse by governments for not doing their constitutional duty.[6]

In judgment upon judgment, High Courts have spelt out the specific steps that need to be taken to enable courts in their jurisdiction to discharge their functions. There are Law Commission reports urging governments to take steps to ensure that the infrastructure in courts is improved. In 2013, there was a joint conference of Chief Justices and chief ministers on the matter, and they unanimously passed a resolution about the steps that would be taken to improve conditions in courts forthwith. While ensuring that the states would have greater discretion over a much higher proportion of resources devolving to them, the 14th Finance Commission specifically recommended that the states set aside higher amounts to improve

6 See, for instance, *Brij Mohan Lal v. Union of India,* (2012) 6 SCC 502; *Hussainara Khatoon v. State of Bihar,* (1980) 1 SCC 98; *Imtiyaz Ahmed v. State of Uttar Pradesh,* decided on 2 January 2017 in Criminal Appeal Nos. 254-262 of 2012; *All India Judges Association v. Union of India*, op. cit.

the infrastructure in courts. In April 2015, the prime minister did his part—he wrote a letter! A letter to the chief ministers to set aside funds for completing tasks that the Fourteenth Finance Commission had mandated ...

And yet you just have to visit any of our local courts to see how little has been done in comparison to what is needed. You just have to read any recent judgment—for instance, *Mumbai Grahak Panchayat v. State of Maharashtra*[7]—to drive yourself to tearing your hair in helpless frustration. Courts are overcrowded. There is no place even to house records. Fire prevention equipment is wholly inadequate. Courts are functioning from premises rented from private parties. Repairs are urgently needed, the landlords refuse to carry these out. There is no drinking water. The washrooms 'stink'. Some buildings have become structurally so unstable that they have had to be evacuated at a moment's notice. When judges are transferred to a city, there is no place for them to stay—often they are put up 'in makeshift hostels'. Acts, rules are not being published in physical form; they are not being uploaded—especially the amendments to them; and versions published by private parties are neither up-to-date nor complete—to say nothing of litigants and lawyers, even the courts do not have the requisite bare acts. The situation is 'very grim'. Projects are sanctioned for building new accommodation; court staff has to run to the finance department for funds; clearances take long; in the meantime, costs have escalated; the court staff have once again to 'run from pillar to post' to get sanctions for the higher amounts that are by now required...[8]

This neglect, this 'pronounce and move on' disposition, harms individuals and communities, of course—to take one instance, their fundamental rights remain on paper. But eventually the neglect in

---

7 LiveLaw.in—PIL 156 of 2001, Civil Appeal 155 of 2015, Civil Appeal 157 of 2015, and several others, decided on 5 May 2017 by division bench of the Bombay High Court, Coram Justice A.S. Oka and Justice A.A. Sayed.

8 For details in regard to the position in Maharashtra, see the judgment of Justices Oka and Sayed just cited—each of the expressions in the paragraph is taken from this judgment.

following up and verifying that the decisions that have been handed down are actually being adhered to boomerangs on the court itself.

Consider the consequences of the Supreme Court neglecting to follow up on Prakash Singh's pleas to reform the police forces. Cases remain unsolved. False cases get filed. Riots incinerate life and limb. But consequences do not stop at individuals and groups. Take one right: the freedom of speech. Our Supreme Court has been among the most zealous protectors of this right. But while ringing judgments are a source of hope and protection, everyone in the field is also confronted by the brutal fact that fifty-six persons have been killed merely because they sought information under the Right to Information Act and the justice system has not been able to bring any of the murderers to book: that stark fact has all the 'chilling effect' that the Supreme Court has so often spoken about.

A new situation has arisen. Some years ago, when the pro-reservationists in Tamil Nadu declared that they would burn down theatres that screened a film that they insisted was against the government's reservations policy, the Supreme Court delivered a landmark judgment. It is the duty of the state to protect those who are merely exercising their fundamental right, the court declared. If those who are exercising their constitutionally guaranteed fundamental right are imperiled, what are fundamental rights for, it asked. But the screening of the film will create a 'law-and-order' problem, the government argued. The court had an unequivocal answer. The 'reasonable restrictions' that the Constitution permits are, to stick to the present example, in the interest of 'public order'. And 'public order' is not affected by a mere affray, it held. 'Public order' cannot be said to have broken down merely because there is a 'law-and-order problem'. When the state claims that there is the danger of a breakdown of 'public order', it must demonstrate that there is every likelihood of a breakdown of general order.

Such judgments were a bulwark in more innocent times. They were our shield when someone sought to prevent the publication or circulation of a book, or the screening of a film. But today we have two new developments. First, we have posses hunting for issues. And, second, these posses have the sub rosa protection and encouragement of politicians and parties controlling the state. What is the result? The Supreme Court once again upholds the screening of a film—*Padmaavat/i*—in ringing terms. The state governments ruled by the BJP just look the other way. Little bands intimidate and threaten. The police, not having been reformed, stands by and does nothing. The Supreme Court's ringing words are reduced to a nullity. The iqbal of the court—and, after all, institutions run on the esteem and awe in which they are held—drains.

Two general points

The first thing that leaps at one is that the political class as a whole, and not just one party or another, strives to keep the judiciary down. After all, different parties have been in power at the Centre over the last three decades, and yet the attitude towards the directions of the courts—be these regarding the number of judges or the infrastructure of courts—has remained the same. Similarly, at any given time, different parties are in power in different states, and yet non-compliance is a feature common across several states.

The second point is a lesson for the judiciary itself. The courts, especially so overburdened a court such as the Supreme Court, have to proceed on the assumption that good faith and conscience would lead everyone to instantly and to the fullest extent abide by its directions. Moreover, the assumption is that if governments or others do not abide by its instructions, those aggrieved by their non-compliance will bring the infraction to the notice of the courts. As instances such as the forgoing show, the twin assumptions are not entirely in sync with reality.

The lesson is obvious. The court must, from time to time, and suo motu as the expression goes, do a sort of random check whether its directions are being obeyed or not. There is a special reason for doing so now. When a judgment is declaratory of law or of what is lawful and constitutional, in a sense that is the end of the matter. But when a judgment prescribes that the executive or others take certain steps, in a sense, it is the *beginning* of the matter. And such judgments are more and more common these days as all of us rush to the courts beseeching them to step in and direct government and others to do their duty.

Moreover, consequences must be visited upon individuals—the senior-most in a department, etc.—for the dereliction. For, when its directions are disregarded, it isn't just that the goals that, say, the Supreme Court had sought to achieve in that particular case are set back. Its authority in general is damaged. And every act of noncompliance or partial compliance that goes unpunished emboldens those who will do wrong, and thus makes the next one that much more likely.

Even more vital than ensuring that its orders are carried out to the letter, the judiciary must ensure that its good name remains free of the slightest taint.

6

When one of our own is involved

Today, the judiciary is among the few institutions—perhaps one of just two or three—that still commands respect. It is one of the few from which the people at large still expect something. And it has many, many sterling achievements to its credit.

First of all, such accountability as survives in public life does so only because of the judiciary and sections of the media—more accurately, because of a few judges, and a few journalists.

Second, for seventy years, the judiciary—in particular, the Supreme Court—has been the dyke that has preserved free speech.

Third, the singular check that exists today against misuse of its power by Parliament is in place solely because of what the Supreme Court decided in *Kesavananda Bharati*[1]. Similarly, one has only to recall how frequently and with what impunity Article 356 used to be unleashed by the executive before the Supreme Court's judgment in *Bommai's*[2] case and how few the attempts to misuse it have been since to realize what a salutary check the judiciary has been on excesses of the executive.

Fourth, some of the most salutary improvements, however limited they may be, that have occurred in the last few years in our public life, have occurred because of initiatives taken by the courts, indeed, by the courts reaching beyond what many would argue are

---

1 *Kesavananda Bharati v. State of Kerala*, (1973) 4 SCC 225.

2 *S.R. Bommai v. Union of India*, (1994) 3 SCC 1.

its proper limits. Recall, for instance, the change that the Supreme Court brought about in the nomination form that candidates must file when they stand for elections. I was in government at the time, and can testify from personal knowledge how intensely ever so many politicians, among them prominent ministers, opposed the Supreme Court's suggestion to the Election Commission that the nomination form include both the educational background and the criminal antecedents of candidates. Similarly, the more recent change by which those who have been convicted are barred from holding office or contesting elections would never have come about if the matter had remained in the hands of the political class. As we have seen, it is only because of the Supreme Court that today, several conspicuous politicians are not able to sit in legislatures and decide the laws under which we shall live, indeed to decide the ways in which our Constitution itself will or will not be amended.

Fifth, several of the 'excesses' for which the judiciary is criticized have been necessitated by the executive or our legislatures not doing their duty. The shameful way in which the self-serving sub-section, which enabled those convicted even of heinous crimes to continue as legislators, remained on the statute book is a ready example. Its perverse consequences were highlighted time and again. Legislatures did nothing. And that for the all-too-obvious reason: the decision to undo it lay in the hands of the very ones who would be the first to suffer were the law to be changed. It is only because legislatures failed for decades to excise the perverse provision that the Supreme Court stepped in.

Therefore, I am among those who feel deeply indebted to the judiciary—both as a citizen and as one whose work is to read and write. And I am among those who look ever more expectantly to the judiciary because of the alarming deterioration in the standards of our legislatures, and therefore of the executive. We look all the more to the judiciary because of the unique opportunity that lies in its hands today. The number of judges one has to convince to bring about a change is far fewer than the number one must convince to bring about the same change via legislatures, for instance. Moreover, judges as a class are far better informed than, say, our legislators or even ministers as a class. There is also an opportunity for another reason: today, twenty- to thirty-odd prominent politicians are arrayed before one court or another. If fifteen or twenty of them end up in jail serving seven- to eight-year sentences, thousands will come to feel that, despite all the perversions that have taken place in the last thirty years—for instance, in spite of the extent to which investigating agencies have become the private posses of whoever is in office—the corrupt *can* be brought to book. That single fact will give heart to millions to do their bit to rein in the wicked. Today, just a handful of judges can indeed trigger a new beginning.

All this is true, but it is equally true that there are grounds for concern.

Recall, for instance, the direction that the discourse on the collegium of judges has taken over the last few years. After bitter experience, an instrument was devised to wrest back the key from the robber, if I may use a phrase I had to use in regard to the second *Transfer of Judges*[3] judgment—an instrument to limit the power of the executive to determine the selection and postings of judges. Over the years, the very authors of the device came to feel that the collegium had become a forum for judges—and that too, the senior-most judges—to strike bargains over nominees. The executive used the criticisms to try and grab back the power. To every thinking person's relief, the Supreme Court defeated that effort. But that the field could be prepared for such an attempt to be made showed that all had not been well. And that in future the collegium would have to be guided even more by manifest merit of the candidates than has been the case in the past.

Second, while it is true that there *is* a once-in-a-lifetime opportunity for the judiciary to trigger a new beginning—for instance, consider stemming corruption—it is equally true that the opportunity is not being grasped as firmly as it needs to be. Every so often, cases in courts wax and wane in accordance with the convenience of those who happen to be in power. And not just in regard to corruption—recall the way several cases of terrorist blasts, or of inciting riots, or of fake encounters have gone. That evidence is being diluted or perverted is evident to all—it must be even more so to the judges who are hearing the case from day to day and are, therefore, so much better placed to discern the changes. And yet right in front of their

3 *S.P. Gupta v. Union of India*, (1981) Supp. SCC 87.

eyes the prosecution emphasizes one thing one day and buries it the next. And the judges sit and watch silently.

Third, while each judge as an individual must be as compassionate as the rest of us, there is little doubt that the system taken as a whole has become heartless—recall the instance with which I began the book.

Fourth, it is indeed sad to see that as is the case with other institutions, there continues to be a secular decline in the excellence of the judiciary: one has only to read the judgments of the 1950s and those being given today to see this, and we will come to a few examples of the latter in a moment.

Being above suspicion

Few would today say that the judiciary is 'above suspicion'. Every time one hears allegations about how a magistrate or judge has been suborned, one's heart breaks. I say this from personal experience, having worked in *The Indian Express* that was often set upon by the rulers. I realized that while we could indeed turn to the courts for protection as we did, ultimately the only protection for a paper or a writer was the reader's faith. Ultimately the only thing that would—and did—save us was the fact that the readers saw that what we were doing was in the public interest. One's work must be so manifestly in the public interest that, when rulers raise a hand against one, the readers must know, they must *feel* that the paper or writer is being set upon because of what it has done or the writer has written in their interest, they must instinctively feel that the paper is in the right and the rulers have something to hide. It is because *The Indian Express* was seen to be acting in the public interest that, every time Rajiv Gandhi's government raided us or filed cases and set up inquiries against us, our circulation went up. I was able to request our cartoonist to draw a cartoon—a truthful one—with the prime minister slumped on one of our broken-down desks, with a banner '*Indian Express*' behind him, and a small board lying on the desk in front of him with the legend 'Circulation Manager'. If people begin to feel that judges are not above board, if they get convinced that, the compassion of judges as individuals notwithstanding, the system has become heartless, they will not stand by the judiciary when the executive or legislators of the day raise their hand against the institution.

That points to three requisites. First, of course, the judiciary must stand firm against the slightest attempt to whittle its powers and ambit—as it has recently done in thwarting the attempt of the political executive to appropriate greater power for itself by tilting the membership of the proposed Judicial Appointments Commission. Second, it must deliver justice—swift, certain, unambiguous—so that the people see the judiciary as their shield, so that when the executive raises a hand against the judiciary the people feel that it is raising a hand against *them*. Third, and most important, the reputation of judges must be such that—even in our times when everyone is only too ready to believe the worst about everyone else—no one should even entertain the allegation that they will ever do anything for any collateral purpose or consideration.

An institution does not run, the state itself does not run, on danda, on the threat that it can heap punishment on those who do not abide by its decrees. The judiciary cannot run on, say, the powers it has under the Contempt of Courts Act. Institutions run, the state runs, on iqbal, on the esteem in which people hold it. That is why the slightest tear in reputation brought about by the misconduct of a single judge is so injurious: it taints the reputation, and therefore whittles the power of the judiciary as a whole.

And one must remember that nothing remains hidden. The tout who would have engineered or mediated the deal will let it be known far and wide that he has a special relationship with Judge X: it is only by broadcasting that fact that he will get more business. In fact, the infirmities in the resulting judgment are manifest, they are enough to suggest that something has happened. In any case, the biggest litigant—the government—keeps an eye on weaknesses, and gets to know. From then on, the judge is under its sway.

This entails three things at the least. Of course, every judge must be absolutely straight. Second, and I am sorry to record that this is so often lost sight of, judges must never accept an ounce of extra privilege from the executive. How well I remember the day Justice V.D. Tulzapurkar retired. Anita and I had gone to his house to bid Mrs Tulzapurkar and him goodbye. The house was bare except for governmental furniture—all their personal belongings had already been sent to Bombay. We accompanied Justice and Mrs Tulzapurkar to the railway station. Both took their seats in the chair-car bogey. He had vacated the government house and left Delhi the day he had retired. Months later, I was in Bombay. I contacted him, and sought time to meet him. When I went to the address, I found him in a little cubby-hole of an office. Seeing my surprise, he said, 'This is where I began, this is where I have returned.' What a contrast it is today, and how disheartening to hear of judges angling for appointments to commissions.

A lemma follows. Judges must take the swiftest action whenever even the slightest allegation is made against a colleague. One of the factors that has drained the political class of all legitimacy has been a perverted sense of loyalty: 'O, he is our brother, he is from our party, we must stand by him.' Unfortunately, judges do not always act with the swiftness that the matter demands when some inconvenient fact erupts about a colleague. Two examples will suffice to illustrate both—the course such instances take, and the injury that the procrastination inflicts on the good name of the judiciary.

A wrong delivery brings a reality to light

On 13 August 2008, a person came and delivered a packet to the guard at the residence of Justice Nirmaljit Kaur, a judge of the Punjab and Haryana High Court. A member of her staff brought it to her saying that a person had brought case papers from Delhi. She asked him to open the packet, and was shocked to see that in fact the packet contained money—Rs 15 lakh. She had her staff seize the courier. Police were called. The man was taken into custody. The judge also immediately informed the Chief Justice of the High Court.[4]

---

4 I am grateful to Saurabh Malik of *The Tribune* and Varinder Bhatia of *The Indian Express* for recalling the details of the episode. But for Saurabh, I would have missed an important turn in the case. In this section, all material which is within quotation marks or indented is taken from the exemplary judgment of Justice Permod Kohli of the High Court of Punjab and Haryana in *Mrs. Nirmal Yadav v. Central Bureau of Investigation,* Criminal Misc. Number M-14289 of 2011.

Interrogation of the courier and further inquiries revealed five things:

- The courier was the junior munshi of the then additional advocate general of Haryana, Sanjiv Bansal.
- The money was meant for another judge of the High Court—Justice Nirmal Yadav: one explanation is that the munshi was told to deliver the money to 'Nirmalji', he heard 'Nirmaljit' and thus helped the cause of probity.
- The money was a bribe in lieu of a favourable judgment that had been handed down earlier in regard to a property case, a case in which the then additional advocate general, Sanjiv Bansal, was an interested party.
- According to the CBI, the judgment had been delivered 'under the influence of' a businessman, Ravinder Singh, 'who had close association' with the judge.
- The businessman had paid the money through a hotelier based in Delhi.[5]

The case was first taken up by the state police. It was later transferred to the CBI. According to the CBI, the money not having reached her, Justice Nirmal Yadav again demanded Rs 15 lakh. This amount was delivered to her the next morning, 14 August 2008.

As we know, a judge can be prosecuted only after obtaining sanction of the appointing authority, in this case the president of India. In *Veeraswami's* case,[6] the Supreme Court ruled that, in determining whether to sanction prosecution, the president must consult the Chief Justice of India. In a host of judgments, the court has also laid down that the 'consultation' must be 'full and effective'. In the matter at hand, namely whether a judge should be prosecuted, in *Veeraswami,* the Supreme Court had in fact laid down that:

---

5 Whom Varinder Bhatia describes as being one who is 'considered to be a well-entrenched businessman in New Delhi, Punjab and Haryana judiciary'.

6 *K. Veeraswami v. Union of India,* 1991 (3) SCC 655.

> ...the Chief Justice being the head of the judiciary is primarily concerned with the integrity and impartiality of the judiciary. Hence it is necessary that the Chief Justice of India is not kept out of the picture of any criminal case contemplated against a Judge. He would be in a better position to give his opinion in the case and consultation with the Chief Justice of India would be of immense assistance to the Government in coming to the right conclusion. We therefore, direct that no criminal case shall be registered under Section 154, Cr. P.C. against Judge of the High Court, Chief Justice of High Court or Judge of the Supreme Court unless the Chief Justice of India is consulted in the matter. Due regard must be given by the Government to the opinion expressed by the Chief Justice. *If the Chief Justice is of opinion that it is not a fit case for proceeding under the Act, the case shall not be registered.* If the Chief Justice of India himself is the person against whom the allegations of criminal misconduct are received the Government shall consult any other Judge or Judges of the Supreme Court. *There shall be similar consultation at the stage of examining the question of granting sanction for prosecution and it shall be necessary and appropriate that the question of sanction be guided by and in accordance with the advice of the Chief Justice of India.*

There was a difference of opinion within the CBI between the Director, Prosecutions, who felt that prosecution was not warranted, and the Director, CBI, who felt that it was. Accordingly, in accordance with what its manual prescribes, the CBI wrote to the government to seek the opinion of the attorney general.

From this point on things began to get curiouser and curiouser.

The attorney general was Milon Banerjee. He rendered an opinion that can only be described as Nelsonian. Remember that by now the CBI had already established the key facts. Apart from the Rs 15 lakh having been delivered, apart from the statements of the munshi and others, the CBI had uncovered additional indications of the close acquaintance of Justice Nirmal Yadav and Ravinder Singh—for instance, telephonic conversations, as well as air tickets, mobile phone, etc., that had been gifted to the judge by this person. Furthermore, the CBI found out that Justice Nirmal Yadav, her brother (then the finance minister of Haryana), Ravinder Singh and others had joined together to acquire land in Solan, Himachal Pradesh, and for this undue influence had been used. Banerjee was not moved. Please read the opinion he rendered as it shows how much the foremost law officer of the country can strain not to see what is manifest. Banerjee wrote:

> 9. Therefore, even assuming for the sake of argument that Justice Nirmal Yadav had demanded Rs.15 lakhs, *there is absolutely no evidence to prove that Shri Ravinder Singh was in any manner or was likely to be in any manner concerned in any proceedings or business transacted or about to be transacted by Justice Yadav or that accused Ravinder Singh was having any connection with the official function of Justice Yadav.* The amount had admittedly originated from Shri Ravinder Singh and was being merely delivered by Sanjiv Bansal. Therefore, the prosecution is required to establish that there was some connection between Ravinder Singh and Justice Yadav because of which this amount was demanded or delivered. Even if the entire evidence is to be believed, such a connection is not even remotely established. *There may have been, as alleged by the CBI or may not have been some connection between Justice Yadav and Sanjiv Bansal in the past. This is a matter which cannot be a subject matter of investigation in the present FIR.* In any event, that is absolutely no evidence to indicate, far less to prove that this amount was demanded or delivered for any official connection relating to the work of Justice Yadav or to confer a benefit on Ravinder Singh or Sanjiv Bansal or any other person. Therefore, on the material on record no offence under Sections 11 and 12 is made out against Justice Nirmal Yadav. Consequently, the charge under Section 120-B read with Sections 11 and 12 of the PC Act would be baseless.
>
> 10. At this stage I may indicate that from the notes it appears that the Deputy Legal Adviser was of the view that an offence under Section 11 is made out against Justice Yadav because she had received mobile phone, air ticket etc., from Ravinder Singh and Sanjiv Bansal. In my view, since there is *no evidence of any official relations between Justice Yadav and Ravinder Singh*, Section 11 is not attracted in the present case.

> 11. In so far as the alleged offences under the Indian Penal Code are concerned, there is not even an iota of allegation that Justice Yadav was involved in any manner in the statements made by accused S/Shri Sanjiv Bansal, Nirmal Singh, Rajiv Gupta or the documents which were tendered by them to the local Chandigarh Police. *It appears that once Rs.15 lakhs were seized, the said accused persons allegedly made up a story of delivery of Rs.15 lakhs to accused Nirmal Singh. As rightly pointed out by the Additional Legal Adviser such statements or documents were given to the local police prior to the registration of FIR and therefore, the ingredients of Sections 192/193 IPC are not attracted.* The Additional Legal Adviser has rightly pointed out that since the statements made to the police are not evidence in the eyes of law, Section 199 IPC also is not attracted. Therefore, there is grave doubt as to any offence under Sections 192 read with 193, 199 or 200 of IPC was committed by accused S/Shri Sanjiv Bansal, Rajiv Gupta and Nirmal Singh. *In any event of the matter in so far as accused Justice Yadav is concerned, there is not a shred of evidence that the said alleged offences were committed by Sanjiv Bansal, Ravinder Singh and Nirmal Singh in conspiracy with accused Justice Yadav.* There is definitely no material to prosecute Justice Yadav for a charge under Section 120-B far less for substantive offences under Sections 192/193 of IPC.

Are 'official relations' between a judge and the source of money necessary? Does the source of the money need to have a connection with 'the official function' of the judge? To refute what the CBI had uncovered, is it enough to say, 'It appears that'—without indicating the basis on which 'it appears that'—'once Rs. 15 lakhs were seized, the said accused persons allegedly made up a story of delivery of Rs. 15 lakhs to the accused Nirmal Singh.' And in how many cases is that criterion—that statements made before the police are 'not evidence in the eyes of law'—deployed?

The CBI gave detailed answers to the conclusions that Banerjee had formulated. Apart from recounting the evidence that it had uncovered, it noted that one reason the attorney general had concluded that no case was made out was his premise that the FIR had related only to the delivery of Rs 15 lakh to the house of Justice Nirmaljit

Kaur, and that, as the Chief Justice had not given any concurrence to investigate transactions relating to the land in Solan, it could not be brought into consideration of the matter. The CBI recorded that, in point of fact, the Chief Justice of India *had given his concurrence* in this regard—and it furnished a communication dated 4 September 2008 from the secretary general of the Supreme Court to this effect.

And then came another twist. Indeed, three.

By now a series of changes had taken place fortuitously. Chief Justice K.G. Balakrishnan had been succeeded by Justice S.H. Kapadia. Law Minister H.R. Bharadwaj had been succeeded by Veerappa Moily. And Milon Banerjee had been succeeded by Goolam E. Vahanvati as attorney general, another officer of law committed to probity.

Media published reports that the CBI had been refused permission to proceed with the cash-at-the-doorstep case. On 15 July 2009, the law minister recorded on file:

> The allegations made herein are quite serious in nature. These allegations cannot be brushed aside only on technical grounds. The case in question, if not pressed will erode the faith of people in the judiciary.
>
> In view of the above, I strongly feel that the matter may be referred to the present Attorney General for opinion and examine the matter on merits.

On 19 November 2009, the CBI sent its detailed response to the Ministry of Personnel, and requested that the matter be examined again and the opinion of the new attorney general be sought.

Vahanvati too shut an eye: whereas Milon had ensured that, in addition to other aspects of the matter, he would not see the transactions relating to the purchase of land by Nirmal Yadav, Ravinder Singh and others, Vahanvati ensured that he would not see the main question—the Rs 15 lakh that had been wrongly delivered. He dealt with the transactions relating to the purchase of land at Solan and disposed of them as follows:

> It is stated that one Ravinder Singh had purchased the plots of land at Solan jointly with Justice Nirmal Yadav, and this is linked to para

5 of that letter, where it is mentioned that according to Shri Sanjiv Bansal, an amount of Rs.15 lakhs was to be delivered to Justice Nirmal Yadav at the instance of his close friend Shri Ravinder Singh. It therefore appears that the reference to Ravinder Singh and the purchase of land in para 6 of the letter is to show the connection between Ravinder Singh, and the cash of Rs.15 lakhs with Justice Nirmal Yadav. I do not find any reference in the letter dated 4.09.2008 to any irregularities in relation to purchase of land at Solan.

4. The letter received from the Hon'ble Chief Justice of India in relation to grant of permission for investigation is not on the file. I assume that it was written with reference to the letter dated 04.09.2008. As mentioned above, there is nothing in the letter dated 04.09.2008 which seeks to investigate the alleged irregularities in relation to the purchase of land at Solan. It therefore cannot be said that the learned Chief Justice had granted permission to investigate into alleged irregularities in the purchase of land at Solan.

5. Incidentally, this seems to be the understanding of the SP himself since in his report dated 13.01.2009 in para 15.12, the following has been stated:

'15.12. The scrutiny of the files related to the grant of permission to Mrs. Justice Nirmal Yadav (A-6) and 17 others for purchase of land in District Solan, Himachal Pradesh reveals prima facie commission of offences of forgery, cheating and abuse of official position by Mrs. Justice Nirmal Yadav (A-6), officers of Himachal Pradesh Government and others. As this is a separate offence, committed in different territorial jurisdiction, it requires to be investigated separately, for which permission of Hon'ble Chief Justice and Himachal Pradesh Govt. is required as laid down in *K. Veeraswami vs. Union of India* (1991 SCR (3) 189) as well as notification under Section 5 and 6 of the DSPE Act respectively.'

6. This clearly shows that even according to the SP, the allegations relating to the alleged offences of forgery, cheating and abuse of official position with regard to purchase of land at Solan constitute a separate offence and committed in different territorial jurisdiction which was required to be investigated separately and for which the permission of the Hon'ble Chief Justice of India would be required in accordance with the judgment in K. Veeraswami's case.

On 7 December 2009, D.R. Meena, secretary, Ministry of Law and Justice, wrote to the director, CBI, that 'sanction for prosecution has been declined on the grounds that after analysis of the available evidence, the learned attorney general of India has observed that there is not a shred of evidence that the said alleged offences were committed by Sanjiv Bansal, Ravinder Singh and Nirmal Singh in conspiracy with Justice Yadav' and that 'the matter had been discussed with the CJI, who had observed that no action was required for the present'.

Accordingly, the CBI filed a 'closure report' in the court of the special judge on the ground that sanction for prosecution had been refused by the competent authority.

This too hit the headlines—that sanction had been refused after consultation with the Chief Justice of India. On 10 February 2010, the secretary general of the Supreme Court wrote to newspapers that the matter had *not* been referred to the Chief Justice, and that he had *not* recommended that sanction for prosecution be refused.

On 26 March 2010, the special judge turned down the 'closure report', and directed the CBI to investigate the matter further.

The question was now properly referred to the Chief Justice of India. Since May 1997, a procedure had been laid down for dealing with such instances. In accordance with that the Chief Justice set up an internal committee of three judges—the Chief Justices of the High Courts of Allahabad and Gujarat and a judge of the Delhi High Court. The committee examined nineteen witnesses, including Justice Nirmal Yadav, Justice Nirmaljit Kaur and others. It examined documents as well as records of telephonic conversations. The examination led it to infer that the Rs 15 lakh was indeed meant for Justice Nirmal Yadav.

Eventually, on 1 March 2011, two-and-a-half years after the misdelivery, the president accorded his sanction for prosecuting Justice Nirmal Yadav.

A year after her name figured in the case, Justice Nirmal Yadav was transferred to the High Court of Uttarakhand where, of course, she continued to dispense justice.

It is only on 4 March 2011—*two-and-a-half years* after the incident—that the CBI filed a charge sheet. Justice Nirmal Yadav was accused of corruption, and, along with others, of criminal conspiracy. The charge sheet also mentioned land that she, her brother (then finance minister of Haryana), and other relatives had purchased in Himachal Pradesh the day after the money was delivered—to the wrong address! March 4, 2011 happened to be the last day of her tenure as a judge: she retired that day.

Filing of the charge sheet was challenged.

After detailed hearings, on 14 November 2011, the High Court rejected the challenge. The principal ground for the challenge was that the sanctioning authority, having once refused sanction, could not proceed to reverse his opinion and grant sanction. In an exemplary reconstruction of the law and events, the High Court showed that (i) there is no bar to the sanctioning authority reversing its opinion when new evidence is put to it; and (ii) that the consultation with the Chief Justice of India that is required by various judgments of the Supreme Court was gone through only once, and so there was no ground to maintain that he or the president had reversed their opinion.

Further twists and turns took place. It was only on 31 July 2013—*five years* after the misdelivery—that the CBI court in Chandigarh accepted the charge sheet against Justice Nirmal Yadav and the others.

And it was only on 3 May 2016—*seven-and-a-half years* after the delivery—that the special judge framed charges in the case.

The case is still in the trial court.

The additional advocate general whose munshi had misheard and thus misdelivered the money has died of brain tumour.

Justice Nirmal Yadav has retired.

Justice Nirmaljit Kaur who raised the alarm is currently a judge in the Rajasthan High Court.

Nine years, and the case is still in its first lap.

Several lessons leap up from the sequence:

- The exemplary role of the special judge who refused to accept the 'closure report' of the CBI
- The deftness with which the High Court disposed of the challenge

- The role of lawyers who—as in the case of Jayalalithaa before the Karnataka High Court—pressed arguments that can only be described as arguments of convenience
- The role of the highest law officers of the country: were they acting as the judicial conscience of governments, and of counsellors to the judiciary itself, or as the handmaidens of the influential?
- The role of civil servants: the record clearly showed that the sort of consultation with the Chief Justice mandated by law had *not* taken place, and that the file had *not* been sent to the authority that has the power to accord or refuse sanction for the prosecution of a judge, namely the president of India. Hence, on what consideration—of law and facts—did the law secretary write that sanction had been refused? On what basis did he insinuate the impression that this refusal had occurred after consultation with the Chief Justice?
- The odd decision of transferring Justice Nirmal Yadav to the High Court of Uttarakhand even as she was under such a dark cloud. Why saddle courts—whether it be the Calcutta High Court in the case of Justice Karnan, or, as has happened ever so frequently, the courts of Sikkim and other hapless states in the Northeast, or that of Uttarakhand for that matter—with such eminences? And notice too that the fact that the judge was transferred to the High Court of Uttarakhand became one of the arguments that was urged in her favour. It was argued in the High Court that the very fact that the collegium had transferred her showed that, after examining the facts and consulting the Chief Justice, the sanctioning authority had refused sanction. After all, if the Chief Justice and the president had concluded that, yes, she deserved to be prosecuted, would the collegium, of which the Chief Justice was himself a member, have allowed her to assume charge in another High Court?

And, of course, above all these is the central question: what does such a sequence—one in which nine years after it burst into the public arena, a case involving a judge of a High Court is still in the first stage—do to the image of the judiciary as a whole? Are people liable to conclude that the system is geared to swiftly excise a tumour or that it is designed so that a fellow judge will get the most indulgent consideration?

Judges and I are taken to be fools

In the same year in which this misdelivery happened in Chandigarh, 2008, after an investigation lasting three years, the CBI had registered a case against a member of the Income Tax Appellate Tribunal (ITAT) for delivering 'pre-decided' judgments in favour of the clients of one firm of chartered accountants based in Kolkata. The house of the member had been raided and Rs 28 lakh had been recovered. By January 2012, *The Indian Express* was reporting that the text of judgments—some of which had not even been delivered—was found in the computers of that firm. Clearly, some members had outsourced their decisions, so to say. The paper reported that the CBI had come upon reasons to doubt at least sixty-nine judgments delivered by twenty-three members in favour of the firm's clients. The racket was obviously widespread. In May 2012, the paper reported, 'The agency seized 75 pre-dated judgments from the hard discs' of the firm. 'Of these, 57 were learnt to be delivered by ITAT benches in Chennai, Mumbai, Kolkata and Hyderabad.' In the case of twelve judgments, the text was found even before they had been delivered. When they were delivered, they turned out to be identical to the ones that were lodged in the computers of the firm.

In February 2012, the paper reported that the CBI was still awaiting permission to investigate a sitting High Court judge and sixteen others. The CBI had registered preliminary enquiries against eight members—they had retired, and so no permission from the government was needed. But for the rest, the CBI had applied to the law ministry for registering preliminary enquiries against fifteen members of ITAT and four officials of the income tax department. The law ministry sent the file to the attorney general. Four years went by. At last, in May 2012, the CBI received permission to proceed further in regard to the remaining members and officers.

By May 2014, one case was under trial. The CBI had closed all the other cases! The evidence was insufficient, it maintained ... there was no direct evidence of quid pro quo. And, lo and behold, the CBI, the *Express* reported, had concluded that 'the charge that the judgments were "pre-written" cannot be proved, and it is a normal practice for the benches to seek assistance from the accountant firms due to shortage of staff'.[7]

I got direct evidence, so to say, of that alibi. I had been invited by the National Judicial Academy at Bhopal to deliver a lecture. Judges from the Supreme Court, High Court judges, sessions judges and other judges from four states and senior officials from the law ministry were participating in the conference. I mentioned the Income Tax Tribunal case to illustrate the point that the judiciary must act swiftly when one of its own is implicated in a matter, that the consequence of letting the matter drag or be derailed by legalisms or legal ploys is to raise doubts about the judiciary itself.

Later in the day, the senior-most official explained, 'Sir, you don't quite follow the matter. That draft judgments were found in the computers of the accountants' firm does not mean that they were being prepared there. You see, to earn a little extra money, our stenos take up part-time work after office hours in such firms. The tribunal members would have dictated the judgments, the stenos would have taken the dictation pads to the firm and, between typing work for the firm, they would have been typing what the members had dictated. That is all.'

How well this tallied with what *The Indian Express* had reported: 'The agency [the CBI] has also concluded that the charge that the judgments were "pre-written" cannot be proved, and it is a normal practice for the benches to seek assistance from the accountant firms due to shortage of staff'—just that instead of the benches seeking assistance of firms of chartered accountants, in this official's version the stenos were seeking to make a little extra money! I had to tell him that he must be taking me and the judges who were sitting at our table to be fools. First, stenos are barred from taking drafts out

7 On all this, see reports by Rahul Tripathi and Ritu Sarin, in *The Indian Express* of 11 January 2012, 9 February 2012, 14 May 2012 and 5 May 2014.

of the office. Second, they are barred from doing part-time work—certainly at firms that service clients who are arraigned before the tribunal. And, third, how is it that *sixty-nine* judgments had turned up in the computers of these firms, that *twelve* judgments which had yet to be delivered had turned up in the computers of one firm? The officer focused more intently on the food on his plate.

Clearly, whenever a judge is found or even suspected of having done wrong, the judiciary must ensure that the investigation and the case proceed with maximum speed. Second, the attitude must not be one of false loyalty, 'O, he is our brother judge.' The judiciary must proceed with the conviction that if there is a tumour, it must be excised immediately lest it infect the body as a whole.

After all, the judiciary is 'a house set on a hill'—it is being looked upon, and not just looked up to, by everyone. Does it reinforce belief in itself when it rejects a request for information on a matter as simple as the medical expenses that have been incurred on individual judges and been reimbursed by the Supreme Court? Does it reinforce belief in itself when it decides not to take up the request for information on assets owned by judges and their immediate family members? Does it lessen or enhance the belief of citizens that it is serious about delivering justice swiftly when it rejects a petition seeking information about cases, arguments on which have been concluded but judgments on which have yet to be delivered?[8]

Second, all of us, and that includes judges, must always remember that institutions come down not so often by the sudden, great blow but by corrosion—over decades. Every dilution, every departure from the highest standard accustoms us to the next lower level. And soon we are hurtling down a steep and greasy slope. What has happened to the political class should be ample warning.

Nor is it just that the procedures that are prescribed and the systems that are in place for dealing with allegations against judges are the only ones that need to be examined afresh. A recent case, and a tragic one at that, showed how procedures and systems for dealing with far graver infirmities too must be thought through again.

---

8 C.f., Anjali Bharadwaj and Prashant Bhushan, 'A transparency deficit,' *The Indian Express*, 22 February 2018.

7

Bane hain ahl-e-havas muddai bhi munsif bhi...

Developments of the recent past leave one disheartened in the extreme—for the highest court itself has been proceeding in ways directly antithetical to the lessons that became apparent in the preceding chapter. Three cases that caused much public unease will illustrate both what has been happening, as well as the consequences that have ensued, not in the least for the court itself.

A suicide note

Kalikho Pul had been an elected representative in Arunachal Pradesh since 1995. He became chief minister of Arunachal in February 2016. A series of events so tragically common in the Northeast—trading, switching sides—took off. The matter was taken to the Supreme Court. On 13 July 2016, the court's judgment ended his government.

Pul's body was found hanging on 9 August 2016. The additional district magistrate found a sixty-page handwritten note next to his body. Each page had been signed and initialled by Pul. The last signature was dated the very day that Pul had committed suicide—8 August 2016.

To anyone who is even in the least bit familiar with the Northeast—and I had occasion to learn about the region in detail both during the All Assam Students Union (AASU) agitation in Assam, and during Mr Vajpayee's government, as the Northeast was one of the ministries that I handled—the note had the ring of truth. The corruption that he detailed, the devices by which money allocated to the state had been and was being siphoned off by politicians of the region—these have indeed been the bane of the Northeast, and the appalling misfortune of the good and simple people of the region. Other than paragraphs that dealt with his personal life, every paragraph stated facts and contained figures.

For our present purposes, what is of importance is that during the course of his narration of how the matter had reached the Guwahati High Court and eventually the Supreme Court, and the events that had followed, Pul had made specific and far-reaching allegations against persons in high office, including those of the party, the Congress to which he had belonged, as well as against two former Chief Justices, the then Chief Justice, the then second senior-most judge of the Supreme Court, and senior advocates. The gravamen of these statements was that he had been asked for—huge—sums of money to get the Supreme Court to decide in his favour. He wrote that he had had neither the resources nor the disposition to pay the amounts; that his rivals had both in abundance, and that is how they had secured the verdict in their favour.[1]

The former governor of Arunachal Pradesh, Raj Khowa, affirmed that the allegations that were made in the note were of a very serious nature, and needed to be investigated thoroughly.

The widow of Pul, Mrs Dangwimsai Pul, wrote to the then Chief Justice requesting that an independent inquiry be instituted to examine the charges. We have seen that since *Veeraswami's* case,[2] an inquiry into the conduct of a judge cannot be initiated without the permission of the Chief Justice. As the then Chief Justice had

---

1 Pul wrote the note in his own hand in Hindi—a language in which he was proficient. For the complete text—translated into English—see the website of the Campaign for Judicial Accountability and Reforms: http://judicialreforms.org/cjar-covering-note-along-with-mr-kalikho-pul-former-arunachal-pradesh-cms-complete-suicide-note-without-redactions/. In the text of the note, see, in particular, paragraphs 9.7-8, 15.19-27.

2 *K. Veeraswami v. Union of India,* (1991) 3 SCC 655.

himself been named in Pul's note, and as the judge next in line to become Chief Justice too had been named, the matter should have been referred to one or more of the other senior judges. That was not done. Moreover, the matter was of an administrative nature, dealing as it did with the functioning of the court. Instead, the Chief Justice took the matter in his own hands, converted the letter into a petition and assigned it on the judicial side to Court Number 13. On legal advice, Mrs Pul withdrew the petition and instead wrote to the next three senior-most judges for permission to have an FIR registered.

Various turns occurred after that. The material point is that nothing came of all the efforts. Did the judges and advocates, more important did the court, win or lose?

Three things stand out. First, it is wrong to presume that nothing happened in the end. For in the end, the allegations levelled by Pul have survived. Is that good for the repute of our courts and judges?

Second, even a week's work would have established whether the suicide note was at all worthy of examination. It was replete with references to specific events, dates, governmental schemes, outlays and the rest. A check would have established whether the statements had any basis in fact. If statements about these schemes, programmes, outlays, etc.—all unconnected with the judges and the courts—were found to be inventions, one could have concluded, at least prima facie, that one need not examine assertions about the judges and courts. On the other hand, if these statements tallied with facts—if the schemes that Pul had mentioned, the outlays that he had listed, the devices by which monies were being siphoned off, etc.—had indeed been as he had listed them in his note, further inquiry into other statements he had made would have been warranted. Even this simple exercise was never undertaken.

Third, there is the law. A dying declaration is assigned great weight in our courts. And, in this regard, under the relevant sections of the Indian Evidence Act, a suicide note is akin to a dying declaration. It has evidentiary status—all the more so if the person has recorded facts of which he is liable to have had personal knowledge, and which implicate himself. Consider Section 32 of the Indian Evidence Act:

> 32. *Cases in which statement of relevant fact by person who is dead or cannot be found, etc., is relevant.* — Statements, written or verbal, of relevant facts made by a person who is dead, or who cannot be found, or who has become incapable of giving evidence, or whose attendance cannot be procured without an amount of delay or expense which under the circumstances of the case appears to the Court unreasonable, are themselves relevant facts in the following cases: —
>
> (1) When it relates to cause of death.—When the statement is made by a person as to the cause of his death, or as to any of the circumstances of the transaction which resulted in his death, in cases in which the cause of that person's death comes into question.
>
> Such statements are relevant whether the person who made them was or was not, at the time when they were made, under expectation of death, and whatever may be the nature of the proceeding in which the cause of his death comes into question.
>
> ...(3) or against interest of maker.—When the statement is against the pecuniary or proprietary interest of the person making it, or when, if true, it would expose him or would have exposed him to a criminal prosecution or to a suit for damages.
>
> (4) or gives opinion as to public right or custom, or matters of general interest.—When the statement gives the opinion of any such person, as to the existence of any public right or custom or matter of public or general interest, of the existence of which, if it existed, he would have been likely to be aware, and when such statement was made before any controversy as to such right, custom or matter had arisen.

Now, Pul was indeed dead. The facts he had set out were such that he would 'likely to have been aware' of them personally. The note certainly set out the circumstances in which he was being compelled to take his own life. Many of the disclosures exposed him, and were, therefore, against his own interest. The matters that he had set out were most certainly of general as well as public interest.

Going by the lessons that we have gleaned from the cases considered above, far from letting the matter 'die a natural death', the prudent course would have been for the judiciary to institute the most independent inquiry as soon as the note had surfaced.

A possible murder

The next case, and the judiciary's reaction to it, was of much, much greater consequence—for it involved not money but possible murder. A person, Sohrabuddin, had been murdered in Gujarat along with his wife in 2005. He was said to have been killed in an 'encounter' with the Gujarat police. And the poor wife? Could she too have been in the 'encounter'? Amit Shah, then home minister of the state, and later president of the BJP, was among those who were charged with having engineered the deaths. The higher courts came to the conclusion that there was every prospect that the case would not be tried fairly in Gujarat, so they directed that the case be shifted to Maharashtra. The Supreme Court also directed that the case be tried by one judge from its commencement till it was brought to a conclusion. The case was assigned to the special court in Mumbai that handles CBI cases. The judge was J.T. Utpat. He issued a succession of summons directing Shah to appear in court. Shah did not. On 20 June 2014 he reprimanded Shah's counsel about their persistent efforts to have Shah exempted from appearing in court, and fixed 26 June as the next date, a date on which, he directed, Shah *must* appear. Lo and behold! He was transferred on 25 June! This in spite of the fact that the Supreme Court had directed in its order of 27 September 2012 that the case shall be heard from start to finish by one judge. And who transferred him? The very committee—the Administrative Committee of the Bombay High Court headed by the court's Chief Justice—which had been directed by the Supreme Court to ensure that the case will be heard from start to finish by the same judge.

A new judge, Brijgopal Harkishan Loya, was posted to handle the case. He was repeatedly pestered to discharge Shah without delay. He told the interlocutors that he could not do so—the record of the case ran into 10,000 pages by then, and he could not pass any order till he had studied the documents. Shah continued to not appear in his court also. Loya demanded the reasons for this non-appearance. He set the next date for appearance as 15 December.

He was persuaded to attend a marriage in Nagpur. A man in excellent health, with no consequential medical history, indeed not a trace of any heart ailment, he was said to have suddenly had a massive heart attack on the night of 30 November/1 December 2014, and died early in the morning of 1 December.

By some magic, two persons—wholly unconnected with the family—had got the phone numbers of the judge's wife, sisters and father, all of whom lived in distant towns and villages—Mumbai, Latur, Dhule, Jalgaon, Aurangabad—and had begun calling them from 5 in the morning that the judge had died, and they should proceed to Gategaon, a distant village about 30 kilometres from Latur, as the body was going to be sent there.

Not just the calls, but the choice of Gategaon was a mystery. In the normal course, the judge's body should have been taken to Mumbai where his wife and his family had been living. The family members said later that, even in their state of shock, they were astonished that the body had arrived unaccompanied. The family was persuaded to cremate the body posthaste.

A courageous journalist, Niranjan Takle, had pursued the death for a year and a half. All sorts of inconsistencies had become apparent. After much dilly-dallying, the magazine for which the journalist worked, *The Week*, decided not to publish the journalist's findings. He resigned, and continued to gather additional facts. Eventually, the account was published by the *Caravan* online.[3] It became a sensation.

Loya had phoned his wife around 11 at night. They had talked for forty minutes. He had not complained of any uneasiness. He had been lodged at a government guest house that is used by high-ups in government. He is said to have complained of chest pain around 4 a.m. There would have been several vehicles at the place. He was not taken to either of the two well-known hospitals that were nearby, and could provide specialist care. Instead, he was taken to an orthopaedic hospital—the owner had connections with several right-wing organizations. The journey from the government guest house to the hospital was said to have taken forty-five minutes. When the *Caravan* reporters traversed the same road, it took them six minutes. Several judges were said to have been present at the hospital—but no one seemed to know the name of their colleague. In stories that

3 3. C.f., Niranjan Takle, 'A Family Breaks Its Silence: Shocking Details Emerge in Death of Judge Presiding Over Sohrabuddin Trial', *Caravan,* 20 November 2017; and Atul Dev and Anosh Malekar, 'Death of Judge Loya: Possible Manipulation of Records and Inconsistent New Testimonies Raise Further Questions', *Caravan*, 21 December 2017.

appeared in leading newspapers, ostensibly to refute the *Caravan* account, the ECG was actually reproduced. The machine had printed the time and date of the ECG as 5.11 a.m., 30 November 2014—that is, one full day *before* Loya was said to have had his heart attack and died! Questioned, the hospital authorities maintained that this had happened because of a 'technical glitch'. No other ECG had suffered the glitch. Furthermore, even this ECG did not show the massive heart attack which Loya was said to have suffered. The time of death had been recorded as 6.15 a.m. But the family had started receiving calls around 5 a.m. telling them that the judge had died. Two sources—one at the Government Medical College and the other at the police station—told the follow-up team of *Caravan* that they had been informed around midnight that the judge had died.

The post-mortem was said to have been conducted between 10 and 11 a.m. on 1 December. Even a cursory glance at the report showed that the date had been overwritten. The report was signed by a police sub-inspector and someone who had identified himself as the paternal cousin of the judge; but the judge had no paternal cousin. Had the post-mortem been conducted at the time mentioned, the body could not have been delivered to the distant village when it was. The occupancy register at the guest house had clearly been tampered with. The entries would indicate that three judges had slept in one room that had just two beds.

The sister of the judge, herself a doctor, told Takle that the body bore injuries and blood at the back of the head, that his clothes were bloodstained, in particular his shirt had blood from the left shoulder to the waist—the post-mortem and police reports were not just silent about these facts, they stated the contrary ... And so on.[4]

But to revert to what was happening in the court. A new judge, M.V. Gosavi, was appointed to take the place of Loya. And within days, on 30 December 2014, without hearings that could be said by any stretch of the imagination to have gone into the details of evidence, he discharged Amit Shah. Shah had been discharged without facing trial—something that was again in complete disregard of the law and of specific directions of the Supreme Court.

---

4 On all this, the *Caravan* accounts listed above, and my conversations with Niranjan Takle before the account was published by the *Caravan*.

The CBI had hitherto been maintaining—through the FIRs it had registered, through the charge sheets it had filed—that Sohrabuddin, his wife Kausarbi and Tulsiram Prajapati, a key witness to the abduction of the couple by the police, had been murdered in fake encounters. It had strenuously opposed the order of the Gujarat High Court granting bail to Shah, and had filed a petition in the Supreme Court against it. It had maintained in its charge sheet that Shah was, in fact, presiding over an 'extortion racket'; that there had been 'a larger conspiracy' behind the killings; that Shah 'was the lynchpin of the conspiracy' as a result of which the killings had been executed; that he had 'constantly obstructed any proper investigation' into the killings, that 'it was at his behest and under his pressure that the top-ranking police officers tried to cover up all signs of his involvement in the killings of Sohrabuddin, Kausarbi and Tulsiram Prajapati and systematically suppressed and even tried to mislead this Court [the Supreme Court]'; that call records showed that during the killings Shah was 'in regular touch with the policemen' ... But now, the same CBI did not so much as raise a finger against Shah's discharge.

What had happened? Dushyant Dave nailed the answer: the BJP had come to power at the Centre in May 2014, and in Maharashtra in October 2014.

Here was a case not of mere corruption, but of probable, at least possible murder. Going again by the lessons that spring from the cases we have gleaned above, I would have thought that the Supreme Court or High Court would immediately take note of the facts that had surfaced and ensure that the mysterious death was promptly and thoroughly investigated—they do, after all, take up all sorts of matters suo motu.[5] Instead, for three years, there was radio silence. Even after the disquieting details were published in the third week of November 2017, and the video recordings of interviews with the relatives of Judge Loya were released, the judiciary kept looking the other way. Eventually, on 4 January 2018, the Bombay Lawyers

---

5 And for that I don't have to look far for examples. I can give a ready example from my own experience. I wrote an editorial in *The Indian Express*. The then Chief Justice took suo motu notice of it, and a case of contempt of court was registered against me. The case lingered over my head for *twenty-six years*. I was acquitted by a five-judge bench, and all submissions that were made on my behalf were upheld.

Association took the matter up at the Bombay High Court: it filed a petition praying that the death be investigated. The court took the petition on board, and issued notices.

Within days of the Bombay High Court issuing notices, another petition, in the 'Public Interest', suddenly appeared in the Supreme Court. The petitioner claimed to be a Mumbai-based journalist.[6] This 'journalist' did not endeavour to join the case that had been taken on board by the High Court in Mumbai. He approached the Supreme Court. In the normal course, as the Bombay High Court had already taken the matter up, the Supreme Court would have told the petitioner to join those proceedings. But this time the Chief Justice took up the writ. He didn't just 'take up the writ'. He took it up posthaste, and posted it for the very next day! And then the next exceptional thing happened. If the court in the person of the Chief Justice had suddenly awakened—three years and more after the death of Loya—to the enormous importance of the matter, the matter ought to have been assigned to some senior judges. Instead, the Chief Justice assigned it to Court Number 10 of Justice Arun Mishra.

History was repeating itself—but the roles of the courts were reversed! For this device of pre-empting a court that you think you may not be able to control and, with utmost dispatch, commencing proceedings in another court had been the standard operating procedure in the Sohrabuddin case from the beginning. Apprehensive that the Supreme Court might step in, the Gujarat government twice tried to pre-empt its doing so by hurriedly filing the charge sheets in courts in Gujarat. Recalling what happened after it directed that all records of the Prajapati death be handed over, the Supreme Court noted what had been happening:

---

6 The *Caravan* recounted the background of the 'journalist': he turned out to hardly be a practising journalist; instead, persons who knew him told the magazine that he used to claim to be close to and doing jobs for the president of the BJP in Mumbai. A second writ was filed—this one by a person who claimed to be a Congressman. The party functionaries said that they did not know of him or of his writ. After interacting with him, Dushyant Dave, the senior advocate who had been pursuing the case, concluded that both writs were put-up jobs to pre-empt the hearings in the Bombay High Court. C.f., Atul Dev, 'The backgrounds of the Loya petitioners in the Supreme Court raise questions about the legitimacy of their petitions,' http://www.caravanmagazine.in/vantage/backgrounds-loya-petitioners-supreme-court-raise-questions-legitimacy-petitions

> ...Gujarat Police, however, would neither hand over the records of Prajapati case to CBI nor allow it to make any independent investigation in Prajapati case. On the contrary, Gujarat Police purported to complete its investigation and, like in the case of Sohrabuddin, rather hurriedly filed the charge-sheet in the case on 30-7-2010, followed by a supplementary charge-sheet on 31-7-2010, before the Judicial Magistrate, First Class, Danta, Banaskantha District. The Magistrate, equally quickly committed the case to the Court of Session in two days' time on 2-8-2010 even without proper compliance with the provisions of Section 207 of the Code of Criminal Procedure.

After examining further facts relating to the course that matters had taken in the Sohrabuddin and Prajapati cases, the Supreme Court observed:

> ...It is, thus, to be seen that Prajapati case also followed exactly the same pattern as the case of Sohrabuddin. Initially, there was a complete denial by the State that he was killed in any kind of a fake encounter. But, when it became impossible to deny that the story of the encounter was false, an investigation was swiftly made by Gujarat Police and charge-sheet was submitted. On the basis of the charge-sheet, on the one hand an attempt was made to proceed with and conclude the trial proceedings as quickly as possible and on the other hand this court was told that after the submission of charge-sheet it was denuded of authority to direct any further investigation. There was thus clearly an attempt not to allow the full facts to come to light in connection with the two cases...[7]

The same devices were being deployed again—except, and how sad it is to record, this time round the dramatis personae seemed to feel that the forum they would be able to put to work in their favour was the Supreme Court rather than the lower courts!

---

7 On the contents of CBI's charge sheets and the observations of the Supreme Court on the Sohrabuddin and Prajapati cases, see *Central Bureau of Investigation v. Amitbhai Anil Chandra Shah* with *Central Bureau of Investigation v. Dahyaji Gobarji Vanzara*, (2012) 10 SCC 545.

In the unprecedented press conference that they, along with Justice Madan B. Lokur and Justice Kurian Joseph, addressed on 12 January 2018, Justice Chelameswar and Justice Ranjan Gogoi acknowledged that it was this decision of the Chief Justice that was the final trigger that compelled them to take the extraordinary step of directly drawing the people's attention to the ways in which the functioning of the Supreme Court was being bent.

What ensued in Court 10 is best described by Senior Advocate Dushyant Dave:

> Once it became public that the Bombay High Court, on January 23, was likely to hear cases seeking an inquiry into the mysterious death of Judge Loya, wheels started moving...
>
> The matters were listed on 12th January, 2018. When I made a fervent prayer to the Hon'ble Bench not to hear it in view of the forthcoming Writ Petitions before the Bombay High Court, my request was sternly declined. The Writ Petitioners were represented by Advocates on Record and not by any Senior Counsel, clearly showing that there was no seriousness on that day or maybe because of the confidence in the Court.
>
> The hearing was brusque, nothing was argued, nothing was discussed and the Court merely enquired as to whether the Government of Maharashtra was present. Shockingly, the counsel for the Government of Maharashtra—a BJP Government—was present, despite there being no notice.
>
> In the Court and outside, many lawyers representing various BJP State Governments were present and so was the Additional Solicitor General of India, who is known to be close to Shri Amit Shah. It all looked too good to be true. The Court asked the counsel for the Government of Maharashtra to produce documents, including the 'Post Mortem Report', on Monday, January 15.
>
> If this was not enough, what transpired on the next date of hearing on January 16, when the following order was passed, was sufficient to shock the judicial conscience of any Judge or lawyer of respect: '*Let the documents be placed on record within seven days and if it is considered appropriate copies be furnished to the Petitioners. Put up before appropriate Bench.*'

What a contrast the step presented to what happens all the time: when petitioners go the Supreme Court, every so often the judges direct them to go first to the concerned High Court.

But the lessons do not end there. Dave's account illustrates a malaise to which we will turn later on, 'the lawyer's disease':

> A careful reading of the above order shows the appearance of Shri Pallav Sisodia, Senior Advocate, for one of the petitioners, and Harish Salve for the Respondent, State of Maharashtra. Shri Pallav Sisodia, a respected lawyer, had appeared for Shri Amit Shah in Special Leave to Appeal (Crl) No 9003/2010 filed by the CBI challenging the grant of bail to Shri Amit Shah in the very same Sohrabuddin encounter case by the Gujarat High Court, before it was transferred to Mumbai. He had appeared on 27.09.2011, 28.09.2011 and 29.09.2011 along with Shri Ram Jethmalani, Senior Advocate, as the Record of proceedings of Supreme Court discloses. Subsequently, he appeared in the same matter on 30.11.2011 and 06.09.2012 apparently for some other accused in the same case.
>
> Shri Harish Salve first appeared for Rubabuddin, brother of Sohrabuddin, in Writ Petition (Crl) No 6 of 2007 on more than one occasion and subsequently successfully defended Shri Amit Shah in opposing the Special Leave Petition (Crl) No 5000 of 2016 filed by Harsh Mander against the judgment and order of the Bombay High Court upholding discharge on the ground that since State has not filed appeal, Harsh Mander was not the person who could maintain the petition.[8]

The remarks of the four judges, the intense public controversy that had ensued, must have had some impact. It was reported that at the ritual morning tea for which judges meet before heading to their courts, Justice Arun Mishra had broken down. He had been working hard and sincerely, he is reported to have said, and now

8 C.f., Dushyant Dave, 'Death of a Judge: There is much more than meets the eye', *Bar and Bench*, 19 January 2018. Sisodia responded: he did not understand how arguing for an independent investigation constituted a conflict of interest, he maintained: *Bar and Bench*, 21 January 2018. The question, of course, was different: '*Who* will select the "independent" investigators?'

his competence and integrity were being questioned. The Chief Justice and Justice Chelameswar were said to have consoled him: 'It isn't personal, it is institutional...' In the event, Justice Mishra and his companion judge in Court Number 10 had directed that the matter be placed before the 'appropriate Bench'. The Chief Justice, his deft decision having been turned back, assigned the case to a bench headed by himself. The bench had changed but the other component of the decision had remained—the case would be heard on 22 January 2018, a day before the Bombay High Court was to have heard the matter...

Kaidi kaa dil behlaane ko
Durbaan badaltey jaatey hain...

If this is how the judiciary handles the possible murder of one of its own, what protection can the average citizen hope for?

As this book closes, arguments are going on before the three-judge bench in the Supreme Court. One thing that Dave had predicted has already come to pass: the Bombay High Court having been prevented from proceeding with the matter, the Mumbai-based 'journalist' has told the Supreme Court that he does not intend to pursue the case, as he no longer feels that any independent inquiry into the death of Loya is needed!

MIDDLEMEN AND INTERCEPTED CALLS[9]

Medical colleges are big business—and so is the granting of permission to set up the colleges. That many a party which has neither the infrastructure nor expertise to impart medical education is able to secure permission to set one up has long been a matter of grave public concern. In 2015, based on assessments of the

[9] The following two sections are based on irrefutable facts set out in writs and petitions filed by the Campaign for Judicial Accountability and Reforms and the documents annexed to these writ petitions, including the transcripts of tapped conversations and the CBI's Preliminary Enquiry Report. All the relevant documents are available on the website of the CJAR. See, in particular, http://judicialreforms.org/cjar-complaint-cji-house-procedure/; http://judicialreforms.org/wp-content/uploads/2018/01/Final-Review-1.pdf

Medical Council of India, the government refused permission to around forty-six parties which had applied for admitting students to medical courses. Among these was the Prasad Education Trust which had sought permission to set up a new medical college in Lucknow. However, three days later, an Oversight Committee which had been set up on the directions of the Supreme Court overruled the decision of the government, and the trust secured permission to set up the college.

The Medical Council of India—which itself has had a chequered reputation—conducted inspections of the college. The college had failed to implement the undertakings it had given while securing permission; it woefully lacked the expertise and infrastructure to impart medical education. The government took two decisions: it debarred the college from admitting students for two years—presumably the college would firm up the facilities and faculty during this interval; second, the bank guarantee that the college had given—Rs 2 crore—would be encashed.

The trust filed an appeal in the Supreme Court against these decisions. The court—speaking through a bench headed by Justice Dipak Misra—directed the government to re-examine the assessment of the Medical Council in regard to this college as well as others which had been refused permission. This happened on 1 August 2017.

Two days later, the government decided to stick by its earlier decisions.

The sponsor of the college contacted a retired judge of the Orissa High Court, I.M. Quddusi, and, presumably on his advice, withdrew the petition that the trust had filed in the Supreme Court. Instead, it filed a petition to similar effect in the Allahabad High Court. On the very day that it filed the application—25 August 2017—a two-judge bench of the Allahabad High Court consisting of Justice Narayan Shukla and Justice Virendra Kumar passed an interim order: the college could continue counselling till the next hearing, and the encashment of the bank guarantee is stayed.

It was now the turn of the Medical Council to approach the Supreme Court. During the hearing, the counsel for the trust affirmed that the only relief they were seeking was that the bank

guarantee not be encashed: they would not continue the counselling, etc. The Supreme Court—the bench was again headed by Chief Justice Misra[10]—was most trusting. It disposed of the petition filed by the Medical Council. It disposed of the writ that was pending in the Allahabad High Court. It permitted the trust to come back to the court—i.e., the Supreme Court—with a fresh writ under Article 32.[11] The trust promptly came back with the recommended writ—it did so on 31 August 2017, that is, within just a day of the permission granted by the Supreme Court bench. It prayed that the government's decisions—preventing it from enrolling students, and encashing the bank guarantee—be quashed.

From now on the dates tell a tale. The trust had filed its writ on 31 August 2017. The writ was listed for being heard on 4 September 2017. On that day, the Supreme Court bench headed by Chief Justice Misra stayed the encashment of the bank guarantee till the next date of hearing—this was fixed for Monday, 11 September.

The CBI had evidently got wind of the efforts being made by the sponsors of the trust, and their having contacted former Justice Quddusi. They had begun tapping their phones. In conversations that took place on 3 and 4 September, there were the most damaging exchanges between a person pushing the trust's case, the ex-judge

---

10 Justice Dipak Misra assumed the office of Chief Justice on 28 August 2017. His term extends to 2 October 2018.

11 The article has a wide sweep and specifies the right to seek constitutional remedies for the enforcement of Fundamental Rights guaranteed by the Constitution. It reads:

32. Remedies for enforcement of rights conferred by this Part.-

(1) The right to move the Supreme Court by appropriate proceedings for the enforcement of the rights conferred by this Part is guaranteed.

(2) The Supreme Court shall have power to issue directions or orders or writs, including writs in the nature of habeas corpus, mandamus, prohibition, quo warranto and certiorari, whichever may be appropriate, for the enforcement of any of

(3) Without prejudice to the powers conferred on the Supreme Court by clauses (1) and (2), Parliament may by law empower any other court to exercise within the local limits of its jurisdiction all or any of the powers exercisable by the Supreme Court under clause (2).

(4) The right guaranteed by this article shall not be suspended except as otherwise provided for by this Constitution.

of the Orissa High Court, Quddusi, and a middleman, a resident of Bhubaneswar, Orissa. 'Prasad had to be delivered to the Temple in Delhi' ... The work was '100 per cent guaranteed' as 'our person who is our captain, it is being done through the captain' ... [This in the conversation of 3 September: the writ was admitted by a bench headed by Chief Justice Misra on 4 September.] The 'luggage would *have* to be delivered—'; 'nothing will happen if the prasad is not given'—but there can be no meeting as the government is watching everyone ... Haggling over the amount that must be given as advance ... Haggling over the total amount that has to be given ... How the middleman has brought the demand down, now the amount is settled: 'Yes, conversation was clear. Calculated as per three. They/he won't do it for less than three.' And the amount will ensure not just the order in the present case: '...Sir, I don't want to take any risk here, because it is a 100 per cent guarantee. No ifs and buts. Once work is done, sir will sit for 10-15 months. Get 14-15 jobs done, even you will believe it. He will do it 101 per cent' ... 'Now only one thing father is saying, one thing he is saying that, this captain of ours has ... all over India ... whatever work there is, he is willing to do.' The ex-judge from Orissa, 'I am saying that I have someone I know from before or I am saying that someone I know from before has approached me' ... The ex-judge again, 'No, he is saying that if money is there, then someone should go inside the house, someone should talk' ... The difficulty of arranging the entire amount immediately: hence, the case has been listed for Monday—11 September—get it postponed by three to four days ... 'If you give two people then we will extend the date by 3-4 days...' At last, the sponsor to the middleman: 'Listen, you take two from us now and as the order is given, we will get admission, we will send one crore to the judge. Your place, Quddusi sir's place, do it this way.'

The CBI raided the houses of Quddusi and the others. It recovered around Rs 2 crore in cash. It arrested the ex-judge as well as others—the one pushing the trust's case and the middleman from Bhubaneswar among them.

Reliable sources told the Campaign for Judicial Accountability and Reforms that two days after this second conversation, the CBI took the material it had gathered to the Chief Justice with the request that he permit them to register a regular FIR against Justice

Narayan Shukla of the Allahabad High Court. Chief Justice Misra refused permission and, instead, opted for an 'internal inquiry'. But the inquiry that he instituted was to be in regard to a related case, one relating to the GCRG Institute of Medical Sciences, and not in regard to the case relating to the Prasad Educational Trust. He decided on this course even though source information pointed to questionable decisions of Justice Shukla in both instances. Refused permission, the CBI registered a preliminary enquiry. Its report recorded in part:

> Source also informed that Shri I.M. Quddusi and Shri B.P. Yadav met Hon'ble Justice Shri Narayan Shukla in the morning on 25.08.2017 at his residence in Lucknow regarding the matter and delivered illegal gratification. Source has further informed that on 25.08.2017, an order was passed in petition, Misc. Bench No. 19870 of 2017 filed by Prasad Education Trust, by a Bench, which included Hon'ble Justice Shri Nayaran Shukla. The order directed that the petitioner's college shall not be delisted from the list of colleges notified for counselling till the next date of listing, i.e. 31.08.2017. Further the encashment of bank guarantee was also stayed till the next date of listing. It was further clarified that on the basis of the order, the petitioners shall have no right to claim any admission of the students...
>
> Sources informed that Justice Shri Narayan Shukla assured Shri I.M. Quddusi that he will return a part of illegal gratification previously received by him shortly.
>
> The aforesaid acts prima-facie reveal that Hon'ble Justice Shri Narayan Shukla of Lucknow Bench of the High Court of Allahabad in collusion with Shri I.M. Quddusi, Retired Justice of the High Court of Odisha; Smt. Bhawana Pandey; Shri B.P. Yadav and Shri Palash Yadav of Prasad Education Trust and Shri Sudhir Giri of Venkateshwara Medical College and unknown others, committed gross misconduct while discharging duties as a public servant.

Permission to proceed against Justice Shukla having been refused, the CBI registered its preliminary enquiry report on 8 September. On 11 September, the Supreme Court directed that the trust's writ be listed for the 18th—recall how the one pushing the trust's case had asked the middleman to have the hearing postponed by 'three-four days'.

On the 18th, the bench presided over by Chief Justice Misra directed that the bank guarantee shall not be encashed, and it directed the Medical Council of India to yet again inspect the college. For reasons that are not evident, the order, issued though it was on 18 September, was put up on the website of the Supreme Court only on 21 September.

Soon enough, the internal inquiry into decisions regarding the related case—of GCRG Institute of Medical Sciences—revealed that indeed, Justice Shukla had been guilty of gross impropriety. It seemed that a week after the Supreme Court had directed that this 'Institute' would not be allowed to enrol students for 2017/18, Justice Shukla had altered by his own hand the High Court decision, thus enabling the 'Institute' to evade the Supreme Court prohibition and enrol students for 2017/18.

Given the conclusions of the internal inquiry, the Chief Justice of the Supreme Court advised the Chief Justice of the Allahabad High Court to stop assigning any work to Justice Shukla. The latter proceeded on leave.

But what about the case relating to the Prasad Educational Trust, and those conversations about the 'captain' who was going to stay in place for the coming ten to fifteen months? As this book goes to press, the matter remains shrouded. Will the CBI move afresh to seek the Chief Justice's permission? Will it conclude that, permission having been refused once, it cannot go back to the Chief Justice and ask him to reconsider his decision? The only thing that is publicly known is the record of the CBI, and especially its recent record—that it will act in accordance with the convenience of its political masters.

Shooting the Messenger

The Campaign for Judicial Accountability and Reforms—the CJAR—had received information about the CBI's findings, the contents of the tapped conversations as well as about the fate of their request to the Chief Justice for taking the next steps against Justice Shukla of the Allahabad High Court.

Accordingly, on 6 November 2017, the CJAR filed a writ in the Supreme Court. The gravamen of the writ was that leaving the matter in the hands of the CBI would endanger the independence of the judiciary: the political executive would certainly have access to what the CBI uncovered, and it could use the information to pressure individual judges; hence the prayer that a Special Investigation Team be formed under a retired Chief Justice of the Supreme Court to investigate the allegations which had been recorded by the CBI in the FIR, and the evidence that was reproduced in its preliminary enquiry. On 8 November, as the Chief Justice was sitting in a Constitution Bench, in accordance with settled convention, Prashant Bhushan mentioned the matter in Court Number 2 before the bench presided over by the judge next in seniority, Justice J. Chelameswar. Justice Chelameswar and his companion judge, Justice Abdul Nazeer, directed that the matter be listed before them on 10 November. Later, on the 8th itself, the registry of the Supreme Court informed Prashant Bhushan that the Chief Justice had passed an order that the writ be listed before another bench.

On 9 November, another advocate, Kamini Jaiswal, filed a writ along the same lines. It too was mentioned in Court 2. Justices Chelameswar and Nazeer directed that the matter be listed before them at 12.45 p.m. The Constitution Bench in which the Chief Justice was sitting normally adjourns for lunch around 12.45 or 1 p.m. The Chief Justice adjourned it unexpectedly at noon, saying that he had to attend to some domestic business. In Court Number 2, after hearing submissions, Justices Chelameswar and Nazeer directed that, given the seriousness of the matter, Kamini Jaiswal's writ be listed before a bench of the five senior-most judges of the court on 13 November.

The next day, 10 November 2017, the first writ which the Chief Justice had in a sense taken away from the bench of Justices Chelameswar and Nazeer came up before a bench consisting of Justices Sikri and Ashok Bhushan. Prashant informed them that the bench of Justices Chelameswar and Nazeer had already directed that the writ of Kamini Jaiswal, which sought reliefs similar to the ones sought by Prashant's writ, be placed before a bench of the five senior-most judges. The natural thing would have been to tag Prashant's writ to that of Kamini Jaiswal's so that both would be heard together by that larger bench. Instead, Justices Sikri and Bhushan directed that the writ be placed before the Chief Justice for directions.

With unheard-of promptness, on that very day, that is 10 November, at 2.45 p.m. a notice was put up that the writ filed by the CJAR would come up for hearing at 3 p.m.—that is, *within fifteen minutes*—before a seven-judge bench presided over by the Chief Justice. When lawyers rushed to Court Number 1, they found two things. The names of two of the seven judges and the chairs meant for them—Justices Sikri and Bhushan who had heard the matter earlier in the day—were being hurriedly removed. And, second, a host of lawyers—in particular, office bearers of advocates' associations whom we shall encounter again—were crowded in the forefront. Prashant Bhushan who was representing the CJAR—the writ which was to be heard was the one filed by it—was shouted out by the advocates who were not even party to the proceedings. In raised voices they kept saying that the order of Justices Chelameswer and Nazeer in regard to Kamini Jaiswal's writ was bad in law. The Chief Justice let them have their say. Soon enough, the bench handed down a decision: the Chief Justice was the sole master of the roster, no one else could constitute benches. In short, even though Jaiswal's writ was not even listed before them, the Chief Justice and his companion judges struck down the order of Justice Chelameswar and Justice Nazeer that Jaiswal's writ be heard by a bench consisting of the five senior-most Judges. Instead, this hurriedly assembled bench decided that the writ would be heard by a bench that the Chief Justice would constitute.

On 14 November, Kamini Jaiswal's writ came up before a three-judge bench constituted by the Chief Justice. The judges dismissed the writ, holding that her plea—that the matter relating to the CBI's findings and the imperative need to constitute a Special Investigation Team should not be heard by a bench of which the Chief Justice was a member—was bad in law. Furthermore, that the concerns she had raised regarding the FIR—about bribes being paid for securing favourable orders—were wholly without merit, wholly unethical and unwarranted, and were just intended to bring the Supreme Court into disrepute.

On 27 November, the same three judges heard the writ of the CJAR. On 1 December, they dismissed the writ, holding it to be 'wholly contemptuous', 'scandalous' and unwarranted. They imposed a penalty of Rs 25 lakh on the CJAR for pursuing the writ even after Kamini Jaiswal's writ had been dismissed.

Naturally, the CJAR filed a petition to review the order. The facts that it had stated in its writ were wholly based on the conversations that the CBI had recorded and the FIR which it had registered. The matter to which it had drawn attention was manifestly of the highest public importance, not the least for the esteem of the Supreme Court itself. The judges had held that the CJAR had scandalized the court by stating that judges of the Supreme Court had been named in the writ: in fact, the writ had not stated this at all. The judges had said, 'We wonder as to what favourable orders have been passed' in the interest of the trust: but these could be easily seen, and the CJAR listed them order by order. To hold that, as the writ of Kamini Jaiswal had been dismissed, the effort of CJAR to pursue its writ was contempt was unwarranted: earlier, in spite of a specific request to that effect, benches of the same court had not agreed to club them together; moreover, a petitioner is fully within his rights to present arguments in favour of his writ—it may well be, and this is just one consideration, that vital arguments may not have been satisfactorily presented when the other writ was heard; in any case, the courts, including the Supreme Court, do change their mind ... The penalty of Rs 25 lakh had been levied without hearing the CJAR at all: indeed, during the hearings, at no time was the counsel told that he was opening himself for such heavy penalty; furthermore, no penalty had been imposed on Kamini Jaiswal even though, and on the saying of the judges themselves, the two writs were similar. As for requesting that the matter be heard by a bench of which the Chief Justice was not a member, the fact was that the Chief Justice had presided over every bench that had heard the medical college matter—the doings of whose sponsors, pushers and middlemen were the subject of the CBI's FIR; it was a well-settled principle that no one could be a judge in his own cause...

Soon, on 15 January 2018, the CJAR filed a formal complaint against the Chief Justice with the five senior-most judges. The complaint was one of the most persuasive and one of the most courageous documents that I had read in a long, long time. It set out various acts of commission and omission. These included, of course, a list of the ways that the matter relating to the Prasad Education Trust had been handled. It set out the facts that the CBI had uncovered during its investigations and raids. It set out the tapped conversations. It made new points: the order by which the decision of the Chelameswer–Nazeer Bench had been nullified, for instance, seemed to have been antedated. There was also the question about the way land had been acquired by Mr Misra, as he then was, several years earlier in Orissa by filing an affidavit which an inquiry by the officials concerned had held to be fraudulent; and how, in spite of this, Mr Misra had held on to the land for twenty-seven years, that is, literally till the time he became a judge of the Supreme Court. The complaint requested that an internal inquiry be instituted against him.

Clearly, judges too are subject to Newton's Third Law: 'When one body exerts a force on a second body, the second body simultaneously exerts a force equal in magnitude and opposite in direction on the first body.'

'But can I end this account on this hopeful note?' I wondered. I asked Prashant Bhushan what course his petition for review of the contempt is to follow. It would be placed before the same three judges who had held that his writ was 'wholly contemptuous', 'scandalous' and unwarranted, he explained, and who had imposed that fine of Rs 25 lakh. And there would be no open hearing, Prashant would not have any chance to present the facts or law before them; the judges would merely discuss it among themselves, in private. If they reconfirmed what they had held, he would have the opportunity to file a curative petition. And who would hear that? The Chief Justice, the three senior-most judges and the three judges who imposed the penalty in the first instance. Four to three! *Kyaa karen, kahaan jaayen...*

Bane hain ahl-e-havas muddai bhi munsif bhi
Kise vakil karen kis se munsifi chahen...

All this was bad enough. But soon the country was jolted into realizing that there was much worse, indeed that practices that would prove disastrous for the institution and, therefore, for the country, had come to be adopted. They transcended individual judges, they struck at the very heart of the Supreme Court itself.

Dilutions and their consequences

Public disclosure by the senior-most judges of the Supreme Court in January 2018 gave us a glimpse of what has been happening inside the court, and it awakened us to another source of mischief that had crept back in. That like the rest of us, judges have predilections is well-known, and in a sense quite natural: to take an example from far away, some judges of the US Supreme Court have been 'strict constructionists'—you had to prove everything to their satisfaction from the plain words of the Constitution itself; others, equally distinguished, were more expansive in their interpretations. In India also, especially from the 1970s onwards, while most judges would go back to the plain text of the Constitution, some felt it their duty to read deeper and wider meanings into the text—witness the way the ambit of Article 21 was expanded in the ensuing years. Those who saw themselves as 'progressive' felt that they had not just the right but a mandate to change the way the Constitution had been interpreted: one judge of the Supreme Court, Justice D.A. Desai, as we saw, went so far as to proclaim that he had joined the system so as to wreck it from within. These differences in perspective translated into specifics. Some judges were almost self-consciously pro-labour—'Bonus is a deferred wage', and the rest—others were conservative. Gautam Bhatia reminded us recently that in the first decade of the new millennium, one bench of the Supreme Court confirmed almost all the death sentences that came to it in appeal while another bench commuted almost all the death sentences.[12] Therefore, the impression got around that the outcome would not depend so much on the facts or even the law as on the bench before which one's case landed. The lemma was ineluctable: many a litigant did whatever he could to deflect his case to one bench and keep it away from another. The registry of the court and the Chief Justice's office became the focus of special deference and attention.

To counter this practice, methods and conventions developed. Benches would be formed subject-wise—the background of the judge, if he had acquired special competence in a particular branch of law, for instance, would naturally be one of the considerations in constituting the subject-wise benches. As cases came up, they would in the first instance be channelled to the set of benches that had been assigned the general area of law in which the case fell and, in the second step, within that set of benches the case would be assigned to a particular bench at random, 'by the computer' as the practice came to be known.

Other conventions also evolved. Sensitive cases—like those involving interpretations of the Constitution or those involving holders of high office—would be assigned to larger benches, and these benches would be manned by senior judges. Similarly, once some judges had begun hearing a case, it would not be snatched away from them and assigned to some other set. If a bench maintained that the case ought to be heard by a larger bench, it *would be* referred to a larger bench. And those judges who had been hearing the case in the first instance would be included in the larger bench. Decisions handed down by larger benches would be adhered to as precedents by benches consisting of fewer judges. Smaller benches would not reopen a question that had been settled by a larger bench, certainly not merely by remarks made in passing: I remember well how in his judgment in the *Minerva Mills* case, Justice P.N. Bhagwati criticized the way in which deliberations and drafting in the case had proceeded—the remarks were clearly directed at the way the then Chief Justice, Y.V. Chandrachud, had handled

---

12 Gautam Bhatia, 'Master and the Roster', *The Indian Express,* 15 January 2018.

the matter; the executive seized upon these remarks and sought to use them to reopen cases of foundational importance.[13] But such

13 Even after all these years, it is instructive to read—and bear in mind as a warning—the observations that provided such a convenient rationalization for the political executive to seek to reopen settled cases that were the very dykes of liberty. Here is what Justice P.N. Bhagwati wrote: 'I may point out at this stage that the arguments on this question were spread over a period of about three weeks and considerable learning and scholarship were brought to bear on this question on both sides. The hearing of the arguments commenced on 22nd October 1979 and it ended on 16th November 1979. I hoped after the completion of the arguments on questions of such momentous significance, there would be a "free and frank exchange of thoughts" in a judicial conference either before or after the draft judgment was circulated by my Lord the Chief Justice and I would either be able to share the views of my colleagues or if that was not possible, at least try to persuade them to agree with my point of view. But, I find myself in the same predicament in which the learned Chief Justice found himself in *Kesavananda Bharati v. State of Kerala*. The learned Chief Justice started his judgment in that case by observing:

> "I wanted to avoid writing a separate judgment of my own but such a choice seems no longer open. We sat in full strength of 13 to hear the case and I hoped that after a free and frank exchange of thoughts, I would be able to share the views of someone or the other of my esteemed brothers, but we were overtaken by adventitious circumstances",

namely, so much time was taken up by the counsel to explain their respective points of view that very little time was left to the Judges "after the conclusion of the arguments, for exchange of draft judgments". Here also, I am compelled by similar circumstances, though not adventitious, to hand down a separate opinion without having had an opportunity to discuss with my colleagues the reasons which weighed with them in striking down the impugned constitutional amendments. Somehow or other, perhaps owing to extraordinary pressure of work with which this Court is over-burdened, no judicial conference or discussion was held nor was any draft judgment circulated which could form the basis of discussion, though, as pointed out above, the hearing of the arguments concluded as far back as 16th November, 1979. It was only on 8th May, 1980, just two days before the closing of the Court for the summer vacation, that I was informed by the learned Chief Justice that he and the other three learned Judges, who had heard this case along with me, had decided, to pass an order declaring the impugned constitutional amendments *ultra vires* and void on the ground that they violated the basic features of the Constitution and that the reasons for this order would be given by them later. I found it difficult to persuade myself to adopt this procedure, because there had been no judicial conference or discussion amongst the Judges where there could be free and frank exchange of views nor was any draft judgment circulated and hence I did not have the benefit of knowing the reasons why the learned Chief Justice and the other three learned judges were inclined to strike down the constitutional amendments. If there had been a judicial conference or discussion or the draft judgment setting out the reasons for holding the impugned constitutional amendments *ultra vires* and void had been circulated, it would have been possible for me, as a result of full and frank discussion or after considering the reasons given in the draft judgment, either to agree with the view taken by my Lord the Chief Justice and the other three learned judges or if I was not inclined so to agree, then persuade them to change their view and agree with mine. That is the essence of judicial collectivism. It is, to my mind, essential that a judgment of a Court should be the result of collective deliberation of the judges composing the Court and it would, in my humble opinion, not be in consequence with collective decision-making, if one or more of the judges constituting the Bench proceed to say that they will express their individual opinion, ignoring their colleagues and without discussing the reasons with them and even without circulating their draft judgment so that the colleagues have no opportunity of participating in the collective decision-making process. This would introduce a chaotic situation in the judicial process and it would be an unhealthy precedent which this Court as the highest Court in the land—as a model judicial institution which is expected to set the tone for the entire judiciary in the country—should not encourage. Moreover, I felt that it was not right to pronounce an order striking down a constitutional amendment without giving a reasoned judgment. Ordinarily, a case can be disposed of only by a reasoned judgment and the order must follow upon the judgment. It is true that sometimes where the case involves the liberty of the citizen or the execution of a death sentence or where the time taken in preparing a reasoned judgment might pre-judicially affect the winning party, this Court does, in the larger interests of justice, pronounce an order and give reasons later, but these are exceptional cases where the requirements of justice induce the Court to depart from the legally sanctioned course. But, here the court had in fact waited for about 5 ½ months after the conclusion of the arguments and there was clearly no urgency which required that an order should be made though reasons were not ready, the delay of about 2 months in making the order was not going to injure the interests of any instances were rare, and, as happened in response to *Minerva Mills*, they always triggered a strong reaction within the legal community.

In recent years, the conventions have got diluted. Perhaps the convention that has suffered the most is that of smaller benches adhering to what larger benches have held. Apart from some viewing themselves as 'progressive' and, therefore, having a duty, so to say, to change the direction of rulings, there is by now such a plethora of judgments, and so many of the judges have been so prolix, that it has become easier and easier to find the passage one requires for buttressing the position one has set out to affirm. This has compounded uncertainty.

But in the last two years, mere uncertainty has given way to apprehension that a pattern is afoot. Sensitive case after sensitive case—in particular, cases in which the current rulers have had a stake—have come to be assigned to a bench headed by a particular judge. Cases that were part-heard have been taken away from a set of judges and reassigned to others, often they have been taken over by the Chief Justice himself. Judges who had been hearing the case, and these cases again happened to be ones in which the current rulers had special interest—Justice Gogoi in the instance of the appointment of a director of the CBI, Justices Chelameswar and S.A. Bobde in the matter of Aadhaar—would suddenly find themselves pointedly excluded from the bench which would henceforth hear the part-heard case. When, say, a bench of two judges felt that the issues in a case were so important that it

---

party, since the order was not going to dispose of the writ petition and many issues would still remain to be decided which could be dealt only after the summer vacation. Thus there would have been no prejudice to the interests of justice if the order had been made on the re-opening of the Court after the summer vacation supported by a reasoned judgment. These were the reasons which compelled me to make my order dated 9th May, 1980 declining to pass an unreasoned order pronouncing on the validity of the impugned constitutional amendments and stating that I would "prefer to pass a final order in this case when I deliver my reasoned judgment". This order unfortunately led to considerable misunderstanding of my position and that is the reason why I have thought it necessary to explain briefly why I acted in the manner I did.' C.f., *Minerva Mills v. Union of India*, (1980) 3 SCC 625.

ought to be heard by a larger bench, the larger bench would indeed be constituted but, in the face of well-settled convention, the new bench would exclude the judges who had been hearing the case. Senior judges in particular came to be excluded from sensitive cases: the Sahara-Birla diaries case was assigned to a bench headed by Justice Arun Mishra overlooking *ten* benches that had judges who had more experience and seniority—this was a case about which the rulers were deeply apprehensive, for their names, along with those of several other prominent persons, figured as having received huge piles of monies; similarly, the Kalikho Pul case which we have encountered earlier was assigned to a bench overlooking *eleven* benches consisting of judges of higher seniority and experience.[14] Worse, senior judges began to be conspicuously excluded even from constitutional cases—Justice A.P. Shah, the former Chief Justice of the Delhi High Court, gave a telling example: Chief Justice Dipak Misra had constituted constitutional benches in seven cases; each of these was headed by himself, and not one of the four senior-most judges figured in any one of them.[15]

As such occurrences became more and more frequent, an alarming breach, reminiscent of the *Minerva Mills* episode, occurred in a case. A lawyer, R.P. Luthra, filed a petition in the Supreme Court asserting that he had been deprived of his right to be appointed as a judge of the Supreme Court. He said that as the Memorandum of Procedure for the appointment of judges had not been finalized, all appointments that had been made in the preceding months were void. The case was assigned to two judges. They rejected the claim of Luthra, but in the course of their judgment, they remarked that, indeed, the Memorandum of Procedure ought to be finalized without further delay.[16] But the matter had already been settled by

---

14 C.f., Dushyant Dave, 'Chief Justice of India—Above or under the law?', *The Indian Express,* 10 January 2018. For several examples, see the note that the Campaign for Judicial Accountability and Reforms issued on 12 January 2018 in the wake of the press conference held by Justice Chelameswar and his colleagues.

15 Ananthakrishnan G, Kaunain Sheriff, Liz Mathew, Manoj CG, Ravish Tiwari, 'Division and Bench', *The Indian Express*, 21 January 2018.

16 *R.P. Luthra v. Union of India,* decided on 27 October 2017, (2017) SCC Online 1254. As a consequence of the letter of judges to which we shall

a Constitution Bench of the Supreme Court.[17] After that judgment, there had been detailed discussions in the collegium of the five senior-most judges. Justice Chelameswar and his senior colleagues wrote to the Chief Justice about this peculiar observation by the two judges to whom he had assigned Luthra's case. Seven months have passed since the procedure that was finalized was sent to government, they pointed out. Its silence must be construed as consent, and the court must proceed on this basis.[18]

No genius was required to see that the observation that had fallen from the two judges would be grabbed by the rulers to proclaim that, on the saying of the Supreme Court itself, the Memorandum of Procedure had *not* been finalized. The question would be reopened and the rulers would try a second time within two years to wrest a larger say in the selection of judges.

Two months passed and there was no response from the Chief Justice.

And then the case of Judge Loya's death in which, as we have seen, the rulers were not just apprehensive, they were mortally apprehensive, was also assigned to Justice Arun Mishra, bypassing all the seniors: he may have been the most upright of judges but his family's proximity to the ruling party was well known and, on the incessantly repeated maxim that justice must not only be done but be seen to be done, this seemed just too much to disregard as a mere coincidence. The deflection of this case became the last straw.

The judges were confronted by what Gandhiji used to call 'an intolerable wrong'. They had tried other methods: they had written to the Chief Justice, they had met him. To no consequence. They were left with no alternative: they made known their misgivings to the people.

---

just turn, the Chief Justice took over the case in a three-judge bench. The bench upheld the decision of the two judges to reject R.P. Luthra's claim, but held in effect that nothing other than this rejection would survive from the earlier judgment.

17 *Supreme Court Advocates-on-Record Association,* (2016) 5 SCC 1.

18 On all this, the letter to the Chief Justice of India released by Justices J. Chelameswar, Justice Ranjan Gogoi, Justice Mohan Lokur and Justice Joseph Kurian at their press conference on 12 January 2018.

As this book goes to press, a small change has been made: the registry has put up on the Supreme Court website the list setting out which judges will hear cases relating to which subject. But clearly it is but a small change. No institutional mechanism for assigning cases has been put in place: the four judges had suggested that a committee of the Chief Justice and of those who are in line to be Chief Justices decide the benches—nothing like that has been instituted. The prerogative has been retained solely in the hands of the Chief Justice. The assignments of subjects to specified judges is 'till further orders'. Furthermore, the order is to apply only to future cases. And, most significantly, all cases originating from PILs, all cases relating to elections and all cases relating to the appointment of constitutional functionaries—that is, precisely all cases in which the current rulers are most liable to have a stake—have been retained by the Chief Justice.[19] The optimistic feel that the change is but the first step, that the Chief Justice will see the gravity of the matter and will eventually put in place institutional mechanisms. Others go by the record thus far—including the record of the executive.

19 C.f., *The Indian Express*, 2 February 2018.

8

What if he had not written that letter?

On 23 January 2017, a sitting judge of the Calcutta High Court, Justice C.S. Karnan, shot off a letter to the prime minister. He named twenty judges—starting with the Chief Justice of the Madras High Court—as being corrupt. He told the prime minister that this was 'an initial list', and that the corruption of the judges 'can be proved through some competent agencies'. He furnished no evidence to substantiate his allegation.

On 25 January, he shot off another letter—this time to the Chief Justice of the Madras High Court, whose name, like Abu Ben Adam's, had led all the rest in the list that Karnan had sent to the prime minister. The reason Karnan was writing to him, it seems, was that in his mind the Chief Justice, Madras High Court, was the origin of his troubles. Karnan recalled that having been called by them, on 16 February 2016, he had met the Chief Justice of India and other members of the Collegium in the chambers of the Chief Justice. The Chief Justice had told him that there were many complaints against his conduct on the bench; he narrated how he had then fallen at the feet of the Chief Justice and entreated him to institute an inquiry into the allegations. He recalled that his troubles had started when, sitting alongside a senior judge, he had objected to a case being taken up that had not been listed; he recalled how he had later taken the case bundle to the senior judge and touched *his* feet. 'Thereafter,' he continued in his letter to the Chief Justice of the Madras High Court, 'Mr. Justice Ibrahim Kalifulla and most of the other Judges started their continuous ragging of myself.' He recalled that the Chief Justice, Madras, had maintained that no such case had been taken up, and that 'Now the collected documents have been misplaced somewhere...'

He recounted another instance. 'On one occasion you and Mr. Justice Akbar Ali came up to me at the second floor of the Additional Block of the High Court wherein High Tea was provided for the small function at the meeting hall, during the social function you and Mr. Justice Akbar Ali barged in front of my seat and indecently confronted me with wicked postures and gestures, which is the lowest form of indecency exhibited from respected gentlemen like both of you especially from the fraternity of Judges...'

He recounted that in his meeting with the Chief Justice and other Collegium judges, he had requested the Chief Justice to cancel the order by which he had stopped all judicial and administrative work from being assigned to him. He concluded his letter to the Chief Justice, Madras, by maintaining, 'Now it is pertinent to ask—who is the culprit? It has to be decided. My view is that you wantonly, deliberately and continuously insulted me. Therefore, you should be prosecuted under the SC/ST [Prevention of] Atrocities Act.'

On 8 February 2017, the Supreme Court issued a suo motu contempt order against him, and directed the Calcutta High Court to ensure that no judicial or administrative work was assigned to him. On 11 February, Karnan dashed off a letter to the registrar general of the Supreme Court. He accused the Chief Justice of India and the six other judges who had sat on the bench that had prevented work from being assigned to him 'with *mala fide* intention in order to protect the Corrupt Judges' whom he had named. He maintained that he had sent the list of judges he regarded as corrupt only in accordance with the exhortation of the previous Chief Justice of India who had exhorted that, if you believe any judge to be corrupt, 'then take an open stand by publicly naming him'. 'Hence, a question of contempt does not arise absolutely since the [previous] C.J.I.'s advice does not come under the purview of the current Court, nevertheless the advice is in tandem with Natural Justice.'

On 16 March, he addressed a letter to the Chief Justice of India and the six other judges who had been on the bench, telling them that they had been part of an 'unconstitutional Bench after breaking the Indian Constitutional Law' and passed the order holding him in contempt and stopping all work from being assigned to him. He again maintained that they had done so to protect the corrupt judges whom he had named in his letter to the prime minister. 'Therefore, I am calling upon all seven Judges to pay compensation since you have disturbed my mind and my normal life, besides you have insulted me in the general public consisting of 120 crore in India due to lack of legal knowledge ... Now all the seven Judges will pay compensation within a period of seven days from the date of receipt of this order, failing which on the same stand of yours (same footing), I will restrain Judicial and Administrative work of yours.'

On 17 March, he again charged the Chief Justice and his six colleagues with having 'deliberately and wantonly failed due to lack of judicial knowledge', and warned that 'this kind of worst type of acrimonious behaviour will only endanger ultimately the General Public'. Hence, he declared, close the contempt proceedings, lift the order preventing work to be assigned, etc.

Later in the day, he shot off another epistle to the Chief Justice and his colleagues: policemen had come to his residence to execute the bailable warrant that the Supreme Court had issued against him, he recounted: 'I rejected the same after assigning valid reasons ... This kind of demeaning acts from your Lordships and further perpetrating the Atrocities Act is absolutely out of law to the utter embarrassment of a Dalit Judge. Hence I request you to stop your further harassments in order to uphold the dignity & decorum of our Courts.'

As the Supreme Court remained firm in its orders, on 13 April, Karnan, functioning from his house which he had declared to be his 'make-shift Court', passed a lengthy '*Suo Motu* Judicial Order in the interest of the Nation to protect the General Public of their life, property and justice to all'. In this he charged the Chief Justice of India and his six colleagues of passing their order 'without following due procedure of law while violating the Principle of Natural Justice and the Prime Articles 14 and 21 of the Constitution further after breaking the Indian Constitutional Law'. In addition, he charged them with constituting 'an unconstitutional Bench due to extreme malice and vengeance, which amounts to violating Article 219 of the Constitution'. He termed the directions that the Supreme Court had issued to be 'Atrocities' [with a capital 'A'], and thus being in violation of the Scheduled Castes and Scheduled Tribes (Prevention of Atrocities) Act, 1989, and the subsequent amendment act. He maintained that in moving against him, the judges had violated, among others, the clause that holds a person guilty if he 'Forces or intimidates or obstructs a member of a Scheduled Caste or a Scheduled Tribe, who is a member or a Chairperson or a holder of any other office of a Panchayat under Part IX of the Constitution or a Municipality under Part IXA of the Constitution, from performing their normal duties and functions'—a clause pertaining to panchayats and municipalities invoked in the case of a judge of a High Court? In addition, he held them to have violated the clause that holds a person to have committed an offence who 'intentionally insults or intimidates with intent to humiliate a member of a Scheduled Caste or a Scheduled Tribe in any place within public view'. He held them guilty also of promoting feelings of enmity, hatred and ill-will against members of the Scheduled Castes and Tribes.

He recorded that he had pronounced a judgment on 31 March in which the seven judges stood accused under the 1989 Act, and added, 'Now I am directing the Hon'ble 7 Judges to give replies in person or through your Council [sic] regarding declaration of guilt and quantum of punishment by 28.04.2017 at 11.30 AM at my residence which has now become my make-shift Court...'

He charged them with having insulted him and harassed him by their orders. He directed the Airports Authority to ensure that they did not travel abroad. He directed the judges to surrender their passports ... He prohibited them from approaching any court against his order. 'Further the Registry of the Supreme Court is not to clear the pension benefits of the said Judges till the recovery of Rs. 14 crores as compensation mentioned in my earlier attachment order which has become final and upheld.'

He declared them to be 'National Offenders by showing caste prejudice'. And he issued 'a general appeal to all foreign countries' not to allow any one of the seven judges to enter their shores 'because if allowed entry into a particular Country they could spread the virus of Caste discrimination'.

The Chief Justice had adjourned the contempt hearings for a month, saying that Justice Karnan did not seem to have a clear mind. Karnan saw in this 'an additional big insult'. The Chief Justice suggested that Karnan engage an advocate to represent his case. Karnan replied that he was much more competent to defend himself, that he had disposed of 'about 25,000 cases during my tenure of service with the Court'. The Chief Justice had inquired—perhaps half in jest—whether all the cases had been dismissed. 'This kind of language also insulted me in the open Apex Court.' All these events established that the seven judges were guilty of having committed atrocities on a Dalit.[20]

In addition to asking the judges to appear at his residence or send their advocates, Justice Karnan requested the Speaker of the Lok Sabha to initiate impeachment proceedings against the seven judges 'who have committed a major National Offence'. And he requested the Foreign Secretary, 'Please do not allow the above mentioned 7 erring Judges to visit any foreign Country until the serious heinous crime on discrimination is finalized by the Parliament.'

The Supreme Court directed that a medical examination be conducted to determine whether Justice Karnan was of sound mind. He refused to subject himself to the examination. Instead, on 8 May, he passed an order sentencing the Chief Justice of India and his six colleagues, plus an eighth judge whom he added to the list for good measure, to five years' rigorous imprisonment. In addition

---

20 'Is there any way to substantiate that claim—of having disposed of 25,000 cases?' I asked my friend, the advocate Rahul Unnikrishnan in Chennai. His response: 'It is very difficult to find the exact number of cases disposed of by Justice Karnan. Manupatra (the database of court judgments) has reported 1,068 decisions in delivering which he was a part. Out of 1,068, he wrote 915 while sitting by himself. The remaining 153 were ruled when he was a part of various division benches. However, this does not mean that he authored all the 153 division bench decisions.' Rahul added, 'All of us are of the view that his judgments were erratic and not very well-reasoned...'

to paying Rs 2 crore to him as compensation, he directed each of the seven judges to pay Rs 1 lakh to the National Commission on Scheduled Castes and Scheduled Tribes as fine for having committed 'Atrocities' under the SC/ST [Prevention of Atrocities] Act.

The Supreme Court had run out of options as well as patience. On 9 May 2017 the seven-judge bench ordered that he be arrested and serve six months in jail for contempt of court. By this time, Justice Karnan, still a sitting judge of the Calcutta High Court, had fled Kolkata.

After a search by several agencies, a search that lasted over a month and covered many cities and sites, he was caught near Coimbatore. Taken back to Kolkata, he was lodged in Presidency Jail. What had begun as an amusing farce had by now become a tragedy. Many felt sorry for the judge. He was manifestly in need of help.

At the personal level, yes, it was a tragedy. But the episode raised questions far wider than the fate of an individual. A few passages from the cover story that *Frontline* carried upon his arrest will refresh our recollection of the facts and help us glean the lessons:

> ...The beginnings of the current controversy can be traced to the elevation of 65-year-old Chinnaswamy Swaminathan Karnan from the Bar to a judge on the bench of the Madras High Court on March 30, 2009, after he had served as a lawyer in the Madras High Court for more than a decade. He was made a permanent judge two years later.
>
> Until then no one seemed to have heard about him. His elevation to the bench surprised many then. Justice Karnan, a Dalit hailing from a village in Cuddalore district in Tamil Nadu, has been in the limelight since then for courting controversy.
>
> In the view of many observers of the judiciary, only a thin line separated his unusual behaviour from an abnormality. The unpredictability in his character is too obvious to be missed. The latest was the claim of 'mental frustration' in his letter to the apex court after he was transferred to Kolkata. Besides, when he appeared before the Supreme Court in person in response to a

contempt notice, he told the bench that he 'has lost his physical and mental balance'. And he has always used his caste identity to claim victimhood and intimidate fellow judges and extricate himself from embarrassing situations his actions created.

When he was serving on the bench in the Madras High Court in 2011, he accused brother judges of harassing him since he was a Dalit. He sent a written complaint against a few fellow judges and the then Chief Justice of the Madras High Court, R.K. Agarwal, to the National Commission for Scheduled Castes (NCSC), accusing them of 'harassing and victimizing' him since he was a Dalit.[21]

The sequence raises several questions:

- How had Karnan been picked up from the Bar and made a judge of the High Court? After all, it isn't that he was a leading and distinguished advocate. Quite the contrary, explains one of most respected senior advocates who has practised at the Madras High Court for thirty years: he was unknown. He was picked up and made judge in 2009. His conduct was evident from his very first days on the bench. How was he confirmed as permanent judge two years later, in 2011? Furthermore, remember that every few weeks, some antic of his or other would cause consternation among fellow judges, and yet Karnan continued as a High Court judge for *seven to eight* years.
- It turns out that as complaint upon complaint was brought before Mr R.K. Agarwal, then Chief Justice of the Madras High Court, he recommended to the then Chief Justice of India that Karnan be transferred to another High Court. This 'remedy' was adopted only years later upon the insistence of the next Chief Justice of the Madras High Court. Karnan was transferred to the Calcutta High Court. In what way did, in what way *could* shifting him to the Calcutta High Court solve the problem?

21 Ilangovan Rajasekaran, 'Justice C.S. Karnan: A controversial career,' *Frontline*, 10 June 2017.

Does shifting hazardous waste from the left side of an ICU to the right side mitigate the danger?

- Had Karnan not, to use his expression, 'published' the names of those twenty judges he alleged were corrupt, had he not kept shooting off letters and making them available to the press, he would have continued to dispense judgments—judgments that would have affected the lives and fortunes of numerous individuals. Would that have been just?
- The Supreme Court had little choice but to move against him in the way it did. But several of the senior-most advocates I talked to felt that Karnan should have been handled in some other way. That points to a basic design defect. The process that the Constitution provides for dealing with erring judges, of disciplining a judge, in the end of impeaching him, is just not an adequate one. Apart from other things—like the time that the process takes—in a body such as the Parliament, the eventual decision becomes a *political* decision. For instance, recall the case of Justice V. Ramaswamy which went up for impeachment. Could it be that not one Congressman saw merit in the evidence that had surfaced against him, and, correspondingly, not one member of the other parties felt the evidence to be inadequate? I fear that if the Karnan case had gone to Parliament for impeachment, the fact of his caste would have weighed just as heavily with many an MP and the controller of many a party as it did with Justice Karnan himself.
- There is the obvious lesson in how every 'posture and gesture', to use his expression, seemed to Karnan to be an insult, an insult hurled at him because he is a Dalit: could it be that a predilection so strong of seeing everything in Dalit/non-Dalit terms would not have affected the way arguments and facts that were presented before him would strike him? And then there is a lesson in the felicity with which Karnan invoked the Scheduled Castes and Scheduled Tribes (Prevention of Atrocities) Act. This came to nothing because in this instance, the act was being hurled at the Chief Justice of India and six of his colleagues. But what would have been the case if the target was an ordinary citizen? Would the citizen be able to ward off the misuse of

the act? Moreover, the point transcends the injustice that the targeted individual would have suffered. Would a Karnan-type misuse of the act not foment a backlash against what many would regard as an essential remedy for the protection of Scheduled Castes and Tribes?[22]

22 After detailing Justice Karnan's erratic ways, and showing how completely justified the Supreme Court was in holding him guilty of having committed contempt of court, Arvind Datar pointed out that the case nevertheless raised a series of questions in regard to law and court procedure. He listed these as follows:

1. Would it have been proper to first convict Justice Karnan and then adjourn the case for sentencing? (This was done in the case of Vijay Mallya who was also convicted on the same day but his case had been adjourned to a later date for imposing a sentence.)
2. Can a High Court sentence a district judge to imprisonment by adopting a similar procedure?
3. Can a division bench of two Supreme Court judges pass a similar sentence? What should be the strength of a bench that passes such a sentence?
4. The Constitution enables the removal of a High Court judge only by the process prescribed under Article 124(4)—by what is popularly termed as the 'impeachment process'. In the present case, Justice Karnan would have retired on 11 June 2017. If he had several years to continue, can a conviction for contempt result in his removal as a High Court judge in view of the mandatory provision of Article 124(4)?
5. Will it be necessary for Parliament to pass a resolution for his removal under Article 124(4) *after* the sentence of imprisonment is passed? What happens if Parliament does not pass any resolution for his removal? Will the convicted judge continue in service even if no work is allotted to him?
6. Is it not necessary to set-up an in-house correction mechanism to deal with judicial misconduct or other cases of impropriety?

C.f., Arvind Datar, 'Justice C.S. Karnan—an ignominious end,' *Bar and Bench*, 11 May 2017, https://barandbench.com/justice-cs-karnan-ignominious-end-arvind-datar/

9

Eloquence

Mr Jayaprakash Narayan had passed away—weakened as much by the failures and breakup of the Janata Party as by the collapse of his kidneys. Mr V.M. Tarkunde, one of our most distinguished and public-spirited judges and advocates, was the president of the People's Union for Civil Liberties. I was its general secretary. We had instituted an annual lecture in honour of JP. That particular year, it was decided that we should request Justice V.R. Krishna Iyer to deliver the lecture. He was known for his progressive views, and had delivered many a judgment that opened new vistas for citizens. Mr Tarkunde spoke to him about the lecture, and told him that he would send me over to explain more about the series.

I was a bit nervous: I had expressed myself strongly against some of Justice Krishna Iyer's judgments—among these were his judgments on reservations, and other issues dear to progressives at the time. I had been particularly harsh about the conditional stay that he had given on Justice Jagmohan Lal Sinha's judgment against Mrs Indira Gandhi. He had gone so far as to indicate from the bench to Mrs Gandhi and her supporters a way out of the bind: this is as much as I can do with the law as it stands, he had said in effect; but, of course, if you amend the law, the Supreme Court will have to go by the amended law. That is exactly what Mrs Gandhi's troopers proceeded to do.[1]

I had found him sitting in the veranda, wearing a Kerala-lungi and shirt, dictating to a steno. My apprehension had been completely misplaced. He greeted me warmly: 'Come on, Shourie, come on. Tarkunde told me you will be coming. Just sit down: I will finish this in a moment, and then we will talk.' As I sat listening to him dictate, I noticed that in addition to the pile of case papers lying around, there were two or three dictionaries, and a thesaurus. The judge would pause mid-sentence, look up the thesaurus, sometimes consult the dictionary and resume dictation with an abstruse word or expression. In two editions of his critical exposition of our Constitution, Mr H.M. Seervai had included a special annexure on Justice Krishna Iyer's prose and the perils it could pose in interpreting what he had meant.

Alas! Grandiloquence still bursts forth from time to time. The opening paragraph of the judgment of Justice Dipak Misra in the defamation case[2] has often been cited in this context, and many a passage from it has become famous. The question at hand was whether defamation is just a civil offence against an individual or, in addition, is it a criminal offence: in the sense, in part because the person defaming another deserves, in addition to paying a fine, to be jailed; and in part because defamation disrupts social relations and is thus a crime against society and state as a whole. Justice Misra[3] opened his exposition thus:

---

1 For an appreciation of Justice Krishna Iyer's contributions to Indian jurisprudence, a view stressing how he had his heart in the right place, and how his enlargements of the law and creative interpretations brought relief to millions, see Fali S. Nariman, *Before Memory Fades: An Autobiography,* Hay House, New Delhi, 2010.

2 *Subramanian Swamy v. Union of India and Ors.,* (2016) 7 SCC 221. Tunku Varadarajan was the one who first drew attention to Justice Misra's prose in this case. C.f., Tunku Varadarajan, 'Judgment by Thesaurus, Or a "Proponement in Oppugnation" to the Supreme Court's use of language,' *The Wire,* 16 May 2016.

3 As he then was. At the time of writing, he is the Chief Justice of India.

> This batch of writ petitions preferred under Article 32 of the Constitution of India exposits cavil in its quintessential conceptuality and percipient discord between venerated and exalted right of freedom of speech and expression of an individual, exploring manifold and multilayered, limitless, unbounded and unfettered spectrums, and the controls, restrictions and constrictions, under the assumed power of 'reasonableness' ingrained in the statutory provisions relating to criminal law to reviver and uphold one's reputation. The assertion by the Union of India and the complainants is that the reasonable restrictions are based on the paradigms and parameters of the Constitution that are structured and pedestaled on the doctrine of non-absoluteness of any fundamental right, cultural and social ethos, need and feel of the time, for every right engulfs and incorporates duty to respect [the] other's right and ensure mutual compatibility and conviviality of the individuals based on collective harmony and conceptual grace of eventual social order; and the asseveration on the part of the petitioners is that freedom of thought and expression cannot be scuttled or abridged on the threat of criminal prosecution and made paraplegic on the mercurial stance of individual reputation and of societal harmony, for the said aspects are to be treated as things of the past, a symbol of [the] colonial era where the ruler ruled over the subjects and vanquished concepts of resistance; and, in any case, the individual grievances pertaining to reputation can be agitated in civil courts and thus, there is a remedy and viewed from a prismatic perspective, there is no justification to keep the provision of defamation in criminal law alive as it creates a concavity and unreasonable restriction in individual freedom and further progressively mars voice of criticism and dissent which are necessitous for the growth of genuine advancement and a matured democracy.

The judge moved to recapitulating the submissions that the counsel had made to the court: 'We may immediately state that the effort would be to record the submissions in fullest, may be [sic] sans elaborations and individualistically crafted and sculptured nuances during the oral hearings...'

Paragraphs followed summarizing the arguments of the counsel who argued that defamation is just a civil wrong against a person, and not a crime against the state. And this was followed by a section that set out what Justice Misra characterized as '*Proponements In Oppugnation*'.

And so on. Yet, such flights of eloquence are to a pattern. In *Manoj Nirula v. Union of India*,[4] the petitioner had urged that no one who is guilty of a heinous crime should be allowed to be inducted into the Council of Ministers. Justice Misra opened his oration with customary eloquence:

> A democratic polity, as understood in its quintessential purity, is conceptually abhorrent to corruption and, especially corruption at high places, and repulsive to the idea of criminalization of politics as it corrodes the legitimacy of the collective ethos, frustrates the hopes and aspirations of the citizens and has the potentiality to obstruct, if not derail, the rule of law. Democracy, which has been best defined as the Government of the People, by the People and for the People, expects prevalence of genuine orderliness, positive propriety, dedicated discipline and sanguine sanctity by constant affirmance of constitutional morality which is the pillar stone of good governance.

Priyanka Srivastava and Ors. v. State of U.P.[5] dealt with persons who had borrowed from the Punjab National Bank and, instead of returning the loans, had begun filing cases against officials of the bank. Justice Misra began:

> The present appeal projects and frescoes a scenario which is not only disturbing but also has the potentiality to create a stir compelling one to ponder in a perturbed state how some unscrupulous, unprincipled and deviant litigants can ingeniously

4 (2014) 9 SCC 1.
5 (2015) 6 SCC 287.

> and innovatively design in a nonchalant manner to knock at the doors of the Court, as if, it is a laboratory where multifarious experiments can take place and such skillful persons can adroitly abuse the process of the Court at their own will and desire by painting a canvas of agony by assiduous assertions made in the application though the real intention is to harass the statutory authorities, without any remote remorse, with the inventive design primarily to create a mental pressure on the said officials as individuals, for they would not like to be dragged to a court of law to face in criminal cases, and further pressurize in such a fashion so that financial institution which they represent would ultimately be constrained to accept the request for 'one-time settlement' with the fond hope that the obstinate defaulters who had borrowed money from it would withdraw the cases instituted against them. The facts, as we proceed to adumbrate, would graphically reveal how such persons, pretentiously aggrieved but potentially dangerous, adopt the self-convincing mastery methods to achieve so. That is the sad and unfortunate factual score forming the fulcrum of the case at hand, and, we painfully recount.

In the course of the judgment we learn of '...the respondent No.3, possibly nurturing the idea of self-centric Solomon's wisdom...'; we are taken through a matter that seems somewhat removed from the issue at hand, only to learn, '...Though the present controversy is different, we have dealt with the said facet as we intend to emphasize how the Courts have dealt with and addressed to such a matter so that a borrower with vengeance could ultimately exhibit his high-handedness...'; we learn that '...Presently, we are required to sit in the time machine for a while'; we learn how '... At this stage, it is apposite to state that the third respondent, if we allow ourselves to say so, have [sic] possibly mastered how to create a sense of fear in the mind of the officials who are compelled to face criminal cases', in fact that '...The labyrinth maladroitly created by the respondent No.3 does not end here. It appears that he had the indefatigable spirit to indulge himself in the abuse of the process of the Court'; we then learn about 'the devilish design of respondent No. 3'; we are reminded that 'When a citizen avails a loan from a financial institution, it is his obligation to pay back

SC 699, a three-Judge Bench, while dealing with the magnitude of the problem in engagement of the child labour in various hazardous factories or mines, etc., speaking through Hansaria, J., commenced the judgment thus:-

I am the child.
All the word waits for my coming.
All the earth watches with interest to see what I shall become.
Civilization hangs in the balance.
For what I am, the world of tomorrow will be.
I am the child.
You hold in your hand my destiny.
You determine, largely, whether I shall succeed or fail,
Give me, I pray you, these things that make for happiness.
Train me, I beg you, that I may be a blessing to the world.

That turns out to be the quotation of a quotation:

> The aforesaid lines from Mamie Gene Cole were treated as an appeal by this Court and the Bench reproduced the famous line from William Wordsworth 'Child is the father of the man'. I have reproduced the same to highlight that this Court has laid special emphasis on the term 'child' as a child feels that the entire world waits for his/her coming. A female child, as stated earlier, becomes a woman. Its life-spark cannot be extinguished in the womb, for such an act would certainly bring disaster to the society. On such an act the collective can neither laugh today nor tomorrow. There shall be tears and tears all the way because eventually the spirit of humanity is comatosed.

The judge fortified the message further:

> Vishwakavi Rabindranath Tagore, while speaking about a child, had said thus:- Every child comes with the message that God is not yet discouraged of man.
>
> Long back, speaking about human baby, Charles Dickens had said thus:- Every baby born into the world is a finer one than the last.
>
> It would not be an exaggeration to say that a society that does not respect its women cannot be treated to be civilized. In the first

> part of the last century Swami Vivekananda had said:- Just as a bird could not fly with one wing only, a nation would not march forward if the women are left behind.

Next, the exhortation had to be made specific to women who were agreeing to abort the foetus:

> When a female foeticide takes place, every woman who mothers the child must remember that she is killing her own child despite being a mother. That is what abortion would mean in social terms. Abortion of a female child in its conceptual eventuality leads to killing of a woman. Law prohibits it; scriptures forbid it; philosophy condemns it; ethics deprecate it, morality decries it and social science abhors it. Henrik Ibsen emphasized on the individualism of woman. John Milton treated her to be the best of all God's work. In this context, it will be appropriate to quote a few lines from *Democracy in America* by Alexis De Tocqueville:- 'If I were asked ... to what the singular prosperity and growing strength of that people [Americans] ought mainly to be attributed, I should reply: to the superiority of their women.'

If, in turn, I were asked, I would point out that Ibsen, Milton and de Tocqueville are not likely to carry much weight in Haryana: strict and prompt punishments of the offenders will do more. The judge reinforced the quotations by recalling our own judgments:

> At this stage, I may with profit reproduce two paragraphs from *Ajit Savant Majagvai v. State of Karnataka* MANU/SC/0822/1997: (1997) 7 SCC 110:-
>
> Social thinkers, philosophers, dramatists, poets and writers have eulogised the female species of the human race and have always used beautiful epithets to describe her temperament and personality and have not deviated from that path even while speaking of her odd behaviour, at times. Even in sarcasm, they have not crossed the literary limit and have adhered to a particular standard of nobility of language. Even when a member of her own species, Madame De Stael, remarked, 'I am glad that I am

> not a man; for then I should have to marry a woman', there was wit in it. When Shakespeare wrote, 'Age cannot wither her; nor custom stale, her infinite variety', there again was wit. Notwithstanding that these writers have cried hoarse for respect for 'woman', notwithstanding that Schiller said, 'Honour women! They entwine and weave heavenly roses in our earthly life' and notwithstanding that the Mahabharata mentioned her as the source of salvation, crime against 'woman' continues to rise and has, today undoubtedly, risen to alarming proportions.
>
> It is unfortunate that in an age where people are described as civilised, crime against 'female' is committed even when the child is in the womb as the 'female' foetus is often destroyed to prevent the birth of a female child. If that child comes into existence, she starts her life as a daughter, then becomes a wife and in due course, a mother. She rocks the cradle to rear up her infant, bestows all her love on the child and as the child grows in age, she gives to the child all that she has in her own personality. She shapes the destiny and character of the child. To be cruel to such a creature is unthinkable. To torment a wife can only be described as the most hated and derisive act of a human being.

'[Emphasis supplied],' the judge noted. A judgment quoting a judgment quoting Madame de Stael, Shakespeare, Schiller, Mahabharata![9] I did not quite understand how putting *woman* and *female* in quotation marks would carry the message farther. That apart, clearly, and the Mahabharata notwithstanding, the point that women are vital to civilization needed further reinforcement. The judge continued: 'Long back, Charles Fourier had stated,

9 The original judgment concerned the death by strangulation of a lady. Her husband was said to be the one who had killed her. The trial court had acquitted him. The High Court had overturned the trial court acquittal. The Supreme Court upheld the High Court decision. The judge might as well have included the paragraph that preceded the two he reproduced—for it was just as eloquent: 'BATTLE OF SEXES has always been a battle of wits. Today it is denuded of its charms. It has degenerated into a WAR involving physical violence, torture, mental cruelty and murder of the female, including, particularly, the WIFE (caps in the original).' But then, perhaps doing so would have made the context too obvious.

"The extension of women's rights is the basic principle of all social progress."'

Too many foreign authorities? But the judgment had a long way to go as yet:

> Recapitulating from the past, I may refer to certain sayings in the Smritis which put women in an elevated position. This Court in Nikku Ram's case (supra) had already reproduced the first line of the 'Shloka'. The second line of the same which is also significant is as follows: *Yatra tastu na pujyante sarvastatraphalah kriyah*.
>
> A free translation of the aforesaid is reproduced: All the actions become unproductive in a place, where they are not treated with proper respect and dignity.
>
> Another wise man of the past had his own way of putting it:
> *Bhartr bhratr pitrijnati swasruswasuradevaraih.*
> *Bandhubhisca striyah pujyah bhusnachhadanasnai.*
>
> A free translation of the aforesaid is as follows: The women are to be respected equally on par with husbands, brothers, fathers, relatives, in-laws and other kith and kin and while respecting, the women gifts [sic] like ornaments, garments, etc. should be given as token of honour.
>
> Yet again, the sagacity got reflected in following lines:- *Atulam yatra tattejah sarvadevasarirajam| Ekastham tadabhunnari vyaptalokatrayam tvisa||*
>
> A free translation of the aforesaid is reproduced: The incomparable valour (effulgence) born from the physical frames of all the gods, spreading [sic] the three worlds by its radiance and combining together took the form of a woman.

From our sages of the past to a British sage of the present:

> From the past, I travel to the present and respectfully notice what Lord Denning had to say about the equality of women and their role in the society:- 'A woman feels as keenly, thinks as clearly, as a man. She in her sphere does work as useful as man does in his. She has as much right to her freedom—to develop her personality to the full as a man. When she marries, she does not become

> the husband's servant but his equal partner. If his work is more important in life of the community, hers is more important of the family. Neither can do without the other. Neither is above the other or under the other. They are equals.'
>
> I have referred to certain pronouncements of this Court, the sayings of the sagacious ones, thinkers, poets, philosophers and jurists about the child and women only to emphasise that they play a seminal role in the society. The innocence of a child and the creative intelligence of a woman can never ever be brushed aside or marginalized. Civilization of a country is known [by?] how it respects its women. It is the requisite of the present day that people are made aware that it is obligatory to treat the women with respect and dignity so that humanism in its conceptual essentiality remains alive. Each member of the society is required to develop a scientific temper in the modern context because that is the social need of the present. A cosmetic awareness campaign would never subserve the purpose. The authorities of the Government, the Non-Governmental Organisations and other volunteers are required to remember that there has [sic] to be awareness camps which are [sic] really effective. The people involved with the same must take it up as a service, a crusade. They must understand and accept that it is an art as well as a science and not simple arithmetic. It cannot take the colour of a routine speech. The awareness camps should not be founded on the theory of Euclidian geometry. It [sic] must engulf the concept of social vigilance with an analytical mind and radiate into the marrows of the society. If awareness campaigns are not appositely conducted, the needed guidance for the people would be without meaning and things shall fall apart and everyone would try to take shelter in cynical escapism.

In practical terms, how should the camps be conducted? The judge was contextual: 'It is difficult to precisely state how an awareness camp is to be conducted. It will depend upon what kind and strata of people are being addressed to [sic].'

But one thing was clear—persons conducting such camps must be men and women of wide learning:

> The persons involved in such awareness campaign are required to equip themselves with constitutional concepts, culture, philosophy, religion, scriptural commands and injunctions, the mandate of the law as engrafted under the Act and above all the development of modern science. It needs no special emphasis to state that in awareness camps while the deterrent facets of law are required to be accentuated upon, simultaneously the desirability of law to be followed with spiritual obeisance, regard being had to the purpose [sic] of the Act, has to be stressed upon. The seemly synchronization shall bring the required effect. That apart, documentary films can be shown to highlight the need; and instil the idea in the mind of the public at large, for when mind becomes strong, mountains do melt. The people involved in the awareness campaigns should have boldness and courage. There should not be any iota of confusion or perplexity in their thought or action. They should treat it as a problem and think that a problem has to be understood in a proper manner to afford a solution. They should bear in mind that they are required to change the mindset of the people, the grammar of the society and unacceptable beliefs inherent in the populace. It should be clearly spelt out that female foeticide is the worst type of dehumanisation of the human race.

All true. But what did all those quotations add to jurisprudence? Was their place in a judgment or in a public peroration? The judge had his reason: 'I have highlighted the aforesaid aspects so that when awareness campaigns are held, they are kept in view, for that is the object and purpose to have real awareness.'

Repeating for emphasis

But, of course, that could not be the end of the matter. The Supreme Court had been issuing directions for eliminating this terrible practice since 2001.[10] The court had done so again in the judgment that we

---

10 C.f., *Centre for Enquiry into Health and Allied Themes (CEHAT) and Ors. v. Union of India and Ors.* MANU/SC/0291/2001, (2001) 5 SCC 577; and *Centre for Enquiry into Health and Allied Themes (CEHAT) and Ors. v. Union of India and Ors.* MANU/SC/0700/2003, (2003) 8 SCC 398.

have just traversed, a judgment delivered in 2013. Far from the directions being followed with the thoroughness that was warranted both by the gravity of the practice and by the fact that the directions had been given by the Supreme Court, during proceedings in the court in November 2014 it came to light that several states—among them Assam, Bihar, Goa, Gujarat, Kerala and Madhya Pradesh—had not taken even the most elementary step: they had not even filed the affidavits that the Supreme Court had directed them to file.

In 2014, the Indian Medical Association (IMA) filed a writ in the Supreme Court. The lapses for which several medical professionals were being arraigned were merely minor clerical errors in filling up forms. As the relevant act—Pre-conception and Pre-natal Diagnostic Techniques (Prohibition of Sex Selection) Act, 1994—did not classify offences, as all offences had been made non-bailable and non-compoundable, and as it conferred draconian powers on the authorities, the act had become a new way for extorting bribes, the IMA pointed out. As a result, the matter was brought before the court again in 2016.[11] This time the bench consisted of Justice Dipak Misra and Justice Shiva Kirti Singh. Justice Misra delivered the judgment on behalf of both of them. The writ filed by the Voluntary Health Association of Punjab which pointed to lapses in implementation (it had been filed in 2006) and the writ of the IMA were taken up together.

The judgment began with the eloquence which by now we have learnt to expect. The issues that had been raised in the 2006 petition had been raised earlier also, the court observed, 'and been dealt with serious concern and solemn sincerity'. They are being taken up again:

> It is because they relate to the very core of existence of a civilized society, pertain to the progress of the human race, and expose the maladroit efforts to throttle the right of a life to feel the mother earth and smell its fragrance. And, if we allow ourselves to say, the issues have been highlighted with sincere rhetorics and balanced hyperboles and ring the alarm of destruction of humanity in the

11 *Voluntary Health Association of Punjab v. Union of India and Ors.*, MANU/SC/1433/2016, (2016) 10 SCC 265.

> long run. It is not a group prophecy, but a significant collective predication. The involvement of all is obvious, and it has to be.

The court then proceeded to recount the history of judgments and directions for stopping the abortion of female foetuses. As we have seen, in its judgment of 2013, it had reproduced passages from *Ajit Savant Majagvai v. State of Karnataka.*[12] It now reproduced the same passages again, adding, 'We may repeat, the aforestated observation though made totally in a different context but nonetheless, it seemly stated the marrow of the problem'—we thus had the judge quoting from his own earlier judgment passages that he had quoted from another judgment. Next, he reproduced the directions that the court had given in 2001 and 2003. Then he reproduced the directions it had given in 2013. As this last set included that direction on educating the people to the evil inherent in the practice, Justice Misra now observed, 'We may profitably reproduce certain passages from the concurring opinion'—that is, his own opinion delivered in 2013: passages in which, while agreeing with the direction to educate the people, he had felt compelled to dilate upon the vital role and high status of women, of the child and of the female child. Then came a recapitulation and, so to say some discussion of some of the data which had been furnished by the states. This was followed by reproducing at length provisions from the act—something that had been done in each one of the earlier judgments. And then the concluding oration to rival the ones in the 2013 concurring opinion:

> Before parting with the case, let it be stated with certitude and without allowing any room for any kind of equivocation or ambiguity, the perception of any individual or group or organization or system treating a woman with inequity, indignity, inequality or any kind of discrimination is constitutionally impermissible. The historical perception has to be given a prompt burial. Female foeticide is conceived by the society that definitely includes the parents because of unethical perception of life and nonchalant attitude towards law. The society that treats man and woman with

12 (1997) 7 SCC 110.

> equal dignity shows the reflections of a progressive and civilized society. To think that a woman should think what a man or a society wants her to think tantamounts to slaughtering her choice, and [is] definitely a humiliating act. When freedom of free choice is allowed within constitutional and statutory parameters, others cannot determine the norms as that would amount to acting in derogation of law. Decrease in the sex ratio is a sign of colossal calamity and it cannot be allowed to happen. Concrete steps have to be taken to increase the same so that invited social disasters do not befall on [sic] the society. The present generation is expected to be responsible to the posterity [sic] and not to take such steps to sterilize the birth rate in violation of law. The societal perception has to be metamorphosed having respect to legal postulates.

If instead of quoting from earlier judgments, including one's own, if instead of once again listing the provisions of the Act, if instead of once again reproducing directions that the Supreme Court had given repeatedly, the judges had actually brought some consequences to bear on those whose duty it was to implement the directions and who had not done so—would that not have been a real step towards mitigating the evil?

But what about the second writ—that of the Indian Medical Association—which had been clubbed with the one by the Voluntary Health Association of Punjab? After all, it had made far-reaching assertions. Was there any effort to ascertain if its assertion was true—that the act had become an instrument of extorting bribes? Wouldn't that inquiry have taken us to, as the judge would say, the marrow of the problem—the problem why the court's oft-repeated directions were being taken so casually? As the cause is so important, and was of obvious concern to the judges, the assertions of the IMA merited inquiry. If they were false, office bearers of the IMA deserved to be severely punished for trying to mislead the court on so important a matter. On the other hand, if they were true, if indeed provisions of the act were being used to extort bribes, the fact would be of as much significance: it is well-known that misuse of a law ignites a backlash against the law itself—the result being that even a law which is needed loses legitimacy, something that would happen from a Karnan-type misuse of the law to prevent atrocities against members of Scheduled Castes and Tribes. But for the court, the peroration delivered, there was nothing further to be done. After we read of that writ—the one by the Indian Medical Association—in the title of the case, we see nothing of it till the very end of the judgment. In the third-last paragraph, the IMA's assertions are summarized. And in the next paragraph, summarily dismissed.

With no editor to say 'No'

Sometimes it seems that a judge has been devoted to a particular cause or has a pet aversion, or he has some passages, perhaps an essay, that had been prepared for some occasion, and he just bungs it in. No editor to say 'No', after all.

In *Ramlila Maidan Incident*,[13] the judges were dealing with allegations that the police had used excessive force while dispersing people who had gathered for what was supposed to be a yoga shivir. Baba Ramdev's people had obtained permission to hold a day-long shivir at the Ramlila Ground in Delhi. The gathering had taken on a political colour. Baba Ramdev was engaged in negotiations with ministers. Ministers were visiting him. The day stretched into night. Around 1 a.m., the police entered the area and sought to disperse the crowd. Baba Ramdev had been sleeping in a side room. He was awakened. Some policemen went to the dais to serve an order on him to have the crowd disperse. His followers claimed that they climbed to get hold of him and whisk him away. A melee ensued. Ramdev jumped down from the dais, into the gathering, and escaped. He was arrested at the railway station—attired in a woman's salwar-kameez, with his beard hidden under a dupatta: he claimed later that had he not escaped, the police would have killed him. Back at the pandal, there were scuffles—the police claimed that the crowd had hurled stones, the followers of the Baba claimed that it was the police that had started hitting them with lathis, and fired teargas shells ... The judges held against the police. One of the

13 *Ramlila Maidan Incident, in Re, Suo Motu Writ Petition (Crl.) No. 122 of 2011,* decided on 20 June 2011, (2012) 5 SCC 125.

factors that led them to do so was that videos showed the followers to have been asleep at the time.

Of the two judges who heard the case, one wrote the main judgment. The other concurred. But even as he concurred, he felt it necessary to dilate upon the significance of sleep. He came to the subject stressing that the duties of the state—for instance, to prevent disorder—had to be balanced against the rights of individuals:

> No doubt, the law of social control is preserved in the hands of the State, but at the same time, protection against unwarranted governmental invasion and intrusive action is also protected under the laws of the country. Liberty is definitely no licence and the right of such freedom is not absolute but can be regulated by appropriate laws. The freedom from official interference is, therefore, regulated by law but law cannot be enforced for crippling the freedom merely under the garb of such regulation. The police or the administration without any lawful cause cannot make a calculated interference in the enjoyment of the fundamental rights guaranteed to the citizens of this country. As to what was material to precipitate such a prohibitory action is one aspect of the matter, but what is more important is the implementation of such an order. This is what troubles me in the background that a prohibitory order was sought to be enforced on a sleeping crowd and not a violent one. My concern is about the enforcement of the order without any announcement as prescribed for being published or by its affixation in terms of Delhi Police Standing Order 309 read with Section 134 CrPC.

That the videos showed the crowd to have been asleep brought him to the question of sleep:

> It is believed that a person who is sleeping, is half dead. His mental faculties are in an inactive state. Sleep is an unconscious state or condition regularly and naturally assumed by man and other living beings during which the activity of the nervous system is almost or entirely suspended. It is the state of slumber and repose. It is a necessity and not a luxury. It is essential for optimal health and

> happiness as it directly affects the quality of life of an individual when awake inducing his mental sharpness, emotional balance, creativity and vitality.

And then to what was perhaps an unconscious effort to provide an explanation as to why some in the crowd had started hurling stones and bricks at the police: 'Sleep is, therefore, a biological and essential ingredient of the basic necessities of life. If this sleep is disturbed, the mind gets disoriented and it disrupts the health cycle.'

And then back to the significance of sleep:

> If this disruption is brought about in odd hours preventing an individual from getting normal sleep, it also causes energy disbalance, indigestion and also affects cardiovascular health. These symptoms, therefore, make sleep so essential that its deprivation would result in mental and physical torture both. It has a wide range of negative effects. It also impairs the normal functioning and performance of an individual which is compulsory in day-to-day life of a human being. Sleep, therefore, is a self-rejuvenating element of our life cycle and is, therefore, part and parcel of human life. The disruption of sleep is to deprive a person of a basic priority, resulting in adverse metabolic effects. It is a medicine for weariness which if impeded would lead to disastrous results.

And then once again that, perhaps unconscious, urge to explain the crowd's conduct: 'Deprivation of sleep has tumultuous adverse effects. It causes a stir and disturbs the quiet and peace of an individual's physical state.'

And then to laying the ground for enlarging the scope of Article 21 to include the right to sound, uninterrupted sleep:

> A natural process which is inherent in a human being if disturbed obviously affects basic life. It is for this reason that if a person is deprived of sleep, the effect thereof, is treated to be torturous. To take away the right of natural rest is also therefore violation of a

> human right. It becomes a violation of a fundamental right when it is disturbed intentionally, unlawfully and for no justification.

And then the explanation for the crowd's behaviour again: 'To arouse a person suddenly, brings about a feeling of shock and benumbness.'

And then back to the centrality of sleep:

> The pressure of a sudden awakening results in almost a void of sensation. Such an action, therefore, does affect the basic life of an individual. The state of sleeping is assumed by an individual when he is in a safe atmosphere. It is for this reason that this natural system has been inbuilt by our creator to provide relaxation to a human being. The muscles are relaxed and this cycle has a normal recurrence every night and lasts for several hours. This necessity is so essential that even all our transport systems provide for facilities of sleep while travelling. Sleep is therefore, both, life and inherent liberty which cannot be taken away by any unscrupulous action.
>
> An Irish proverb goes on to say that the beginning of health is sleep. The state of sleep has been described by Homer in the famous epic *Iliad* as 'sleep is the twin of death'. A person, therefore, cannot be presumed to be engaged in a criminal activity or an activity to disturb peace of mind when asleep. Aristotle, the great Greek philosopher, has said that all men are alike when asleep. To presume that a person was scheming to disrupt public peace while asleep would be unjust and would be entering into the dreams of that person.

Thence to the way the police sought to implement the order:

> I am bewildered to find out as to how such declaration of the intention to impose the prohibition was affected on a sleeping crowd. There may be a reason available to impose prohibitory orders calling upon an assembly to disperse, but to me, there does not appear to be any plausible reason for the police to resort to blows on a sleeping crowd and to throw them out of their

> encampments abruptly. The affidavits and explanation given do not disclose as to why the police could not wait till morning and provide a reasonable time to this crowd to disperse peacefully. The undue haste caused a huge disarray and resulted in a catastrophe that was witnessed on media and television throughout the country.

Thence to reinforcement by reiteration:

> I fail to find any explanation for the gravity or the urgent situation requiring such an emergent action at this dark hour of midnight. I, therefore, in the absence of any such justification have no option but to deprecate such action and it also casts a serious doubt about the existence of the sufficiency of reasons for such action. The incident in this litigation is an example of a weird expression of the desire of a tyrannical mind to threaten peaceful life suddenly for no justification. This coupled with what is understood of sleep hereinbefore, makes it clear that the precipitate action was nothing but a clear violation of human rights and a definite violation of procedure for achieving the end of dispersing a crowd.

Then back to the significance of sleep:

> It is in view of this fact that, in many countries there are complete night curfews (at the airport i.e. banning of landing and taking off between the night hours), for the reason that the concept of sound sleep has been associated with sound health which is an inseparable facet of Article 21 of the Constitution. It may also be pertinent to mention here that various statutory provisions prohibit the arrest of a judgment-debtor, a woman in the night and restrain to enter in the night into a constructed area suspected to have been raised in violation of the sanctioned plan, master plan or zonal plan for the purpose of survey or demolition. (See Section 55 of the Code of Civil Procedure, Section 46(4) CrPC, and Sections 25 and 42 of the U.P. Urban Planning and Development Act, 1973.)

From this to a concession fraught with dangerous possibilities:

> While determining such matters the crucial issue in fact is not whether such rights exist, but whether the State has a compelling interest in the regulation of a subject which is within the police power of the State. *Undoubtedly, reasonable regulation of time, place and manner of the act of sleeping would not violate any constitutional guarantee, for the reason that a person may not claim that sleeping is his fundamental right,* and therefore, he has a right to sleep in the premises of the Supreme Court itself or within the precincts of Parliament. More so, I am definitely not dealing herein with the rights of homeless persons who may claim right to sleep on footpath or public premises but restrict the case only to the extent as under what circumstances a sleeping person may be disturbed and I am of the view that the State authorities cannot deprive a person of that right anywhere and at all times.

Not a fundamental right, but as important a right as the right to—blink: 'Thus, it is evident that right of privacy and the right to sleep have always been treated to be a fundamental right like a right to breathe, to eat, to drink, to blink, etc.'

Then back to what the courts like to call the fact situation: 'There was no gossip or discussion of something untrue that was going on. To the contrary, it was admittedly an assembly of followers, under a peaceful banner of yogic training, fast asleep. The assembly was *at least, purportedly*, ...'

'*At least, purportedly*'? Perchance a slight nod to what the assembly was actually about? Not really. It was:

> ... a conglomeration of individuals gathered together, expressive of a determination to improve the material condition of the human race. The aim of the assembly was prima facie unobjectionable and was not to inflame passions. It was to ward off something harmful. What was suspicious or conspiratorial about the assembly, may require an investigation by the appropriate forum, but to my mind the implementation appears to have been done in an unlawful and derogatory manner that did violate the basic human rights of the crowd to have a sound sleep which is also a constitutional freedom, acknowledged under Article 21 of the Constitution of India.

Back to the way the police acted:

> Such an assembly is necessarily illegal cannot be presumed, and even if it was, the individuals were all asleep who were taken by surprise altogether for a simultaneous implementation and action under Section 144 CrPC without being preceded by an announcement or even otherwise, giving no time in a reasonable way to the assembly to disperse from the Ramlila Ground. To the contrary, the sleep of this huge crowd was immodestly and brutally outraged and it was dispersed by force making them flee hither and thither, which by such precipitate action, caused a mayhem that was reflected in the media.

And then back to the significance of sleep:

> An individual is entitled to sleep as comfortably and as freely as he breathes. Sleep is essential for a human being to maintain the delicate balance of health necessary for its very existence and survival. Sleep is, therefore, a fundamental and basic requirement without which the existence of life itself would be in peril. To disturb sleep, therefore, would amount to torture which is now accepted as a violation of human right. It would be similar to a third-degree method which at times is sought to be justified as a necessary police action to extract the truth out of an accused involved in heinous and cold-blooded crimes. It is also a device adopted during warfare where prisoners of war and those involved in espionage are subjected to treatments depriving them of normal sleep.

Then begin citations from earlier judgments, a score and more of them are cited and extracts from them are reproduced—on the right to life, on the meaning of 'life', on the right to privacy, on public order. Then follow sections detailing when the state may intervene immediately, and what procedure a force like the police must follow…

Finally, the conclusion: 'For the reasons aforesaid, I concur with the directions issued by my learned colleague with a forewarning to the respondents to prevent any repetition of such hasty and unwarranted act affecting the safe living conditions of the citizens/ persons in this country.'

Such heavy artillery just to concur?

One judgment or six?

Professor Geeta Oberoi of the National Judicial Academy at Bhopal draws my attention to a variant of quoting oneself, of quoting oneself quoting others. Often several petitions come before judges pertaining to more or less the same matter. The general practice is to club them together, and dispose of them through a single judgment. But sometimes it seems that the judge treats each in a separate judgment—each judgment being a replica of the other. She directs me to read two sets of cases as a contrast. In *Kalpana Pundlik Jamdade v. State of Maharashtra*,[14] Justice T.V. Nalawade had before him four petitions. All of them advanced pleas against orders that had been issued holding them guilty of having violated the Pre-conception and Pre-natal Diagnostic Techniques (Prohibition of Sex Selection) Act, 1994. He set out the facts relating to each case, as well as the relevant provisions of the law and the rules, and dealt with all the four in a single judgment. By contrast, Justice A.I.S. Cheema, in the same bench of the same High Court,[15] delivered in effect the same judgment six times over by taking six petitions one by one. In each judgment, he cited at length the same provisions of the act. In each, he cited the same rules. In each, he applied the same reasoning.[16] Result? As far as statistics of performance

14 2015 ALLMR(Cri) 17.

15 The Aurangabad bench of the High Court of Bombay.

16 C.f., *Dr. Dattatraya v. The State of Maharashtra and Taluka Adhikari @ The Medical Superintendent Class-I,* 2014 ALLMR(Cri) 3977; *Vinayak v. The State of Maharashtra,* 2014 ALLMR(Cri) 3393; *Dr. Ravindra and Dr. Sudarshana v. The State of Maharashtra, through Dr. B.R. Sonwane,* 2016 ALLMR(Cri) 1876; *Dr. Sau. Nirmala v. The State of Maharashtra, through its Secretary and Appropriate Authority & Medical Superintendent through Dr. S.A. Sable, Beed,* 2016 ALLMR(Cri) 1034; *Radhakrishna v. The State of Maharashtra,* 2016 ALLMR(Cri) 1556; *Zaheda v. State of Maharashtra*, 2016 ALLMR(Cri) 2049.

are concerned, Justice Nalawade delivered one judgment, Justice Cheema delivered six!

Stenos and search engines

That women are half the population, that mothers shape generations, that they are the fount of love, that killing a foetus because the to-be-born is a girl, is murder—is any of this so obscure that it requires quotations from Mamie Gene Cole, from William Wordsworth, from Charles Dickens, from Henrik Ibsen, from John Milton, from Alexis de Tocqueville, from Madam de Stael, from William Shakespeare, from Schiller, from Charles Fourier, from Lord Denning, not to forget from Vishwakavi Rabindranath Tagore, from Swami Vivekananda, from the Mahabharata, from the Smritis, and, of course, from earlier judgments of the Supreme Court itself: one and all saying the same thing—that women are vital, in themselves and for civilization? It is as if someone had a book of quotations in hand, and looked up 'woman', then 'child', then 'girl'.

There is a parallel trend: to cite one judgment after another in which the Supreme Court has said on earlier occasions what one wants to say now. The judgment we encountered on whether defamation is merely a civil offence or, in addition, a criminal offence, provides a ready example. That for a statement to be defamatory, there must be an imputation, and that it must have been made with the intention of causing harm or in the knowledge that harm will be caused—this is well-known. The examples that Macaulay penned as 'Explanations' are models of clarity. As are the 'Exceptions'. But the judgment invokes six earlier judgments to explain 'Explanations' I to IV—each citation from each of the judgments in effect just repeats what the original text of the section already says. To explain the 'Exceptions', the judgment cites thirty earlier judgments—each of which in effect also just ends up repeating what the original text states. No wonder, the judgment covers all of 268 pages, albeit double-spaced.[17] On reading such passages I am reminded of what a politician said as we stood chatting and the photographers went

17 Of LiveLaw.in

on clicking their cameras: '*Arey bhaai, itnaa kum self-confidence hai kyaa? Jahaan ek photo se kaam chal jayegaa, aap click kiye hi jaa rahey ho.*'[18]

EVEN WHEN THE MEANING IS STRAIGHTFORWARD

Manoj Nirula v. Union of India,[19] the opening oration of which we encountered earlier, shows another facet.

As we noticed, the plea before the court was that those who are guilty of heinous crimes must not be allowed to be inducted into the Council of Ministers. The court held that for it to lay down that even those who have been charged with having committed such

---

18 Like flowery language, this feature too has invited comment, from judges among others. In the articles on judgment writing cited earlier, Justice Jagannadha Rao observed, 'Likewise, sometimes, Case law is set out, referring to one ruling after another. Some Judges make long extracts from judgments of the Supreme Court or High Court cited by both sides. One does not know which aspect of the precedent is being highlighted. One does not know which ruling is followed or applied to the facts of the case nor which is distinguished…' He returned to the theme: 'There are different types of lengthy judgments. Some extract the pleadings extensively and then refer to the arguments of counsel on both sides *in extenso* almost till the end of the judgment and the ultimate conclusion follows soon thereafter without adequate reasons. Paragraph after paragraph would start with the words: "It is contended by…" and one would neither get the facts nor the reasoning anywhere … Yet another form of lengthy judgment is the "tonsorial and agglutinative" as described by Justice Cardozo … It is "shears and paste-pot which are its implements and emblem"; it consists of long extracts from judgments, one after the other, in unending succession. Every paragraph starts: "In A vs. B, it was held" and the mechanical long extract starts. There is no emphasis on a particular aspect nor to the distinctive facts of the cases cited. The cases are not even grouped in relation to identity or close proximity of facts or reasons. After long pages of quotations, towards the end, the result suddenly appears. There is no connecting link between the extracts and results. In fact, the cited quotations may not all be uniform and the Judge does not say which precedent he follows or which precedent he distinguishes. The judgment is naturally reported because of the quotations it contains but has no precedential value.'

19 (2014) 9 SCC 1.

crimes must not be allowed to be in the Council of Ministers would be to interpose a disqualification that is neither provided in Article 75(1) of the Constitution nor implied by it.

Not that complicated, it would seem. But the court took a typically long route to get to this conclusion.

First, it dilated upon the significance of ensuring the purity of elections—and to carry conviction on this point, it invoked what the Supreme Court had said in three earlier judgments.

Next, it bemoaned the criminalization of politics. To carry conviction on this point, it once again invoked what the Supreme Court had said in three earlier judgments. Then what the N.N. Vohra Committee had said on what was in fact happening and what consequences would follow. Then it invoked the Law Commission ... All this, only to affirm: 'The aforesaid vividly exposits concern at all quarters about the criminalisation of politics. Criminalisation of politics, it can be said with certitude, creates a dent in the marrows of the nation.'

Marrow can be *dented*—like the fender of a car? The court then turned to 'Corruption in the present scenario'. It went on to spell out how corruption corrodes institutions, elections, the rule of law. And to carry conviction that this really happens, it invoked what the Supreme Court had said in two earlier judgments.

Next, the court turned to provisions relating to the qualifications and disqualifications for MPs, MLAs and MLCs. It reproduced in full what the Constitution provides in this regard, what the Indian Penal Code says. It then reproduced what the Supreme Court has said in two earlier judgments.

It then proceeded to reproduce the constitutional provisions relating to ministers, and the oaths they have to swear before assuming office.

Counsel had argued that the criteria for selecting ministers should be more stringent than for being elected, that this was an implied limitation, and that the court had accepted the doctrine of implied limitation in *Kesavananda Bharati*.

That became the occasion to reproduce what was said in that case by Justice Sikri; then what was said by Justices Shelat and Grover; then what was said by Justices Hegde and Mukherjea; then what was said by Justice Jaganmohan Reddy; then what was said by Justice Palekar; then what was said by Justice Chandrachud; and, finally, what was said by Justice Khanna in the case.

Then came time for quotations from *Minerva Mills*[20]. Then for passages from *B.R. Kapur*[21]. Then for passages from *I.R. Coleho*[22].

The court then went on to consider the principle of constitutional silence or abeyance: as to what could be construed or advanced when the Constitution does not say anything specific on a point.

Then it felt it necessary to dilate upon the doctrine of constitutional implication.

Then on the 'doctrine' of good governance. Government must be good and clean. For this to be so, persons in government must be ones of good character and competence. To fortify these, surely unfamiliar theses the court invoked what the Supreme Court had said in five earlier judgments. And then a peroration on desirables:

> In a democracy, the citizens legitimately expect that the Government of the day would treat the public interest as primary one and any other interest [as] secondary. The maxim *Salus Populi Suprema Lex*, has not only to be kept in view but also has to be revered. The faith of the people is embedded in the root of the idea of good governance which means reverence for citizenry rights, respect for Fundamental Rights and statutory rights in any governmental action, deference for unwritten constitutional values, veneration for institutional integrity, and inculcation of accountability to the collective at large. It also conveys that the decisions are taken by the decision-making authority with solemn sincerity and policies are framed keeping in view the welfare of the people, and including all in a homogeneous compartment. The concept of good governance is not a Utopian conception or an abstraction. It has been the demand of the polity wherever democracy is nourished. The growth of democracy is dependent upon good governance in reality and the aspiration of the people basically is

20 (1980) 3 SCC 625; (1986) 4 SCC 222; (1988) 4 SCC 130.
21 *Kapur, B.R. v. State of Tamil Nadu*, (2001) 7 SCC 231.
22 *Coleho, I.R. v. State of Tamil Nadu*, (1999) 7 SCC 580.

> that the administration is carried out by people with responsibility with service orientation.

But this cannot be mandated in every particular. It requires trust, 'constitutional trust'—that is, we have to trust the concerned authority, in this case the prime minister or chief minister, to do right. To fortify this leap of faith, the court invokes what Dr Ambedkar said in the Constituent Assembly Debates. It invokes what Dr Rajendra Prasad said. It invokes what the Supreme Court has said in three earlier judgments. It then invokes H.M. Seervai. And then a *Constitutional and Administrative Law*. And then a next *Constitutional Practice*. And then Edmund Burke. And then the Supreme Court again.

Now, these ministers in the collective are to tender 'advice'. That triggers a discourse on 'advice'. The meaning of the word as given in the *New Shorter Oxford English Dictionary* is cited. The meaning of the word as given in Ramanatha Iyer's *Law Lexicon* ('Second Edition') is cited. The meaning of the word as given in the *Webster Comprehensive Dictionary* ('International Edition') is cited. The meaning of the word as given by the Supreme Court in an earlier judgment is cited. Then Ivor Jennings is invoked. Then Lovehead's *Constitutional Law, A Critical Introduction* is invoked. Then what Dr Rajendra Prasad said in the Constituent Assembly Debates is invoked. And yet the word 'advice' continues to mean what you and I would normally understand it to mean without all these quotations.

The conclusion? That the court cannot add another disqualification to ministership—that is, it cannot lay down that a person who has been elected cannot be made minister merely because he has been charged as having committed a heinous crime. We have to leave matters to the good sense of the prime minister and chief ministers:

> Thus, while interpreting Article 75(1), definitely a disqualification cannot be added. However, it can always be legitimately expected, regard being had to the role of a Minister in the Council of

> Ministers and keeping in view the sanctity of oath he takes, the Prime Minister, while living up to the trust reposed in him, would consider not choosing a person with criminal antecedents against whom charges have been framed for heinous or serious criminal offences or charges of corruption to become a Minister of the Council of Ministers. This is what the Constitution suggests and that is the constitutional expectation from the Prime Minister. Rest has to be left to the wisdom of the Prime Minister. We say nothing more, nothing less.

The results—both at the Centre and the states—are there for all to see: 'We say nothing more, nothing less.'

And contrast this reticence with the excellent reasoning on which the same Supreme Court struck down the self-serving sub-section 8 (4) of the Representation of People's Act, 1951, and in effect *legislated* a far-reaching change in our electoral laws.[23] Sub-section 8(1) of the Act lists a series of crimes and provides that if a person is convicted of any of them, he shall lose his seat in the legislature forthwith, that he shall be disqualified for six years from the date of his conviction, and, if he is imprisoned, for a further period of six years from the date of his release.[24] But the very next sub-clause nullified this, and provided an escape hatch: 'Notwithstanding anything [in the earlier sub-sections], a disqualification shall not, in the case of a person who on the date of conviction is a member of Parliament or the legislature of a state, take effect until three months have elapsed from that date or, if within that period an appeal or application for revision is brought in respect of the conviction or the sentence, until that appeal or application is disposed of by the court.' As a result, even those who had been convicted of murder continued as legislators: upon being convicted, all they had to do

23 *Lily Thomas v. Union of India,* (2013) 7 SCC 653.

24 The Constitution Review Commission had pointed to an incongruity. Under sub-section (1), a legislator convicted, say, of rape, was to remain disqualified for six years. He would be sentenced to spend ten years in prison. Hence, in the last four years of his imprisonment, he could again stand for elections from within the prison, and become a legislator!

was to file an appeal, and then stretch the case out forever.[25] The Supreme Court struck sub-section 8(4) down as unconstitutional—the basic ground being that it could never have been the intention of the Constitution-makers and of the legislature to render nugatory the basic disqualification that the law had provided. The court was not restrained by what the law said and how narrow a latitude the 'doctrine of implication' gave it. In effect, it legislated a change in the law.

25 On this and the imperative to overturn the self-serving sub-section 8(4), see Arun Shourie, *The Parliamentary System: What We Have Made of It, What We Can Make of It*, ASA and Rupa, New Delhi, 2007, pp. 100–02.

10

And yet I am taken by surprise

Though I was inured by examples of the kind we have just glanced through, I was jolted by what I read recently. A story in *The Wire* led me to look up the judgments of a judge of the Himachal Pradesh High Court. To check if there was a pattern, I downloaded a few decisions that he had handed down in the first half of 2016, and the second half of 2017. And then opened a judgment at random. It turned out to be *State of H.P v. Narottam Singh and Others,* decided by the judge in May 2016.[1]

'X' had twice struck 'Y' with a sword. The latter had warded off the attacks. In doing so, 'Y's' index finger and thumb had been injured. A lower court had decided that the assailant should be tried under Section 324 of the Indian Penal Code—which deals with 'Voluntarily causing hurt by dangerous weapons or means', and carries a sentence of imprisonment up to three years—rather than Section 302—which deals with 'Attempt to murder', and carries a sentence of imprisonment up to ten years. The High Court judge saw weight in the arguments of the state: 'X' should be tried for attempted murder—one should look at the weapon that had been wielded, and that the accused had struck 'Y' twice, rather than the

1 High Court of Himachal Pradesh, *State of H.P. v. Narottam Singh and Ors.,* decided on 20 May 2016: http://164.100.138.228/casest/generatenew.php?path=data/judgment/2016/&fname=CRCR.R201742015.pdf&smflag=N

fact that the injuries that 'Y' had suffered were merely cuts on a finger and a thumb. Had 'Y' not been able to ward off the assault, he could have been killed. That, more or less, was all that there was to the case, and the judgment.

Now see how the judge put the matter:[2]

> The learned Additional Advocate General has with pain staking efforts contended on the strength of allegations constituted in the FIR recorded in the Police Station concerned with a portrayal therein of the accused wielding a 'Kripan' with user whereof he attempted to strike blows at the victim, blows whereof stood thwarted by the victim twice by putting his hands against the 'kripan' act whereof his to baulk its striking him sequelled his sustaining injuries on his right thumb whereupon the accused repeated his concert to strike a blow of 'kripan' at him which successive blow of 'Kripan' also stood thwarted by the victim projecting his hand sequelling his sustaining injuries on his index finger. The aforesaid echoing in the FIR by the victim of the genesis of the occurrence per se prima facie at this stage stands corroborated by the MLC of the victim prepared in quick spontaneity to the occurrence by the doctor concerned who in the apposite MLC has reflected of the victim sustaining injuries on his right thumb besides on his index finger. On anvill whereof, the learned Additional Advocate General contended of satisfaction standing begotten qua the ingredients of Section 307 of the IPC of the accused endangering the life of the victim constituted by his wielding a 'Kripan' qua user whereof he struck two abortive blows on the person of the victim of hence the learned Additional Sessions Judge committing a gross error in concluding of the offences constituted against the accused respondent rather falling within the ambit of Section 324 of the IPC.

---

2 As I have merely downloaded the passages from the website of the Himachal Pradesh High Court, the syntax, words, the variations in the way a particular word is spelled, the variations in quotation marks are as they occur in the judgment.

What the counsel for the accused had submitted was set out in a similar exposition. And then the reasoning of the judge:

> Having considered the rival submissions addressed before this Court by the learned Additional Advocate General as also by the learned counsel appearing for the accused/respondents herein, this Court is of the considered view that the submissions addressed before this Court by the learned Additional Advocate General ought to merit theirs standing accepted by this Court. There is a palpable display in the FIR lodged qua the occurrence by the victim, of the accused at the relevant time wielding a kripan. With its user as aforestated he struck successive abortive blows on the victim, yet the factum of the victim thwarting the blows of kripan successively struck at him by the accused, begot his hence sustaining injuries initially on his right thumb and later on his right index finger when stands as referred aforestated corroborated by the apposite MLC prepared by the doctor concerned, who subjected the victim to medical examination in quick spontaneity to the occurrence, is of predominant significance. Moreover, since the recovery of the 'Kripan' wielded by the accused stands recovered under a recovery memo, as a corollary, at this stage it would be in-sagacious to accept the submission addressed before this Court by the learned counsel appearing for the accused of the factum of the injuries sustained by the victim being a preeminent factor as stood tenably borne in mind by the learned Additional Sessions Judge for concluding of the penal misdemeanors committed by the accused standing constituted within the ambit of Section 324 of the IPC and theirs not falling within the ambit of Section 307 of the IPC. The reason for discountenancing the submission of the learned counsel for the accused is of his having slighted the effect besides the import of the provisions of Section 307 of the IPC which mandate the preeminent factor relevant for concluding whether the offence as alleged to be committed by the accused stands constituted within its ambit not being the nature of the injuries ultimately sustained by the victim in sequel to the assault perpetrated on her/his person by the accused rather the stark factor for concluding whether the offence stands constituted within its

ambit is of the endangerment emanating or the imminent threat accruing to the life of the victim spurring from the nature of the weapon wielded by the accused dehors the fact that even on its user the victim ultimately sustains simple injuries. In aftermath, at this stage prima facie material when is connotative of the accused wielding a 'kripan' which per se meted on its standing used by the accused an imminent threat to the life of the victim hence aroused endangerment to his life besides when with its user he attempted to inflict fatal blows on the person of the victim which stood thwarted by the latter in the manner aforestated, naturally, the learned Additional Sessions Judge while remanding the case to the committal Magistrate has committed a grave legal fallacy while discarding the factum of the accused at the relevant time wielding a 'Kripan' and its user begetting endangerment to the life of the victim rather his contrarily and inaptly meteing reverence to the injuries meted to the victim by the accused while striking him with blows of kripan has gone off the mark in capturing the subtle nuance and spirit of the provisions of Section 307, IPC, ingredients whereof for reasons aforestated stood satiated. In aftermath, this Court is of the view that the learned Additional Sessions Judge, has committed a legal impropriety by remanding the matter to the Committal Magistrate for framing a charge against the accused for theirs committing an offence punishable under Section 324 of the IPC.

Apart from the question whether the case fell within the jurisdiction of the additional sessions judge, the latter's conclusion was wrong, the judge ruled:

The learned counsel appearing for the accused/respondents has with much vigour on the anvil of the judgement of the Hon'ble Apex Court, the relevant paragraphs whereof stands extracted hereinabove, contended of the learned Additional Sessions Judge having rendered an apt order. However, with the relevant paragraph which stand extracted hereinabove foisting a jurisdiction upon the Court concerned to weigh and sift the evidence, nonetheless, when the manner of weighing or sifting besides appraising the probative worth of the material on record by the learned Additional Sessions Judge suffers from a perversity and absurdity, the contention of the learned counsel for the accused would not stand countenanced by this Court.

What had happened? Had the thesaurus taken over completely? I read a few other judgments. That exercise turned out to be quite unnecessary: the pattern was the same. Hence, it will be enough to go back to the judgment from which *The Wire* had extracted a few sentences—as it had a special ending.

Here is the judgment. Please gather some friends, and read it aloud—don't give up halfway, persevere to the end:

2016 SCC OnLine HP 2699 J1

In the High Court of Himachal Pradesh at Shimla

(Before Sureshwar Thakur, J.)

Shri. Pawan Kumar Sharma ... Petitioner/JD

v.

Sarla Sood and Others ... Respondents/DH

For the Petitioner: Mr. Deepak Bhasin, Advocate.

For Respondents: Mr. B.C. Verma, Advocate.

C.R. No. 184 of 2011

Decided on December 5, 2016

Sureshwar Thakur, J.:— The Judgment debtor/petitioner herein, tenant in the demised premises stands aggrieved by the pronouncement made by the learned Executing Court upon his objections constituted therebefore vis-a-vis the execution petition constituted thereat by the Decree holder/landlord, wherewithin the apposite unfoldments qua his resistance to the execution of the decree stood discountenanced by the learned Executing Court.

2. The learned counsel appearing for the judgment debtor/petitioner herein submits qua the impugned pronouncement made by the learned Executing Court upon the apposite objections preferred therebefore by the JD/tenant manifesting

therein qua the decree put to execution therebefore not warranting recording of affirmative orders thereon, its standing fully satisfied, standing stained with a vice arising from the factum of its palpably slighting the factum of unfoldments occurring in the relevant record existing therebefore comprised in the testification recorded on 29.10.2004 in Rent Petition No. 10/2 of 2003 by the General Power of Attorney of the landlord wherein he made articulations qua all the outstanding arrears of rent qua the demised premises standing liquidated by the judgment debtor excepting conspicuously the one's pertaining to the period commencing from 1.9.2000 uptill 31.03.2003 whereupon he hence canvassed qua the executable pronouncement recorded in rent petition No. 1-2 of 1996 put to execution before the learned Executing Court embodying therein qua the Judgment debtor, falling into arrears of rent commencing from 1.9.1995 upto the date of payment standing fully satisfied, satisfaction whereof emanating from the factum of liability of rent fastened upon the tenant in a verdict recorded in Rent Petition No. 1-2 of 1996, standing acquiesced to stand liquidated more so when the aforesaid verdict stood put to execution. However, the learned counsel appearing for the tenant/JD/petitioner herein cannot derive the fullest succour from the aforesaid acquiescence occurring in the testification of the GPA of the decree holder/landlord, given its sinew suffering partial dissipation from an imminent display occurring in the impugned pronouncement hereat wherewithin unravelments are held qua the rendition recorded by the learned Rent Controller in Rent Petition No. 1-2/1996 standing assailed before the learned Appellate Authority by the tenant/JD by the latter preferring an appeal therebefore whereat he under an application constituted under Section 5 of the Limitation Act sought extension of time for depositing his statutory liability qua the arrears of rent determined by the learned Rent Controller in a pronouncement made by the latter on 6.11.1999, wherefrom an inference spurs of the JD acquiescing qua his not making the relevant deposit qua his liability towards arrears of rent within the statutorily prescribed period, application whereof suffered the ill fate of its dismissal by the learned Appellate Authority under the latter's order recorded on 16.12.2000. Of course, the inevitable ensuing sequel therefrom is qua the tenant/JD acquiescing to the factum of his not depositing the relevant computations of arrears of rent made by the learned Rent Controller concerned in Rent Petition No. 1-2 of 1996 within the statutorily prescribed period for its deposit therebefore whereupon the apposite decree for his suffering eviction from the demised premises on account of his falling into arrears of rent became executable qua him, whereupon, he stands estopped besides forestalled to derive the fullest strength from any acquiescence made by the GPA of the decree holder/landlords, rather stands entailed with the misfortune of the learned Executing Court ensuring his eviction from the demised premises by ordering for issuance of warrants of possession qua him.

3. Even though, this Court has partially blunted the effect of the aforesaid communication occurring in the testification of the GPA of the decree holder qua the tenant/JD not holding any liability qua the landlord vis-a-vis liquidation qua him of rent for the period commencing from 1.9.1995 upto the date of payment, whereupon, this Court concludes qua its entailing the effect of the Executing Court ordering for issuance of warrants of possession upon the judgment debtor yet before ordering, the learned Executing Court to make the aforesaid pronouncement, this Court is enjoined to also not remain oblivious to the factum of the executable decree standing rendered in the year 1999 by the learned Rent Controller concerned in Rent Petition No. 1-2 of 1996, also this Court stands enjoined to not remain unmindful to the factum of the landlord subsequent to his obtaining a verdict in Rent Petition No. 1-2 of 1996 his also qua the demised premises instituting Rent Petition No. 10/2 of 2003 before the learned Rent Controller concerned, during proceedings whereof the GPA of the landlord made a communication displaying his acquiescence qua the tenant liquidating his liability of rent qua the demised premises in sequel to the pronouncement made in Rent Petition No. 1-2 of 1996. Though, the acquiescence of the GPA of the landlord would not erode the play of the dicktat

of the relevant statutory mandatory provisions enjoining the tenant to within the time prescribed therewithin deposit his apposite judicially determined liability of arrears of rent before the Court concerned, whereas, evidently with the tenant not liquidating his apposite liability within the statutorily ordained period for its liquidation whereupon the statutory consequence qua the Executing Court ordering for issuance of warrants of possession qua him is an inevitable ensuing sequel therefrom. However, the acquiescence qua the relevant facet made by the GPA of the landlord in rent petition No. 10/2 of 2003 which stood instituted subsequent to the pronouncement made in rent petition No. 1-2 of 1996 holding bespeakings therein of the tenant making the relevant liquidation holds the sequel of the landlord accepting the attornment of rent to him by the tenant/JD other than the statutory mode for its deposit. The effect of the landlord personally/directly accepting attorning of rent qua the demised premises from the tenant in detraction of the statutory mode does hold the consequence of the landlord waiving his rights to seek eviction of the tenant, right whereof stood bestowed upon him under an executable decree pronounced in Rent Petition No. 1-2 of 1996, inference whereof when stands construed in coagulation with the landlord subsequent to the pronouncement recorded by the Rent Controller in Rent Petition No. 1-2 of 1996, his in the year 2003 instituting another petition seeking eviction of the JD from the demised premises, ultimately also when both the factum aforesaid stand construed in entwinement with the apposite execution petition constituted before the learned Executing Court by the landlord whereupon he sought execution of the executable decree rendered in Rent Petition No. 1-2 of 1996 standing constituted therebefore belatedly on 30.08.2010 does foster an inference of with the landlord receiving rent directly from the tenant, he is to stand construed to not only create a fresh tenancy qua the demised premises upon the tenant besides is to stand construed to concomitantly hence, waive his rights to seek eviction of the JD under an executable decree recorded in Rent Petition No. 1-2 of 1996. Contrarily, it has to be concluded of the landlord by procrastinating the execution of the executable decree rendered on 6.11.1999 in Rent Petition No. 1-2 of 1996 upto 29.09.2005 whereat a pronouncement in rent petition No. 10/2 of 2003 also occurred his also thereupon renewing the tenancy qua the relevant premises vis-a-vis the JD.

4. The summom bonum of the aforesaid discussion is that all the aforesaid material which existed before the learned Executing Court standing slighted besides their impact standing untenably undermined by him whereupon the ensuing sequel therefrom is of the learned Executing Court while pronouncing its impugned rendition overlooking the relevant and germane evidence besides its not appreciating its worth. Consequently, the order impugned suffers from a gross absurdity and perversity of mis-appreciation of material on record. Accordingly, the instant petition is allowed and the order impugned is quashed and set aside. In sequel, the apposite execution petition seeking execution of the verdict pronounced in Rent Petition No. 1-2 of 1996 is dismissed, whereas, the objections instituted thereat by the JD/petitioner herein/tenant are allowed. All the pending applications also stand disposed of.

Did you persevere reading aloud till the end? Beats the merely eloquent for sure! The aggrieved party took the matter to the Supreme Court. Counsel for the two sides argued the matter before a bench of two judges. The judges decided as follows:

> After hearing learned counsel, it is not possible to comprehend the contents of the impugned order passed by the High Court. The order passed by the High Court is, therefore, set aside and the matter is remanded to the High Court for fresh consideration on merits.
>
> The special leave petitions are disposed of. The High Court will hear the matter *de novo*.

For all I know, the judge concerned may be the fairest of them all. But surely, at least to some extent, the language one uses is an index of how one thinks. A person whose flow of thoughts and words is such—and has been for years—is a High Court judge.

In fact, the instance holds a lesson for the method of selecting judges. When we come across a judge like Justice Kumaraswamy of the Jayalalithaa-judgment fame, who rose step-by-step through the lower courts, we urge lateral entry from the Bar. When we come across Justice Karnan who had been elevated from the Bar, we urge an All India Judicial Service, and urge that judges be elevated only from within the service. Well, in the present instance, like Justice D'Cunha—and Justice Kumaraswamy, for that matter—the judge had reached the High Court after having served in various capacities in lower courts. His father had been a judge of the High Court. He himself had joined as additional district and sessions judge in 2001. He had been promoted to the position of district and sessions judge in 2005. In 2013, he had been appointed as the registrar of the Himachal Pradesh High Court. In May 2014, he was appointed additional judge of the High Court. Thereafter, as the website of the High Court records, 'Took oath as Judge of the High Court of Himachal Pradesh on 30th November 2014 (Forenoon).'

To summarize, no mechanical solution will work: neither lateral entry from the Bar, nor elevation from among district judges. Many more things are required. Among these is one that seems to me to be the sovereign remedy.

But not just a High Court

But it would be unfair to single out the judge or even the High Courts for a dénouement of this kind. Readers will recall, and in an earlier study I had set out, what happened in one of the most hotly contested set of cases of recent times, those relating to the rights of minority institutions.[3]

St. Stephen's College v. University of Delhi had given wide latitude to minority institutions.[4] In 1993, an institution by the name of Islamic Academy of Education approached the Supreme

3 I had set out this sequence in *Falling Over Backwards*,(HarperCollins, 2012) from which the following is taken.

4 *St. Stephen's College v. University of Delhi,* (1992) SCC 558.

Court against directions sought to be given by the Government of Karnataka. The matter was assigned to a bench of five judges. At the very outset, the bench felt that just because an institution was a minority institution, it did not, by virtue of Article 30, get the right to choose any old method of selecting students that it thought fit. The bench felt that the decision of the court in *St. Stephen's College* needed to be reviewed. That case had been decided by a bench of five judges—though Justice N.M. Kasliwal had contributed a most cogent dissent. The five-judge bench which had been constituted to deliberate on the writ of the Islamic Academy accordingly recommended that the case be placed before a bench of seven judges. On the basis of what lawyers for the contenders argued, the seven judges recommended that a bench of eleven judges be constituted.

And so a bench of eleven judges was constituted. Their judgment in *T.M.A. Pai Foundation v. State of Karnataka* was delivered in 2002.[5] At around 92,000 words, it is longer than even my articles! Actually, there are four different judgments—five, if you count a concurring opinion as a judgment by itself.

Setting aside what the other judges had said, even the judgment delivered by the majority was taken to say different things by different state governments and, of course, by different institutions that claimed to be minority institutions. Such was the confusion and such the spate of litigation that followed in the wake of *T.M.A. Pai* that the very next year a bench of five judges had to be constituted to clarify what the *T.M.A. Pai* judgment had laid down. This bench delivered a judgment in *Islamic Academy of Education v. State of Karnataka* in 2003.[6]

The clarifications confounded! The very next year, in 2004–05, the matters were again before the Supreme Court. Accordingly, a seven-judge bench was constituted to ascertain once again what the eleven-judge bench had said and, next, to identify the questions on which the five-judge clarificatory-bench, so to say, had done what it could not do, namely where it had departed from what the eleven-

5 *T.M.A. Pai Foundation v. State of Karnataka,* (2002) 8 SCC 481.

6 *Islamic Academy of Education v. State of Karnataka,* (2003) 6 SCC 697.

judge bench had held. And from this we got the Supreme Court's judgment in *P.A. Inamdar v. State of Maharashtra*.[7]

That this is by no means the end of the road is evident from what the five judges themselves said at the very outset in *P.A. Inamdar* about the boundaries within which they had to decide the case. Here it is:

> ...At the very outset, we may state that our task is not to pronounce our own independent opinion on the several issues which arose for consideration in *Pai Foundation* [(2002) 8 SCC 481]. Even if we are inclined to disagree with any of the findings amounting to declaration of law by the majority in *Pai Foundation* [(2002) 8 SCC 481] we cannot; that being a pronouncement by an eleven-Judge Bench, we are bound by it. We cannot express dissent or disagreement howsoever we may be inclined to do so on any of the issues. The real task before us is to cull out the *ratio decidendi* of *Pai Foundation* [(2002) 8 SCC 481] and to examine if the explanation or clarification given in *Islamic Academy* [(2003) 6 SCC 697] runs counter to *Pai Foundation* [(2002) 8 SCC 481] and if so, to what extent. If we find anything said or held in *Islamic Academy* [(2003) 6 SCC 697] in conflict with *Pai Foundation* [(2002) 8 SCC 481] we shall say so as being a departure from the law laid down by *Pai Foundation* [(2002) 8 SCC 481] and on the principle of binding efficacy of precedents, overrule to that extent the opinion of the Constitution Bench in *Islamic Academy* [(2003) 6 SCC 697].[8]

Who would need a clearer hint that the judges would have held differently if only they had not been just five against eleven?

7 *P.A. Inamdar v. State of Maharashtra,* (2006) 13 SCC 293.

8 *P.A. Inamdar v. State of Maharashtra, op. cit.*

11

So much science

On 29 April 2015, twelve peacocks were found dead in the compound of a primary school in a village in Bundi district of Rajasthan. Autopsy reports revealed that some culprit had laced with insecticide the wheat and corn grains that they used to eat. A boy, seventeen years old, was arrested and charged with having poisoned the peacocks. His lawyer argued that he had been picked up on mere suspicion, that there was no direct evidence linking him to the crime. The lower court had rejected the application for bail. The matter had come before Justice Mahesh Sharma, a devotee of Lord Krishna, of the Rajasthan High Court. In his judgment, Justice Sharma noted that the peacock is our national bird, and that it is in danger of extinction. He rejected the bail application, but also directed the juvenile court to try the case expeditiously.[1]

From the lofty podium of the High Court the judge explained the significance of the case, and, hence, the reason for his decision:

> The peacock is the beloved and revered bird of Lord Krishna. The principal attribute of the peacock is that he is a *brahmachari*, a celibate. It is by drinking the tears of the peacock that the

1 Order on *Bunty alias Sandip v. State of Rajasthan,* Writ 71/2016. Justice Mahesh Sharma's orders are written in Hindi. Unless otherwise indicated, the passages are translated from the Hindi original.

> peahen becomes pregnant. It is the feather of so pure a bird that Sri Krishna wears. The killing of such a bird is indeed a matter of national concern. The peacock is a national bird, and it is on the verge of extinction. If such endangered flora, and wildlife and birds are not saved, the entire environmental balance will be brought into jeopardy, and danger will begin to hover over the existence of mankind. In almost all the sacred books of the Hindus, the peacock has been spoken of with reverence. It is imperative that a restraint be placed on those who play with the lives of such animals and birds. It is also the requirement of environmental law.

The judge's knowledge about how the species reproduce, their immaculate conception, the drinking of tears ... these made the headlines.

The science of cows

Later, Justice Mahesh Sharma was disposing of a case relating to a cow sanctuary. Rajasthan is the only state in the country that has a separate ministry for promoting the welfare of cattle. The state banned the slaughter of cows in 1995.[2] As a result, many an owner would just let loose cows that had stopped yielding milk. The government had set up Hingonia Gaushala, a sanctuary for abandoned cows, in 2002. It was placed under the supervision of the Jaipur Municipal Corporation. Allocations were regularly made for the upkeep of the cows. In November 2010, a private organization, the Jago Janata Society, filed a writ pointing out that, while funds were being given to the organization, the gaushala was so poorly managed that cows were dying in large numbers for want of fodder and water.[3]

---

2 Under the Rajasthan Bovine Animals (Prohibition of Slaughter and Regulation of Temporary Migration or Export) Act, 1995.

3 On all this, *Jago Janata Society v. State of Rajasthan,* Civil Writ Number 15585/2010. Judgment of Justice Mahesh Sharma delivered on 31 May 2017.

Between 22 November 2010, when the writ was filed, and 31 May 2017, when Justice Sharma delivered his 139-page judgment, the High Court held *eighty-six* hearings. After each of these hearings, it passed detailed orders: which officer was to do what, which department was to do what, who was to go to the site and inspect how things were in the gaushala, the date by which the report was to be filed...

In the meantime, of course, the cows continued to die. The deaths were regularly highlighted by the media, and they certainly came to the notice of the court. Thus, for instance, the order passed by the court on 20 April 2016 began:

> Today the learned Senior Counsel, Shri S.R. Sarna has in the main submitted before this Court that between 250 and 300 cows have died in the Hingonia Gaushala. Even the cause of their death is not known. News about these deaths are being regularly published in the media also. Today, adopting a humanitarian attitude, the Court alerted [seven senior officers whom the Court named] who are present in Court today...

Similarly, the proceedings of 4 August 2016 begin:

> From the last two days, several news are being published in Print Media. Today also a news has been published wherein it has been mentioned that in Hingonia Gaushala from last two days, 90 cows have been died and in last two weeks more than 500 cows have been died...[4]

In the same order, the court also expressed its anguish at the way its orders were being flouted:

> It is unfortunate on the part of Nagar Nigam Jaipur as they are flouting and disobeying the orders of the Court passed on earlier dates and also not taking care off [sic] the administration of the Government of Rajasthan and by way of their such working

4 Original in English.

> [sic], the reputation of the government is being damaged for not making compliance of the orders passed by this Court earlier in this matter, hence looking to cover all facts and circumstances of the case, this matter has been taken up today.[5]

Again orders were given to officials to visit the gaushala and report back, etc.

Within days the court was dealing with the fact that cows were being clandestinely shifted from the gaushala to other places, including tribal areas. It ordered that no cow shall be moved out of the gaushala without permission of the court. Five days later, the court commissioner was again reporting to the court that, in spite of being informed of the court's order, the concerned officials had not taken the requisite action. He had again submitted several photographs about the conditions in the gaushala, which were being brought on record, the court noted. Let a meeting be held...

Affairs continued the way they were. Hearings kept being held. Orders kept being issued. Cows kept falling dead. On 28 September 2016, an agreement was entered into with the Hare Krishna Charitable Trust: henceforth, the trust would manage the gaushala. The Jaipur Corporation and government would provide the requisite funds, they would ensure the requisite infrastructure ... By now there were 13,400 cattle in the gaushala.

In 118 pages of his judgment, Justice Mahesh Sharma set out the entire history of orders, the woeful nature of compliance right up to the final agreement. He then turned to the general significance of cows.

The cow is so significant an animal, he observed, that Sri Krishna Himself brought it to earth on Gauashtami day. It is believed that 33 crore gods and goddesses reside in its body. That is why it has been said that the cow is the mother of the universe. As Prayaga is the king of sacred places, so is the cow foremost among gods and goddesses. In the churning of the oceans, Surabhi, the cow, is the one who appeared along with Sri Lakshmi. It is the singular animal

---

5 Original in English.

that inhales oxygen and exhales oxygen, the judge recorded in his judgment.

In itself the cow is a pharmacy, the judge observed. Its milk and ghee are comparable to amrit. Its urine confers the following boons:

1. It has the miraculous power to exterminate all pests.
2. It rebalances the tridosh[6] and illnesses are extirpated.
3. By keeping the liver healthy and cleansing the blood, it gives one strength to combat any and every ailment.
4. It has all the elements for combating disease that we lack.
5. It has several minerals, in particular copper, whose deficiency in the body it makes up.
6. It endows strength to the brain and the heart.
7. It is a chemical, it stops ageing and destroys diseases.
8. [Not enumerated in the judgment]
9. It makes up for the desired elements which are deficient in one's diet.
10. It engenders saatvic wisdom.
11. The Ganga has resided in cow's urine, the Ganga destroys sin, and so by drinking cow's urine one destroys diseases that have come upon one because of misdeeds in previous lives.

All this science in a High Court judgment, remember—a judgment dealing with the mismanagement of a government-run gaushala.

The ghee from the cow also confers several boons, the judge noted:

1. It is beneficial for the newborn child. The breast-feeding mother is also counselled to partake of it. It suffuses the mother's milk with health-giving elements.
2. It is also beneficial for the eyes and sight. In Ayurveda, it has been described as one that improves one's eyesight.
3. It helps cure gout and rheumatism also.
4. By curing ulcers in the mouth, it relieves the burning sensation.

6 In Ayurveda, it is the imbalance of vata, pitta and kapha which causes illnesses.

5. It is also used for curing external injuries.
6. It is also useful for one's brain and calming one's mind.
7. It also strengthens one's immune system.

Panchagavya is produced by using the cow's milk, curd, ghee, urine and cow dung, the judge noted. And with panchgavya, one's ability to fight off diseases is fortified, thereby banishing ailments.

From the point of view of science also, the cow has an enormous significance, the judge declared. Agricultural scientists Dr Julius and Dr Book German have said that the cow is the only animal in the world which exhales oxygen. According to the German scientist Rudel Stenner, through its horns the cow assimilates cosmic energy. According to Shirovich, the famous scientist of Russia, houses in which floors and walls are plastered with cow dung are protected from radiation. According to Dr King, the renowned scientist from Madras, cow dung has the power to destroy the pathogens of cholera ... According to Dr Crawford Hamilton of Britain, drinking cow urine cures heart disease, and one's own urine flows with ease. A few days' intake of cow urine stabilizes the flow of blood in one's arteries, one's appetite improves. It is the ideal remedy for endemic skin ailments. According to Dr Simmers of Britain, cow urine destroys impurities in the blood. According to Cornell University's Professor Ronald Rayetey, the *vighman cerebrasais* [sic] in cow's milk is helpful in improving one's brain and memory. At the same time, because of MDGI protein, cancer cannot enter blood cells. According to Dr Anaam, the cow is the only animal whose large intestine is 180 feet long. Because of this, the fodder it consumes is converted into keratin, and this, upon entering the human body, produces Vitamin A which is essential for one's sight.

The cow is also very beneficial for the environment, the judge went on to affirm. According to the Russian scientist Shirovich, germs in the atmosphere are destroyed by the cow's bellowing. Ten grams of cow ghee used in a havan produces one tonne of oxygen. Sprinkling cow urine and gobar are advantageous in the event of plague ... Moreover, one can obtain 4,500 litres of biomass from one cow's gobar ... If cow's gobar is used as fuel, the country can save six crore eighty lakh tonnes of firewood, and thus prevent the destruction of fourteen crore trees…

Of course, that one does not exist in Internet search engines does not mean that one does not exist. But it *is* a strange coincidence that none of the 'scientists' invoked by Justice Mahesh Sharma find any mention there: not 'Dr Julius', not 'Book German', not 'Rudel Stenner', not 'Dr King of Madras', not 'Crawford Hamilton', not 'Ronald Rayete', not 'Anaam'.

We may not find the scientists, true. But the fount of such knowledge is not difficult to locate. Here, for instance, is an interview from the *Indian Express* of 7 August 2016—recall that Justice Sharma delivered his judgment on 31 May 2017:

> *Cellphones suck energy, just put some cow dung: RSS ideologue*
> *'Cow is our mother. Its excreta and urine are nectar and have power to save humans from any disease.'*
>
> Written by Ishita Mishra | Published: August 7, 2016
>
> *On a visit to Agra and Mathura, Shankar Lal, RSS's Akhil Bharatiya Gau Sewa pramukh, 76, explains why he has cow dung on the back of his phone:*
>
> 1. *Why do you have gobar on your phone?*
>   It is fresh cow dung. I have put it to save myself from the harmful radiations of the cellphone. It works, believe me.
> 2. *Do you keep applying fresh cow dung, like people change phone covers?*
>   Cow is our mother. Its excreta and urine are nectar and have power to save humans from any disease. If cow dung can treat cancer, why can't it save us from a phone's microwaves? Haven't you heard that Junagadh scientists (in Gujarat) have found gold in cow's urine (they found traces of it)? I put fresh gobar every week.
> 3. *Do other members of the Gau Sewa also do the same?*
>   Show, show your phones (he says, gesturing to four others, who take out their phones to display the cow dung at the back). All the people in my team, be it children, men or women, have cow

dung on their phone. Why won't they? They know its magical effects.

4. *Can you prove that cow dung can block 'harmful phone waves'?*
   See this pendulum. See how when I place it over the hand of this RSS worker, it starts swinging (he gives it an initial jerk). Look, this man's body has so much energy and the pendulum is swinging because of that. Now, when this man holds a phone in his hand, the pendulum won't move. This is because the phone's harmful waves have sucked all his energy. Now, let him hold a phone with cow dung on it, and hold this pendulum over his hand. See, it's moving again ... His energy is saved!
5. *What else do you do with cow dung?*
   We drink cow urine and have extracts from her dung, which has kept me healthy even at the age of 76. We make pregnant women eat cow dung and urine paste to ensure a normal delivery. We treat all deadly diseases with cow dung. But the gobar should be of our Indian desi cow and not western monsters like Jersey or Holstein. Their dung and milk are nothing but poison.

The news story carried a photograph of this 'ideologue' holding his cellphone with cow dung smeared on it.

A while later, the ideologue soared to greater heights. He declared that the RSS-affiliated gauseva organization would be arranging a fifteen-day 'Gau Jap Mahayagna' to bring into being an 'Apraadh-mukt Bharat'—that is, a crime-free India. He told *The Indian Express* that the crime rate in the country had risen since the time people started drinking the milk of buffaloes and Jersey cows. This milk, he maintained, was tamasic, it foments anger and intolerance. On the other hand, the milk of Indian cows is saatvic. He also disclosed that consuming 40 grams of liquid extract from cow dung along with five leaves of tulsi enables women to give birth through natural delivery. Three thousand women had already done so.[7]

But to get back to the judgment. The judge went on to enumerate the boons that would accrue to agriculture, to the economy. He

7 Lalmani Verma, 'To get masses to yagna, RSS arm to argue cow milk can arrest crime graph', *The Indian Express*, 6 February 2018.

cited the Vedas, the Bhagavata Purana, the Skandha Purana as extolling the virtues of the cow. He recorded how astrology as well as the Dharmashastras have laid down that the time of godhuli, the time of sunset when the cows come home, is the most auspicious time, how the dust rising from the hooves of cows as they tread home banishes all sins. The Shiva Purana and the Skandha Purana affirm that serving the cow removes the fear of death ... When the cow licks the newborn calf out of love, the spittle that falls purifies the soil and removes all impurities from it...

And so on.

So much science in just one judgment.

And yet, the judge noted, it is also true that the orders of the court have not been implemented in letter.

He then turned to another subject. Following the lead given by the Uttarakhand High Court, in *Mohammed Salim v. State of Uttarakhand*[8] in which the High Court had declared the Ganga and the Yamuna as living persons, and legal entities with all the rights accruing to individuals, Justice Mahesh Sharma held that the cow should be declared as our national animal—instead of the tiger, he did not add, which, after all, devours cattle. The Hindu Nation of Nepal in the Constitution adopted on 20 September 2015 has already done so...

The judge concluded with directions. The government will render such-and-such help to the Hare Krishna Charitable Trust to run the Hingonia Gaushala, and fulfil all obligations contained in the agreement signed on 28 September 2016. He listed a number of specific steps that the government must take ... He appointed the chief secretary, Rajasthan government, and the advocate general, Rajasthan, as the 'Persons in *Loco Parentis*' to take all appropriate measures to persuade the Central government so that it declares the cow to be the national animal ... Towards this end, they will comprehensively present the case on behalf of the Rajasthan government, Justice Sharma declared, to every relevant department of the Central government...

This was his last judgment: he delivered it on his last day in court. By that day, armed with such beliefs and such science, Justice

8 2017 (2) RCR (Civil) 636 (PIL) No. 126 of 2014.

Mahesh Sharma had been dispensing justice as a High Court judge for a decade.

As in all such cases, there is a footnote. I was naturally curious to read the writings of the scientists that the judge had cited. Efforts to contact the judge failed. However, a senior advocate in Jaipur got me the number of the judge's son, Aditya Sharma—he also happened to be an advocate. Ten days later, I rang him up. I requested him to ask his father for the publications of the scientists on which the judge had based those 'science-related' passages in his judgment. He first said that everything had been set out in the judgment. When I pointed out that the judgment gave only the names of sundry scientists, and that I had not been able to find any reference to their work or their publications, he said that his father was on tour, and that I should ring him up after a week by which time his father would be back.

I rang him up. His father was back home from his tour. Aditya said that he had checked with his father. The judge had not consulted any of the writings of the scientists directly, and that he had gone by the information given in a booklet that had been put out by the Akshaya Patra. In addition, he said, there was a video put out by Zee TV which also contained information on the benefits that accrued from products of the cow, like its urine, dung, ghee, etc. He said that he would forward the video on WhatsApp.

Could he please get me a copy of the booklet? I asked. He said that he had already got a copy. He promised to send it by post the following day. I sent him my postal address. Two days later, he sent an SMS: that day had been a holiday; he would send the booklet the next day.

I never received the booklet. I rang him up after a few weeks had passed. He did not answer the call. I requested a senior journalist of the *Rajasthan Patrika* to contact him. Aditya did not respond to his calls either.

Eyewitnesses to celibacy

I turn to rationalists in Kerala. They are not surprised at the science! As an example, they ask me to read *S. Mahendran v. The Secretary,*

Travancore Devaswom Board.[9] The issue before the High Court was the ban on women entering and praying in the temple of Lord Ayyappa at Sabarimala. Has this ban been decreed by the temple authorities for a reason? the court asked in its judgment. And it proceeded to recount several reasons. In olden days, journey to the temple involved a hazardous trek on difficult paths and through forests. Of course, conditions had improved since, and the trek is reduced to just 5 km, but still ... Moreover, said the court, 'Pilgrims are expected to observe penance. Purity in thought, word and deed is insisted during the period of penance (*Vratham*). A pilgrim starts trekking for Sabarimala only after completing the penance for a period of 41 days. Women of the age group 10 to 50 will not be in a position to observe *Vratham* continuously for a period of 41 days due to physiological reasons.' In any case, the Thantri of the temple has averred that the ban has been in force for long, and customs are not to be lightly overturned.

But that was not all. 'There is a vital reason for imposing this restriction on young women. It appears to be more fundamental,' the court observed. It is important to read this part of the judgment in some detail.

'The *Thanthri* of the temple as well as some other witnesses have stated that the deity at Sabarimala is in the form of a *Naisthik Brahmachari*,' the court observed. '"*Brahmachari*" means a student who has to live in the house of his preceptor and study the Vedas living the life of utmost austerity and discipline.' To make matters more specific, on the authority of a former Chief Justice of India, the court went on to describe not just a Brahmachari but a Naisthik Brahmachari:

> Sri B.K. Mukherjee, the fourth Chief Justice of India, in his Lordship's Tagore Law Lectures on the Hindu Law of Religious and Charitable Trust says at page 16 of the second addition [sic] thus:
>
> 'Ordinarily therefore a man after finishing his period of studentship would marry and become a house-holder, and

9 *S. Mahendran v. The Secretary, Travancore Devaswom Board.* Decided on 5 April 1991: AIR 1993 Ker 42.

> compulsory celibacy was never encouraged or sanctioned by the Vedas. A man however who was not inclined to marry might remain what is called a *Naisthik Brahmachari* or perpetual student and might pursue his studies living the life of a bachelor all his days.'
>
> A Brahmachari should control his senses. He has to observe certain rules of conduct which include refraining from indulging in gambling with dice, idle gossips, scandal, falsehood, embracing, and casting lustful eyes on females, and doing injury to others.
>
> (vernacular matter omitted) Mann [sic] Smriti Chapter II, Sloka 179.

But, assuming that the deity is a Brahmachari, what is the problem? The court explained:

> The deity in Sabarimala temple is in the form of a Yogi or a *Brahmachari* according to the *Thanthri* of the temple ... Puthumana Narayanan Namboodiri, a *Thanthrimukhya* recognised by the Travancore Devaswom Board, while examined as C.W. 1 stated that God in Sabarimala is in the form of a *Naisthik Brahmachari*. That, according to him, is the reason why young women are not permitted to offer prayers in the temple.
>
> Since the deity is in the form of a *Naisthik Brahmachari* it is therefore believed that young women should not offer worship in the temple so that even the slightest deviation from celibacy and austerity observed by the deity is not caused by the presence of such women.

Please read that again: 'Since the deity is in the form of a *Naisthik Brahmachari* it is therefore believed that young women should not offer worship in the temple so that even the slightest deviation from celibacy and austerity observed by the deity is not caused by the presence of such women.'

So much faith in an idol? Such an anthropomorphic conception of an idol? For that is what exists in the temple: that an entity made of stone might deviate from its vows? And so little faith in the deity? Presumably the Lord has divine, therefore by definition infinite powers. And yet a glance at a young woman might cause Him to deviate from His vow of eternal celibacy?

Faith? Science? Jurisprudence?

A GOOD RULE

Acclimatized though I had become to reading such judgments, I was taken completely by surprise when an advocate practising in the Supreme Court told me about an order of the court and asked me to read the lead item in that day's issue of *LiveLaw.in*.[10] On first reading, I thought it to have been a spoof, especially so as I did not find the content to which the advocate had sought my reaction. And yet, there it was in an earlier order.

A person had been accused of murder. To escape incarceration he had done what so many of our political leaders do—he had feigned a medical condition, and got transferred to a hospital. The case was heard by three judges, led by the Chief Justice of India. They decided that the person had thwarted their order. The murder accused apologized unconditionally. The judges ruled that 'considering the fact that the contemner has expressed an unconditional apology, while not accepting the same in entirety, we think it appropriate to impose a sentence of two months so that justice is done'.

So far, so good—though how one wishes that the same sort of justice is done when leaders suddenly develop chest pains the moment they are sent to jail.

But it was a previous order which took my breath away. For it turned out that two doctors had colluded with the accused to certify that he had that medical condition. In an earlier order, the Supreme Court had fined them Rs 1.4 crore. They had duly deposited the amount with the registry of the court.

The question now was how this money should be utilized. Some suggestions were offered during the hearing. The judges did not think them practical. As for what transpired thereafter, it is best to read the order itself:

10 Ashok M., 'SC sentences murder accused to 2-months imprisonment for contempt', *LiveLaw.in*, 4 December 2017.

Today when the matter was listed, a suggestion came that there are lawyers, who need medical assistance because of many a factor. At this juncture, Ms. Nandini Gore, the Secretary of Supreme Court Advocate-on-Record Association (SCAORA), has submitted that there is need for three vending machines for dispensing sanitary napkins and three incinerators for disposal of the used sanitary napkins.

Mr. R.S. Suri, the President, Mr. Ajit Kumar Sinha, the Vice-President and Mr. Gaurav Bhatia, the Secretary of the Supreme Court Bar Association (SCBA) and Mr. Gopal Singh, the President of the Supreme Court Advocate-on-Record Association have submitted that some amount be given to the Bar Associations, which shall be utilized in case of need for the lawyers when medical assistance is required.

At this juncture, Mr. Rishi Malhotra, learned counsel who has filed an application for directions on behalf of the dependents of the victim, has submitted that as the victims are there, they should be given some amount.

Having heard all concerned, it is directed as follows:-

(a) A sum of Rs. 85,00,000/- (Rupees eighty-five lakhs only) be given to the Supreme Court Bar Association, which shall be kept in a fixed deposit and the interest arising therefrom shall be disbursed for medical assistance to the members of the SCBA on proper verification. The aforesaid amount shall be kept in a different account by the SCBA.

(b) A sum of Rs. 45,00,000/- (Rupees forty-five lakhs only) be given to the Supreme Court Advocate-on-Record Association, which shall be kept in a fixed deposit and the interest arising therefrom shall be disbursed for medical assistance to the members of the SCAORA on proper verification. The aforesaid amount shall be kept in a different account by the SCAORA.

(c) From the balance amount, a sum of Rs. 5,00,000/- (Rupees five lakhs only) be used by the Registry of this Court for purchase of three vending machines for dispensing sanitary napkins and three incinerators for disposal of the used sanitary napkins. The Registry shall also fix them at suitable locations.

(d) A sum of Rs. 5,00,000/- (Rupees five lakhs only) be given to Vimla, the widow of the victim and the said amount shall be kept in a fixed deposit in the name of Vimla so that she can utilize the interest of the amount during her life time. The amount granted in favour of the widow of the deceased should be disbursed by way of a bank draft in her name on proper identification.

(e) The interest that has been accrued in the sum deposited before the Registry of this Court, i.e. Rs. 1,40,00,000/- (Rupees one crore forty lakhs only) shall also be distributed on *pro rata* basis keeping in view the above directions.

After distribution, as stated herein-above, if any amount remains, the Registry shall place the matter before the Court for further direction. Needless to say, the contempt proceedings initiated against the doctors-respondent Nos.1 and 2 stand purged.

The first thing to strike one surely is the court's responsiveness to suggestions from the associations of advocates. The second is its concern for personal hygiene—vending machines for sanitary napkins and incinerators to burn used sanitary napkins, a first, I would guess. The third, the comparatively paltry amount—Rs 5 lakh, that is 1/26th of the amount set aside for associations of advocates—set apart for the widow. Finally, it turns out that the poor widow's name was wrongly spelt—it had to be corrected in the next order.[11]

We have all seen political parties that are out of power oppose, block, shout against what the one in office is doing. And when they, once in office, do the same things, the party which had till the other day been trying to push those measures through now opposes, blocks, shouts against the steps. There is a simple and good rule—for personal to political, and I dare say for judicial life also. In the present instance, think of the head of the customs service and his

---

11 On all this, *Sita Ram v. Balbir@Bali,* Conmt. Pet. © No. 374/2014 in Crl. A. No. 1834/2013, Orders of Chief Justice of India Dipak Misra, Justice A.M. Khanwilkar and Justice D.Y. Chandrachud, dated 3 October 2017 and 1 December 2017.

two senior colleagues. Their staff catches a notorious smuggler. In the struggle to catch him, a member of the staff is killed. The head of the service and his two colleagues levy an enormous—and, let us assume, a wholly justified—penalty on that smuggler. When the amount is deposited, the three decide to distribute it between unions of their officers and their staff; and apportion some for conveniences in their offices, and set aside a bit for the widow of the customs man who was killed. How would judges look upon the decision? Once the penalty had been received, was the money the head's and his colleagues' to distribute? Or was it money that belonged to the public exchequer? Hence, my rule: when you are doing something, ask, 'What would I say if the other fellow were doing this?' I would urge it to the judges too.

And then there was the coincidence, but exactly the kind of coincidence that triggers conspiracy theories. The reader will recall the events that resulted from the plea of Prashant Bhushan and Kamini Jaiswal that the Supreme Court appoint a Special Investigation Team to investigate the allegation that a retired judge of the Orissa High Court had offered to fix a judgment through bribes. The matter had been taken over by the Chief Justice's court. Some of the very office bearers of the associations that had received Rs 85 lakh and 45 lakh respectively in this case had gathered at short notice in that court, and were the loudest and most energetic in shouting down Prashant Bhushan and preventing him from speaking. The bench headed by the Chief Justice decreed Rs 85 lakh and Rs 45 lakh to the associations on 3 October 2017. The ruckus was created in the court of the Chief Justice on 10 November 2017. A coincidence, of course. But, as I said, exactly the kind of coincidence that triggers conspiracy theories.

12

Thinking through

In the third week of October 2016, papers carried accounts of how a wheelchair-bound paraplegic was thrashed in a cinema hall for not standing up when the National Anthem was being played. Salil Chaturvedi was forty-eight years old. He had been paralysed waist-down since a road accident in 1984. He had striven hard to overcome his disabilities, and had twice represented India in international wheelchair tennis tournaments in the 1990s. He had won awards for his writing. His brother was a gallantry award winner. His father had been in the Air Force. There was no reason to doubt his or his family's dedication to our country. He had gone to watch a film in a multiplex in Panaji, Goa—a state known for its tolerance. As the National Anthem commenced, the couple seated behind Chaturvedi and his wife started hitting him for not standing up.

A petition was filed in the Supreme Court, requesting it to give directions so that the respect which is its due is shown to the National Anthem. It also stated that 'sometimes National Anthem is sung in various circumstances which are not permissible and can never be countenanced in law'.

The court heard the petition on 28 October 2016—just a week after newspapers had reported the assault on Chaturvedi. Justices Dipak Misra and Amitava Roy heard it. The then attorney general and seven other advocates took part. On 30 November 2016, the Supreme Court issued seven directions.[1] Among these, three pertained to cinema halls:

> (d) All the cinema halls in India shall play the National Anthem before the feature film starts and all present in the hall are obliged to stand up to show respect to the National Anthem.
>
> (e) Prior to the National Anthem is [sic] played or sung in the cinema hall on the screen, the entry and exit doors shall remain closed so that no one can create any kind of disturbance which will amount to disrespect to the National Anthem. After the National Anthem is played or sung, the doors can be opened.
>
> (f) When the National Anthem shall be played in the Cinema Halls, it shall be with the National Flag on the screen.

That a person bound to a wheelchair just would not be able to stand up did not come in the way of the court's determination to ensure respect for the National Anthem. Among others, the attorney general on behalf of the government had been most emphatic: 'We have so directed,' the judges noted, 'as Mr. Mukul Rohatgi, learned Attorney General for India, submits with all humility at his command and recommend [sic] that National Anthem has to be respected.'

Explaining the rationale for its directions, the court observed, 'The directions are issued, for love and respect for the motherland is [sic] reflected when one shows respect to the National Anthem as well as to the National Flag. That apart, it would instill the feeling within one, a sense [of?] committed patriotism and nationalism.'

The judges must have felt that they must re-emphasize the need for the directions so they did so in the concluding paragraphs, and, in the process, in these concluding expressions of the ruling as well as elsewhere in the judgment, the court introduced a new concept, a new dimension of patriotism—'Constitutional Patriotism'; and a new attribute to our character—'inherent national quality':

---

1 *Shyam Narayan Chouksey v. Union Of India,* Writ Petition(s)(Civil) No(s). 855/2016, decided on 30 November 2016.

> Be it stated, a time has come, the citizens of the country must realize that they live in a nation and are duty bound to show respect to National Anthem which is the symbol of the Constitutional Patriotism and inherent national quality. It does not allow any different notion or the perception of individual rights, that have individually thought of have no space [sic]. The idea is constitutionally impermissible.

The best way to instill patriotism? Or just the temper of the times? The attorney general was as emphatic on ensuring the widest compliance with the order as he had been in affirming that the National Anthem must be respected. The court noted:

> Mr. Rohatgi has submitted that the Union of India shall circulate this order to the Chief Secretaries of all the States and Union Territories. That apart, Mr. Rohatgi submits that the order shall be shown in the electronic Media and published in the print media so that everyone knows that such an order has been passed and follow [sic] the same in letter and spirit.

A minor miracle

We were all surprised at the judgment—the passion for drilling patriotism, the premise that this is best done by demonstrative acts, the fervid prose. But for the surprise, we have none but ourselves to blame: we just do not follow what is happening in the courts.

Long ago there was a movie, *Kabhi Khushi Kabhie Gham.*[2] And a gentleman, Shyam Narayan Chouksey: he was, as the court was to record, 'a member of certain social and spiritual organisations and has taken upon himself the burden of canvassing national temper and launch [sic] a campaign, in the name of the "Jeevn [sic] Jagriti Prayas" to inculcate national, [comma in the original] spirit amongst people'.

He told the court that he had gone to see the film. One scene is set in London. There is a school function. Children give performances.

2 For the following, *Shyam Narayan Chouksey v. Union of India*, MANU/MP/0292/2003. Coram Justice Dipak Misra and Justice A.K. Shrivastava.

One of the children is Indian. His parents are in the audience. When his turn comes, his mother announces that he will sing a song from *The Sound of Music*. But when the child gets to the stage, he sings our National Anthem. The parents and other relatives stand up. Seeing that Indians have stood up, others in the audience also do so. As the child gets to the end of the anthem, he forgets the last four or five words. His mother takes over and completes the anthem.

Chouksey maintained that when the National Anthem was being screened, the audience in the cinema hall did not stand up. Thereby they had not shown the requisite respect to the National Anthem. He approached the Madhya Pradesh High Court for various directions—about the film, about the situations in which the National Anthem may be sung or depicted, etc.

His petition came up before a two-judge bench of the High Court. The bench consisted of Justice Dipak Misra and Justice A.K. Shrivastava. The judgment was delivered by Justice Dipak Misra.

Justice Misra began by describing what a cinema is. He recalled the evolution of the medium. He recalled the importance of free speech and creativity. And then the context in which they must be viewed:

> Once we penetrate into the sphere of any medium of mass communication, the concept of democracy, sovereignty, patriotism, nationalism and collective good emerge, some rise like phoenix, some are immediately vibrant. One remembers the saying by Adli [sic] Stevenson that partriotism is not short and frenzied outbrust of emotion but the tranquil and steady dedication of life time. One is also reminded that freedom is not caprice. And further, democracy is word of disciplining oneself so that one need not be disciplined by others. Thus discipline is the sine qua non for democracy though one may conceive the notion that right to do a wrong is the part of democracy.

Next, to get a grasp of the manner and context in which the National Anthem had been sung, the judges did the exceptional thing, something we would all urge—that is, they actually saw the film. This is what Justice Misra wrote he saw in the sequence:

(a) Before the National Anthem was sung by the child, the son of the main protagonist, there is an expression of appreciation by the parents and the mother gets indulged in whistling for inspiration of proper performance of her son.

(b) The mother says the child will be singing a song from the film. 'The sound of music,' an English movie, which was produced decades back.

(c) The child, a student of Class IV, makes an announcement to the following effect 'THIS IS FOR YOU MOM.'

(d) There is an expression of nervousness by the mother which has been taken cognizance of by the father and they sit, in a mood of apprehension.

(e) The child starts singing the National Anthem of India.

(f) The parents of the Child, his father's brother and mother's sister get up immediately.

(g) On seeing the Indian citizens getting up other people who have been watching the programme get up in a phase wise manner. Some people get up after a line, some after two lines and some after three lines after the National Anthem had commenced.

(h) While the National Anthem is sung by the child the parents express their feelings in an apprehensive manner, but such an apprehension has been shown by facial gesture with movements.

(i) Thereafter the child forgets the last part of the National Anthem and says 'sorry' on the microphone. The mother of the child completes the last five words of the anthem.

The judge detected several things in this simple sequence which were derogatory of the National Anthem. To begin with, he stressed, a variety function in a school is not the sort of occasion during which the anthem should be depicted as having been sung. And then for the child to forget the last few words in it. And then for him to say 'sorry' in the middle...

> National Anthem is to be sung with magna cum laude and nobody can ostracize the concept of summa cum laude. In the case at hand, as we have noted earlier the son of the protagonists

> sings the National Anthem as a surprise item. The presentation, according to us, is in *medias res*. The child actor forgets the line and utters the term 'sorry'. To some it may appear *lapsus linguae*, slip of the tongue or a natural forgetting but if the whole thing is perceived, understood and appreciated in complete scenario, it is the script writer's fertile imagination and the Director's *id est*. It is deliberate. A deliberate slip of the pen. It is because there is in a way, deliberation to project a dramatic effort to show that the scene depicted in the film is on an absolute *terra firma*. The writer and director have totally forgotten that they were portraying the National Anthem of a great country.

The judge cited shastras to point out how great was the conception of our country in the minds of the rishis. And the scriptwriter, producer and director?

> They have not kept in mind '*vox populi, vox dei.*' The producer and the director have allowed the National Anthem of Bharat, the alpha and omega of the country to the backseat.
>
> On a first flush it may look like a *magnum opus* of patriotism but on a deeper probe and greater scrutiny it is a simulacrum having the semblance but *sans* real substance. There cannot be like Caesar's thrasonical brags of '*veni, vidi, vici.*' The boy cannot be allowed to make his innocence a parents rodomontrade [sic], at the cost of national honour. In our view it is contrary to national ethos and an anathema to the sanguinity of the national feeling. It is an exposition of *ad libitum*.

The entire sequence was misconceived, it would seem:

> It is quite demonstrable and patently clear that the national anthem was used in a variety show of a school. It was presented as an item on behalf of Class IV students. It is also noticed that when the boy started singing the national anthem the audience do not stand up immediately. The movement is quite slow. The audience in the film is taken by surprise. They are non-plussed. As we have noted, some of the audience stand after three lines, some of the

audience after four lines and some after five lines. The national anthem has not been sung in an uninterrupted manner. The boy says 'sorry' and mother fills up the words.

'Many a question arises when one sees this screen,' the judge recorded:

(a) Whether national anthem can be used in a variety show/ cultural show of an annual school day of a school?
(b) Whether it can be depicted as a surprise item?
(c) Whether dramatis personae be permitted to cause interruption? We may hasten to add here that when in real life at the end of a cultural show when national anthem is sung one may forget or may not be able to complete due to certain unavoidable circumstances but in the film one knows the future. When a particular scene is put into cinematic medium in the silver screen the child is directed, repeated rehearsals are done and multiple takes are taken and, therefore, everyone involved with the script is aware what is going to happen. In view of this the question is important and the concept of permissibility becomes relevant.
(d) Whether the audience in the film can be allowed to stand/get up taking their own time because explanation is given slowly they understand that the national anthem of India is sung?
(e) Whether national anthem of India can be sung in such an atmosphere where people do not understand the honour and dignity of the same and react in a different manner? ...
(f) Next, but a vital question is whether national anthem can be picturised to gain an advantage in a commercial manner? ...

'When these questions arise and what we have rioted [sic] earlier,' the judge concluded, 'in our considered view that the national anthem has been sung in the movie as if it is a song of advertisement for a commercial purpose. It is absolutely discernible...

'The national anthem is pivotal and centripetal to the basic conception of sovereignty and integrity of India. It is the marrow of nationalism, hypostasis of patriotism, nucleus of national heritage, substratum of culture and epitome of national honour...' Justice Misra observed in a typical passage. And from that the next was but a small step: '... National anthem is the symbol of our history, sovereignty, unity, pride and honour. Any person who shows disrespect to the national anthem in a way, has to be regarded involved in anti-national activity.'

The counsel for the film producer, director, etc., had pointed to the regulations that govern how the censor board is to assess scenes, etc., in which the National Anthem is played. These regulations specifically state that when the anthem is played in a documentary or newsreel, the audience is not expected to stand up. The judge squashed the submission: but this is not a documentary or newsreel, it is a film. In any case, he had already pointed out, mere technicalities are not to be allowed to come in the way of our showing proper respect to the National Anthem:

> The dedication of our forefathers, the sincerity of the people who fought for the people and suffered death and sense of patriotism that was shown, cannot be thrown aboveboard [sic] on the ground of hyper technicality when the interest of the nation is involved. When the pride of the nation is in issue and when nationalism has to play an essential part in the role of developing country, though the basic technicality has an entry but they cannot be allowed to govern or dominate primal or pivotal factors. Every citizen should remember that every word, deed and thought by him has to be indicative of the respect for the Constitution and the national anthem. No one is permitted to pave the path of deviancy and introduce the theory of totalistic individualism in the name of freedom of expression. In that event freedom of expression in the name of art or liberty of creativity would amount to, to borrow the terminology of Dr. B.R. Ambedkar 'Grammar of Anarchy'.

The guidelines say that the film has to be seen as a whole, and they must be assessed on the touchstone of what an average person of average sensibilities will make of it, the counsel submitted. So they do, the judge allowed, but...

> Guidelines stipulate that the whole motion picture has to be seen from a general view point. It has to be creative. But a sixty-four million dollar question arises whether in the name of creativity in a feature film the national anthem can be utilized in this manner. National Anthem as has been indicated is the symbol of history, unity, and pride. In the film, the national anthem has been bifurcated into two parts. The boy signs [sic] one part and the mother sings the rest, may be the last five words. Mr. Singh, learned senior counsel appearing for the respondents 4 and 5 with all his forensic skill would submit that the mother immediately thought it appropriate to complete the national anthem as it should not go unfinished. But the fact remains that the boy says 'sorry' in the midst of the anthem and mother after some time completes the same. All this has been done to create a dramatic impact in the picture for the benefit of the producer. This should not be allowed to be done for the popularisation of the national anthem as has been understood in this great country. That apart in our considered view the national anthem which is the glory of the country and portrays the unity of the country cannot be shown in a variety show or a cultural programme of a school as an item.

A child forgets, says 'sorry', and our anthem is split in two! Hence, the comprehensive, not to say, minatory order:

> Being of this view we direct as under:
> (a) The film 'Kabhi Khushi Kabhi Gham' shall not be shown in any theatre unless the scene which depicts the national anthem is deleted.
> (b) Respondents 4 and 5 shall immediately withdraw the film from all cinema-halls and the theatre owners are restrained from showing the film in the present form.
> (c) The respondent No. 3 [the Censor Board] shall withdraw the certificate unless the deletion is effected and deleted feature film is shown to the members of the Board as required under the Act and the Rules.
> (d) The aforesaid film shall not be telecast in national channel and also in any satellite channel without deletion.

(e) If any video cassette/VCD/DVD is sold in the market without deletion of the national anthem the appropriate authority shall take action against the said persons as permissible in law as it would amount to dealing with an uncensored film.

(f) No cable operator shall show the movie as long as the national anthem is not deleted as that would tantamount to showing of an uncensored film.

And the plaintiff was to be awarded Rs 15,000 in costs.

The producer, etc., of the film applied to the judges for leave to appeal against the order to the Supreme Court. By then the article governing the Right to Appeal prescribed that when, upon a judgment being delivered, those aggrieved request leave to appeal the order, the High Court shall grant the appeal forthwith.[3] In this instance, the producer, etc., applied in writing for leave to appeal. The judges refused permission: the very purpose of the change in the law was to expedite appeals; if appeals are allowed to be filed in writing after an interval instead of orally there and then, the very purpose of the law will be defeated, they held. So, no permission to appeal. And no stay either.[4]

In any event, the producer, etc., approached the Supreme Court. A three-judge bench, headed by the Chief Justice, set aside the order of the Madhya Pradesh High Court:

---

3 The relevant Article of the Constitution reads:
134A. Certificate for appeal to the Supreme Court.—Every High Court, passing or making a judgment, decree, final order, or sentence, referred to in clause (1) of article 132 or clause (1) of article 133, or clause (1) of article 134,—
(*a*) may, if it deems fit so to do, on its own motion; and
(*b*) *shall, if an oral application is made, by or on behalf of the party aggrieved, immediately after the passing or making of such judgment, decree, final order or sentence,*
determine, as soon as may be after such passing or making, the question whether a certificate of the nature referred to in clause (1) of article 132, or clause (1) of article 133 or, as the case may be, sub-clause (c) of clause (1) of article 134, may be given in respect of that case.
Clause (b) which applies to the matter being discussed has been italicised.

4 *Shyam Narayan v. Union of India*, M.C.C. No. 591 of 2003, Order of 28 July 2003, MANU/MP/1044/2003.

> We are satisfied that in view of the instructions issued by the Government of India that the national anthem which is exhibited in the course of exhibition of newsreel or documentary or in a film, the audience is not expected to stand as the same interrupts the exhibition of the film and would create disorder and confusion, rather than add to the dignity of the national anthem. We, therefore, set aside the order under challenge.[5]

But, as Mark Tully has taught us, there are no full stops in India. Time flies. Justice Dipak Misra was elevated to the Supreme Court. The same gentleman, Shyam Narayan Chouksey, who had pleaded before Justice Misra's bench at the Madhya Pradesh High Court in 2004, approached the Supreme Court in 2016. By one of these minor miracles, his petition landed up before Justice Misra's court. And we got the National Anthem judgment that we have been studying!

That judgment as we have seen covered not just one *Kabhi Khushi Kabhie Gham,* it covered all films, and all cinema halls. Poetic revenge! Its consequences too were larger, and burst forth in little time.

Predictable consequences

Rahul Unnikrishnan, advocate in the Madras High Court, pointed out that through its judgment on the National Anthem, the Supreme Court had created an offence—of not standing up when the National Anthem is sung, an offence for which there is no legislative backing.[6] He pointed out:

> The Prevention of Insults to National Honour Act, 1971, criminalises an insult to the National Flag, National Anthem and the Constitution. Section 3 of this Act says that whoever

5 *Karan Johar v. Union of India,* Decided on 19 April 2004, MANU/SC/0535/2004, (2004) 5 SCC 127. The judges were: Chief Justice V.N. Khare, Justice S.B. Sinha and Justice S.H. Kapadia.

6 On the following, Rahul Unnikrishnan, 'The Supreme Court's Tryst With Patriotism Lacks Legislative Backing', *The Wire*, 20 December 2016.

intentionally prevents the singing of the National Anthem or causes disturbances to any assembly engaged in such singing shall be punished with imprisonment for a term which may extend up to three years or with fine, or both. While Section 2 discusses in detail the acts that insult the National Flag and the Constitution of India, Section 3 focuses only on one act of insult—prevention of singing of National Anthem. None of the sections of this Act makes it mandatory for a citizen to stand up when the National Anthem is played. Similarly, the Indian Penal Code, 1860, does not criminalise any act that insults the National Anthem.

We saw how just before the Supreme Court gave its order, papers had published accounts of a wheelchair-bound man being badgered for not standing up as the National Anthem was being played in a cinema hall. The Supreme Court had nevertheless decreed that the National Anthem must be played in cinema halls, and everyone must stand up. Unnikrishnan recalled an equally bizarre incident that occurred in the wake of the judgment:

> Things took an ugly turn at the International Film Festival of Kerala (IFFK) when six people—including journalists—were arrested for allegedly refusing to stand when the National Anthem was played before the screening of the Egyptian film *Clash*. The Director General of Police, Loknath Behra, reportedly received a complaint from the members of Bharatiya Yuva Morcha—the youth wing of the BJP and based on the complaint, he directed the Assistant Commissioner of Police to inquire into the matter. Reports also suggest that Police personnel were among the audience.
>
> The organisers of the film festival had earlier moved the Supreme Court to seek an exemption from its order owing to the large number of daily shows scheduled at the festival. Denying the relief, the Supreme Court observed that, '...if there are 40 movies running in different shows, you will have to, well, stand 40 times'.

Unnikrishnan pointed out that as the direction to stand up had no law behind it, the police was put in a quandary: for what offence should they charge the six they had arrested?

> The Police in Thiruvananthapuram who arrested six people at the IFFK have charged them under Section 188 of the IPC which deals with the disobedience of an order duly promulgated by a public servant. Under this section, a 'public servant' includes judges as well. Hence, in the absence of any other provision of law which criminalises an act that insults the National Anthem by not standing when it is sung, the Police had no other option but to resort to Section 188. Legal commentaries on the IPC say that to constitute an offence under Section 188, it is necessary to show:
>
> - A lawful order promulgated by a public servant empowered to promulgate it;
> - Knowledge of the order which may be general or special;
> - Disobedience of such order; and
> - The result that is likely to follow from such disobedience.
>
> It has been held by multiple high courts that a mere disobedience of an order does not constitute an offence in itself. It must be shown that the disobedience has or tends to have a certain consequence, namely annoyance, obstruction, etc. Further, it is also settled law that the annoyance has to be proved as a fact; the mere mental annoyance of the concerned authorities is not enough. The reliance on Section 188 by the Police, thus, lacks legal wisdom.

And soon enough, there was an echo in distant Guwahati. On 2 October 2017, Gandhiji's birthday, *The Times of India* reported:

> *Disabled abused for not standing up during Anthem*
> Date: 02nd October 2017
> Gaurav Das: TNN
>
> Guwahati: A wheelchair-bound man, who has been fighting for rights of the disabled, was abused at a multiplex here on Friday for not standing up when the National Anthem was being played.
>
> Arman Ali (36) said he was in one of the front rows and 'sat upright' during the Anthem 'as a mark of respect'. However, at the end of the Anthem, two men abused him for not standing up. '*Saamne ek Pakistani baitha hai* (A Pakistani is sitting in front),' one of them reportedly said.

> 'When I looked behind, they bore smug expressions on their faces. How easy to call someone Pakistani without even bothering to know if that 'Pakistani' can stand up or not? Maybe, to them, their national duty is done by commenting on my not standing up for the National Anthem,' Ali, executive director of *Shishu Sarothi*, an NGO working for the empowerment of differently-abled people, said. 'This is what our society has come to. I am planning to write to the Chief Justice of India.'

In any case, if cinema halls, why not drama theatres? If at the commencement of cinema shows, why not at the commencement of music concerts? If at these, why not at the commencement of Kathakali performances during Onam celebrations? If at all these, why not before the commencement of proceedings every morning in courts, including, and especially the Supreme Court? Surely, example is the best motivator.

Whether decreeing patriotism is the best way to instil it apart, should one not think through the different circumstances in which one's decree will have to be enforced?

The text of the Supreme Court judgment prompts one more suggestion: that at least when giving directions on a matter which it obviously regards as sacred, such as respecting the National Anthem, one should be as punctilious about grammar and spellings as Tagore would have been.

What the great do...

Of course, the sequence does not end there. As Justice Misra might remind us, no one less than Lord Krishna himself says in the *Gita*, 'What the great do, the rest emulate.' A year had not passed since the Supreme Court legislating 'Constitutional Patriotism' than Justice M.V. Muralidharan of the Madras High Court took up a petition that had been filed in 2013.[7] The petitioner had appeared for a teacher eligibility test in 2013. One of the questions in the multiple-choice paper was: in what language was '*Vande Mataram*'

---

7 *K. Veeramani v. The Chairman, Teachers' Recruitment Board, College Road, Chennai-6*, decided on 25 July 2017.

originally written? Bengali? Marathi? Urdu? Sanskrit? The petitioner had ticked 'Bengali'. The 'answer key' had maintained that it was written in Sanskrit. The petitioner had thereby lost one point in the score. He had appealed to the High Court to direct the Teachers' Recruitment Board to add one point to his score.

At the very outset, the judge emphasized the importance of language. In prose that would remind us of what we have encountered above, he proclaimed:

> A country with a population of more 1.32 billion people with 29 states and 7 Union Territories and extremely different languages and dialects spoken across every part of this nation makes our country a [sic] largest democracy in this world. As Nelson Mandela has remarked, 'If you talk to a man in a language he understands, that goes to his head. If you talk to him in his language, that goes to his heart.'
>
> Language has perhaps been bridge [sic] between people across towns, cities, states, countries and continents. As civilizations developed, so did languages and our country has the pride of having many languages that have been in existence and practice for several thousands of years together.

He then adverted to the complexity of the question that was before him:

> As there are several languages in our country, it is sometimes difficult to ascertain as to what evolved in which language. This Court is now posed with the question as to in what language was our National song originally written. The answer would in fact answer the main issue involved in the present writ petition.

Hence, research was launched. The court directed the advocate general 'to appear and inform the correct answer to the question since there were conflicting answers to the said question. This Court also sought the assistance of any advocate to offer their reply to settle the controversy involved in the present writ petition'. Could it be that a judge who held '*Vande Mataram*' in such reverence did not know the language in which Bankim Chandra Chattopadhyay used to write?

In any event, many in the Bar devoted themselves to finding the correct answer. With the research results in hand, the judge turned to the issue:

> Our Independence struggle to attain freedom from the British has been one of the most toughest [sic] independence struggle [sic] across this world which resulted in loss of numerous number [sic] of lives but still unified this whole nation together in a peaceful way to protest against the British to leave this country and return it to the natives and the sons and daughters of this soil. To unify and to create a feeling of oneness amongst all Indians across the whole country, several renowned leaders and authors have composed several songs, poems, verses and also enacted several street plays and dramas to bring together the people for the sustained independence struggle.
>
> One such songs [sic] that touched the hearts of thousands of people and acted as a unifier was the song 'Vande Matharam' which meant 'I bow to thee, Mother'...

The mass of material which the research had thrown up was brought on record. It convinced the judge that the song was originally written in Bengali. Accordingly, he directed the board to award the petitioner an extra mark for having answered the question correctly. He spelt out other reasons also, and directed the board 'to accommodate the petitioner in any vacancy that have [sic] arisen in the SC(G) category and consequently issue appointment order as B.T. Assistant, if otherwise eligible within a period of four weeks from the date of receipt of a copy of the order'.

That should have settled the matter. But the judge saw fit to cover the wider field, so to say. Having settled the specific question, emulating the Supreme Court, he proceeded to the general imperative:

> Patriotism is an essential requirement for every citizen of this country. The fact that this country is our Motherland should always be remembered by every citizen of this country. Several

people have sacrificed their lives and families to the independent [sic] struggle that prolonged [sic] for several decades. In these tough times, it was songs like our national song *'Vande Matharam'* which created a sense of belief and confidence in the people.

Perhaps in today's modern era where we have marched ahead with technology, our lives have changed a lot. We have become busy with our own lives that sometimes we forget our nation. Sensing this fact the Hon'ble Supreme Court in *Shyam Narayan Chouksey v. Union of India* reported in 2016 SCC Online SC 1411 has directed that National Anthem shall be strictly respected by all citizens and the Anthem shall be played in all cinema halls across the country before the start of the movie.

He proceeded to cite passages from the National Anthem judgment. Next, he recalled that the Madras High Court had itself directed the state government to introduce aphorisms from the *Thirukkural* in school curricula. Hence:

Considering the larger public interest and to instill a sense of patriotism in each and every citizen of the State, this Court in addition to direction already passed in the writ petition, issues the following directions:

(a) The National Song *'Vande Matharam'* shall be played and sung in all schools/colleges/Universities and other educational institutions at least once a week (Preferably on Monday or Friday);

(b) The National Song *'Vande Matharam'* shall be played and sung in all Government Offices and Institutions/Private companies/Factories and industries at least once a Month;

(c) The Director of Public Information is directed to upload and circulate the translated version of *'Vande Matharam'* in Tamil and English thereby making it available in the Government websites and also in social media;

(d) Let a copy of this order be marked to the Chief Secretary of the Government of Tamil Nadu, who shall issue appropriate instructions to the concerned authorities;

(e) In the event, any person/organisation has difficulty in singing or playing the National Song, he or she shall not be compelled

> or forced to sing it, provided there are valid reasons for not doing so.
>
> The youth of this country are the future of tomorrow. This Court hopes and trusts that this order shall be taken in the right spirit and also implemented in letter and spirit by the citizenry of this great Nation.

Is patriotism-by-fiat the way to spur 'The youth of this country [who] are the future of tomorrow' to devote themselves to the country?

Now it was the board's turn to stand firm. It filed an appeal against the judge's order. A division bench of the Madras High Court heard the matter. It decided that [i] both answers—Bengali and Sanskrit—were correct; [ii] that, therefore, the candidate should be given an extra mark; [iii] but that even with the extra mark, the candidate fell short, ever so slightly, of the eligible bar; [iv] that whether to give the candidate the post in spite of this is an administrative matter, and except in exceptional circumstances, courts are not to interfere in administrative matters; [v] that whether '*Vande Mataram*' should be sung compulsorily as ordered by the judge is a policy matter, and is to be left to the government.[8]

Meanwhile, authorities continued to strain to ensure that the Supreme Court's directive about respecting the National Anthem is adhered to by all.

Ambur is a small town in Tamil Nadu. On Independence Day 2017, the local MLA came to hoist the National Flag at the government hospital. As the National Anthem was being sung, the chief medical officer, Dr A. Kennedy, was filmed talking on his mobile. A person filed a complaint with the police. The police registered a case against the doctor for insulting the National Anthem. The accused averred that he had received an urgent call from the office of the DMS—the Directorate of Medical and Rural Health Services—and that he had meant no insult either to the

8 *The Chairman, Teachers Recruitment Board, College Road, Chennai, 600006 v. K. Veeramani*, W.A. No. 1040 of 2017 and C.M.P. No. 14776 of 2017, decided on 12 October 2017.

National Flag or the National Anthem. Apprehending arrest, he applied to the High Court in Madras for anticipatory bail. As evidence of the offence that is alleged to have been committed is at hand, there does not seem to be any need for custodial interrogation, the High Court reasoned, and, on that ground, it granted him anticipatory bail. But while doing so, it laid down seven conditions. Among these is the following one:

> [b] the petitioner shall hoist the National Flag every day at 10.00 a.m. for one week at the Government Hospital, Ambur and salute the flag and sing National Anthem and the respondent police is directed to monitor this and send a report to the Judicial Magistrate Ambur.[9]

Given this kind of enthusiasm, we should be thankful for small mercies. We just about escaped the Supreme Court stepping in to regulate, to the point of banning 'sardar jokes'—only because the Chief Justice who was pursuing the matter retired.

After all that sound and fury

As the months went by, the difficulties of enforcing the Supreme Court's order about compulsorily playing the National Anthem in cinema halls, of closing doors, of everyone standing up, the meaninglessness of standing up again and again as films were screened at film festivals, the ridiculousness of jumping up the moment strains of the anthem came up in a scene or documentary—all these became more and more manifest. The way vigilantes had begun using it to browbeat others, the sheer impossibility of enforcing the order on the handicapped, began to stare everyone in the face. That the court had waded into a matter which was best left to the executive; that it had waded into the sphere of Parliament and legislated a new offence, and on a matter which was not one of such emergent importance—these came to be talked of in legal circles more and more.

9 *Dr A. Kennedy v. The state represented by Inspector of Police, Ambur town Police Station, Vellore District,* Cr. no. 396 of 2017.

At first the court, having penned such ringing words, was unmoved, and, of course, so was the government—uniquely nationalist as it was, in its own eyes. But step by tiny step, apertures began to open. The first aperture was opened in the hearing on 9 December 2016. Everyone agreed that in the cinema halls an exception would have to be made for those who just could not stand up. In its majesty, the court allowed that the handicapped who just could not stand up may remain seated, 'but must show such conduct which is commensurate with respect to the National Anthem'—on reading this, I did feel that the judges just did not know enough about the handicapped, some of whom would, for instance, find it almost impossible to even hold their head still. But one must be thankful for small mercies. And then, the court 'cleared' another matter—the 'clarification' speaks to what was happening as a result of its initial order. 'When we said that the doors shall be closed,' the judges declared, 'we did not mean that the doors shall be bolted as mentioned in the case of *Municipal Corporation of Delhi, Delhi vs. Uphaar Tragedy Victims Association and Ors.* [(2011) 14 SCC 481] but only to regulate the ingress and egress during the period while the National Anthem is played.'

At the next hearing—on 14 February 2017—one more aperture opened up. Recall what had happened in the original case, the one about the film, *Kabhi Khushi Kabhie Gham:* to Mr Chouksey's chagrin, the audience in the cinema hall had not stood up when, in an incident in the film, a young child began to sing the National Anthem in some London school. At the suggestion of the amicus curiae and the then attorney general, Chief Justice Misra and his colleagues ordered:

> In view of the aforesaid [that is, the suggestion of the *amicus curiae* and its endorsement by the Attorney General], it is clarified that when the National Anthem is sung or played in the storyline of a feature film or [as] part of the newsreel or documentary, apart from what has been stated in the order dated 30.11.2016, the audience need not stand.

The case came up on 23 October 2017—again before a three-judge bench. The bench was headed by Justice Dipak Misra, by this time the Chief Justice of India. Justice A.M. Khanwilkar and Justice D.Y. Chandrachud were the other members of the bench. By now, there was a change: the government was still firm, but the court seemed to be wanting to shift the matter out of its hands, and into those of the government.

As the court noted in its Order of 23 October 2017, along with other advocates, the new attorney general, K.K. Venugopal, 'strenuously opposed' the plea that it recall its original order. Recalling the order would send a 'wrong signal' to society, argued thc amicus curiae. The attorney general advanced a new reason. The court recorded this new submission as follows:

> The submission of the learned Attorney General is that because of the vast diversity in the country based on religion, race, caste and even region, it becomes necessary to have uniformity which should be cultivated by playing the National Anthem so that when people come out from the cinema halls, instilling the belief that they are all Indians. Be that as it may. In this context, he has referred to Article 51A(a) of the Constitution of India.

Justice Chandrachud was reported to have questioned both legs of the argument. In response to Venugopal's premise about standing up for the anthem 'instilling the belief that they are all Indians', Justice Chandrachud asked whether viewers, when they came out of the cinema hall, would remember having stood up for the National Anthem or the plot of the film? And what if someone says that standing up is not enough by way of showing respect that is rightfully due to the National Anthem? What if someone says that no one should be wearing shorts when the anthem is played? As for ensuring that everyone must discharge the Fundamental Duties listed in Article 51A, Justice Chandrachud was reported to have inquired how far would the State have to go and how pervasive would its efforts have to be to ensure, for instance, that every citizen was exerting 'to value and preserve the rich heritage of our composite culture'?[10] And rightly too: after all, would everyone in the north have to demonstrate that he was doing enough to revive

10 C.f., *The Wire*, 24 October 2017.

and preserve the Yakshagana; would everyone in the south have to master or at least patronize qawwalis?

As directed, the case came up on 9 January 2018. Arguments flowed to and fro—it speaks volumes to the priorities by which we as a nation and State are seized that the October 2017 order of the court lists, apart from the attorney general and the amicus curiae, *fifty-two* senior advocates and advocates as having appeared in the case. The judges listened patiently to the arguments, and concluded:

> Having heard learned counsel for the parties for some time, we think it appropriate that the Central Government should take a call in this regard and, if necessary, as advised, may bring out the requisite notification or circular or rules. When we say 'take a call', needless to say, the discretion rests with the Central Government. The discretion has to be exercised without being influenced by our interim order. We may further emphasize that the discretion may be utilized to regulate in an inclusive manner or as the Central Government feels fit.

'...the discretion rests with the Central Government', 'The discretion has to be exercised without being influenced by our interim order...', '...or as the Central Government feels fit'—a sea-change from the reverberant words of the original order: the original ringing order had been written and delivered by Justice Dipak Misra, the final judgment was also written by Justice—now Chief Justice—Dipak Misra. The argument that this was something that falls squarely within the sphere of the executive, the argument that the subject is one on which the executive had in fact taken various steps, the argument that by its original order the court had legislated a new crime, and also that the original order of the court had entailed too many unintended consequences seemed to have gone home. The government for its part filed an affidavit that they had set up a committee to study all aspects of the matter. The committee would be headed by the additional secretary (border management)—as if, given the situation on our borders, *this* is what he should be devoting his time to—and would have representatives of *ten* other ministries. This seemed to satisfy the majesty of the court, and therefore, in its turn, while listing its final directions, it reiterated:

> ...(iii) Since the Committee constituted by the Union government is looking into all aspects of the matter, it shall make its recommendations uninfluenced by the interim directions of this Court, as clarified in our order dated 23rd October, 2017. Similarly, the competent authority shall in taking its decision(s) not be constrained or influenced by any of the interim directions.

The attorney general also suggested that the word 'shall' in the original order—the anthem *'shall'* be played in the cinema hall before screening any film—may be substituted by the word *'may'*. The court which had been so absolutely resolute just months earlier, now graciously accepted the attorney general's suggestion.

And thus Chouksey's strenuous efforts to make us patriotic were finally disposed of.[11]

Drivers or roads?

That in our country an appalling number of persons die in motor accidents is well known. That a number of these die because the drivers are under the influence of drugs or liquor is just as well known and just as inexcusable. The obvious remedy is to use Breathalysers and similar devices, and to give exemplary punishments to those who are caught driving after drinking. In the case at hand—*State of Tamil Nadu v. K. Balu*[12]—the Supreme Court itself noted that a driver could acquire liquor before commencing his journey, and

---

11 On these developments, see *Shyam Narayan Chouksey v. Union of India*, I.A. No. 11/2017 in W.P. (C) No. 855/2016, Order of 23 October 2017; and *Shyam Narayan Chouksey v. Union of India*, Writ Petition (Civil) No. 855 of 2016, judgment of 9 January 2018.

12 (2017) 2 SCC 281. To get a sense of relative proportions, it is useful to note what the official studies on which the Supreme Court relied had found. Of accidents in 2015 which could be traced to the fault of the drivers, those which had been caused by drivers having been under the influence of drugs or alcohol accounted for 4.2 per cent. They accounted for 6.4 per cent of the fatalities in accidents which could be attributed to the fault of drivers. Of the 51,204 persons who had been killed in road accidents on national highways, 2,591—about 5 per cent—had been killed in accidents which could be attributed to drivers having been under the influence of drugs or alcohol.

drink along the way. Yet, instead of focusing on drivers, the three-judge bench of the court, headed by the Chief Justice, chose to craft a remedy based on a classification of roads, with predictable results. The court gave a number of directions. Among these were the following:

- No licences shall be given that permit sale of liquor along national or state highways;
- This prohibition 'shall extend to and include stretches of such highways which fall within the limits of a municipal corporation, city, town or local authority';
- No shop for the sale of liquor shall (i) be visible from a national or state highway; (ii) be directly accessible from a national or state highway; and (iii) be situated within a distance of 500 metres of the outer edge of the national or state highway or of a service lane along the highway.

The first problem that arose was that in a city like Chandigarh, a road designated as a 'national highway' passed right through the city. Hotels and restaurants that had been granted liquor licences and which were situated along this road would have either had to shut down or their licences would have had to be revoked. The Chandigarh administration adopted a simple expedient: it reclassified the roads—highways were rechristened: henceforth they would be merely 'major district roads'. The problem was brought to the Supreme Court. The court issued a 'clarification'.[13] Whereas the original judgment had categorically declared that its direction 'shall extend to and include stretches of such highways which fall within the limits of a municipal corporation, city, town or local authority', the court now 'clarified' that the direction shall apply to 'highways properly understood, which provide connectivity between cities, towns and villages'. 'The order does not prohibit licensed establishments within municipal areas,' the court added. 'This clarification shall govern other municipal areas as well.'

---

13 *Arrive Safe Society of Chandigarh v. The Union Territory of Chandigarh*, Special Leave Petition (Civil) Number 10243 of 2017, decided on 11 July 2017.

There was the other predictable development. In its judgment, the Supreme Court had been firm as can be. After setting out its directions, it had recorded,

> All States and Union Territories are mandated to strictly enforce the above directions. The Chief Secretaries and Directors General of Police shall within one month chalk out a plan for enforcement in consultation with the State Revenue and Home Departments. Responsibility shall be assigned, *inter alia*, to District Collectors and Superintendents of Police and other competent authorities. Compliance shall be strictly monitored by calling for fortnightly reports on action taken.

The judgment had but to be given that reports started appearing in the press about the ingenious ways that were being devised to circumvent the directions of the court. A hotel had changed its entrance so that it could not be said to be within 500 metres of the highway. A liquor vend had spent Rs 2 lakh and made a maze so that the distance one had to traverse before entering it from the highway was more than 500 metres. The chief minister of Goa proclaimed that drivers were now drinking even more than they used to do—for they were stocking their cabins with bottles and drinking while driving.[14] The acme of such jugaad was the one adopted by the Government of Punjab. It issued the Punjab Excise (amendment) Ordinance 2017. This provided,

> In the Principal Act, section 26A shall be substituted by the following:-26A(1): *Sale or supply of liquor:* (i) The sale of liquor shall be permitted only through licensed liquor vends which shall not be located within 500 metres from the outer range of the National or State Highway or by a service lane along such

14 For typical reports, and a photograph of that low-cost maze, see, for instance, http://www.huffingtonpost.in/2017/04/08/this-kerala-bar-has-literally-built-a-maze-to-escape-supreme-cou_a_22031228/; http://www.hindustantimes.com/gurgaon/gurgaon-cyberhub-ambience-mall-change-entrances-to-beat-500-metre-sc-liquor-ban/story-YwWUzGQ5EavsZb2DxDc3oM.html

> highway and such liquor vends shall neither be directly visible nor accessible from such National or State Highway.

So far, so good—the ordinance was reproducing the direction of the Supreme Court. But this was followed by,

> (3) Notwithstanding anything contained in any judgment, decree or order of any court, tribunal or authority, every club, hotel, restaurant or any notified place having a licence shall be entitled to engage in the supply of liquor to members, guests or other persons for consumption of such liquor within the premises of such club, hotel, restaurant or notified place, irrespective of whether such club, hotel, restaurant or notified place is located on or near any National or State highway.

In short, even 'other persons' could consume liquor in a 'club, hotel, restaurant or notified place' even if the place was situated 'on or near any National or State Highway' so long as they did so within the premises of the place. It does not require much imagination to see how our jugaad will stretch, to take one example 'members, guests or other persons'. 'Members' as temporary as the mutaah marriage? 'Guests or other persons' to include whoever wants to be included? 'Premises' to include the parking lot of a hotel or restaurant?

Similarly, where the Supreme Court had categorically directed, 'The existing licences which have already been renewed prior to the date of this order shall continue until the term of the licence expires but no later than 1-4-2017,' the ordinance provided:

> (4) Notwithstanding anything contained in any judgment, decree or order of any court, tribunal or other authority, any licence issued to any club, hotel, restaurant or other notified place for the sale of liquor shall be deemed to have been and always be deemed to have been issued for the supply of liquor and all relevant provisions of this Act and the rules made thereunder will continue to apply as they did for sale of liquor.

Are we in for further rounds of litigation? For some more 'clarifications'?

Yet the root of the problem and its remedy were manifest from the moment the judgment was delivered: none of this would have arisen had the court focused not on classification of roads but on the drivers.

Clarifications confounded

This reluctance to think through the consequences of the judgment one is pronouncing has obliged the Supreme Court to issue not just 'clarifications' but 'clarifications' of 'clarifications'. When I was studying judgments that the Supreme Court had handed down on reservations, my friend Arvind Datar pointed to certain features and in their context asked me to look up *Abhay Nath v. University of Delhi*,[15] a judgment delivered in 2009. As I reported in *Falling Over Backwards*, on reading it I learnt that this judgment had to be delivered to 'clarify' what the court had held four years earlier in *Buddhi Prakash Sharma v. Union of India*.[16] On reading *Buddhi Prakash*, I learnt that *that* judgment had to be delivered to 'clarify' what the Constitution Bench of the Supreme Court had held in *Saurabh Chaudri v. Union of India* in 2003.[17] *That* judgment, it turned out, had been necessitated by what the court had decreed in *Dinesh Kumar II*, as it is known, a judgment delivered in 1986.[18] *Dinesh Kumar II* had to be delivered as the scheme which the court had prescribed the previous year in *Dinesh Kumar I* had led to some untenable situations.[19] *That* scheme had been prescribed to 'clarify' what the same bench had actually meant by the judgment it had delivered in 1984 in *Pradeep Jain v. Union of India*.[20]

---

15 *Abhay Nath v. University of Delhi* (2009) 17 SCC 205.
16 *Buddhi Prakash Sharma v. Union of India*, (2005) 13 SCC 61.
17 *Saurabh Chaudri v. Union of India*, (2004) 5 SCC 618.
18 *Dinesh Kumar v. Motilal Nehru Medical College*, (1986) 3 SCC 727.
19 *Dinesh Kumar v. Motilal Nehru Medical College*, (1985) 3 SCC 22.
20 *Pradeep Jain v. Union of India*, (1984) 3 SCC 654.

Of course, there are so many facets to admissions, and the stakes are so high—the entire future of children—that people are bound to approach courts again and again to see if one angle works where another has not. But it does, literally, speak volumes when we learn that by now the judgments of the Supreme Court on educational institutions alone cover seven thick volumes of *Supreme Court Cases*—enough to form a sub-specialization in itself.[21]

There is the other aspect. A three-judge bench of the Supreme Court had, in effect, modified the order made in a judgment delivered by a Constitution Bench of five judges. Further, the court had reviewed its own order years after it was made, in a different proceeding. The review had been called a 'clarification'.

This is but an illustration of a trend in our constitutional jurisprudence. A judgment of five judges is 'clarified' by a bench of three judges. For the Supreme Court, clarification, modification, alteration and variation, even completely nullifying—as has happened in the liquor-outlets-within-a-city-like-Chandigarh order—have all become synonyms.

If one may press the point, this trend shows more than not thinking through the sorts of situations that may arise as a result of one's verdict. Some cases clearly point to a departure from discipline. I have my personal experience as an example. Hindustan Zinc was among the companies that were disinvested during Atal Bihari Vajpayee-ji's tenure as prime minister. Since then the company has done so much better than it was doing when it was under governmental ownership. The disinvestment was challenged in the Rajasthan High Court. The case was withdrawn. The same

21 Arvind Datar also had me 'actually read and not skip through' paragraphs 6 and 7 of *Abhay Nath*. He then showed me that there were two typographical mistakes in that order which, if followed, would turn the position that was decreed on its head! In paragraph 6, the words 'if 22.5% are reserved for SC/ST students' must read as 'if 22.5% are *not* reserved for SC/ST students' since the sentence would be internally inconsistent otherwise. And in paragraph 7, the words 'to the effect that 50% of the seats for all-India quota shall exclude the reservation', must read as 'to the effect that 50% of the seats for all-India quota shall *include* the reservation'.

challenge was then mounted in the Supreme Court. It was rejected by a three-judge bench, presided over by the Chief Justice. Years later, what was virtually an identical challenge was admitted by a two-judge bench. In February 2018, this liberation from discipline entangled the Supreme Court itself. Acquisition of land even for the highest public purposes is a matter of intense contention: for those who own the land, the loss can spell the difference between life and starvation; for the State, the refusal of just a handful to part with their land can stall a necessary project for years. To balance the interests of owners and the needs of the State, the Right to Fair Compensation and Transparency in Land Acquisition, Rehablitation and Resettlement Act was passed in 2013. In 2014, a three-judge bench of the Supreme Court, consisting of the then Chief Justice R.M. Lodha and Justices Kurian Joseph and Madan B. Lokur, held[22] that the acquisition of the land would be valid only if the compensation had actually been deposited in the accounts of the landowners; depositing it, for instance, in a government treasury would not be enough. Lower courts began deciding cases on the basis of this judgment. But on 8 February 2018, by a two-to-one judgment, another three-judge bench consisting of Justices Arun Mishra, A.K. Goel and Mohan M. Shantanagoudar held[23] that the acquisition would be valid if the State so much as offered the compensation or deposited it in, say, the government treasury, and even if the compensation did not get deposited in the accounts of the owners for five years—for instance, because of their refusal to accept an amount they regarded as unfair. With one judge dissenting on the proposition, the bench went further and proclaimed that the decision of the earlier three-judge bench had been passed without due regard to the law. Authorities that had acquired lands swiftly approached the lower courts to now validate their acquisitions on the basis of this new judgment. Naturally, the matter soon came up in the Supreme Court again, before a three-judge bench consisting

22 In *Pune Municipal Corporation v. Harakchand Misrimal Solanki,* (2014) 3 SCC 183.

23 In *Indore Development Authority v. Shailendra (deceased) through LR,* (2018) SCC Online SC 100.

of Justices Kurian Joseph, Madan Lokur—both of whom had been part of the bench that had delivered the judgment which had been pronounced to have been given without regard to the law—and Deepak Gupta. Among others, former Attorney General Mukul Rohatgi apprised the court of what troubles would arise if the situation was allowed to continue: about 5,000 cases had been decided on the basis of the 2014 judgment—all of them could now be sought to be repoened on the basis of Justice Mishra's bench having held that the judgment had been arrived at disregarding the law. During the hearing, Justice Kurian Joseph rightly stressed that the Supreme Court would just not be able to function as one institution unless discipline was observed: it was well-settled that if a bench felt that an earlier decision taken by a bench of equivalent strength needed to be reviewed, it would recommend to the Chief Justice that the matter be referred to a larger bench. How could a bench of three judges pronounce that the decision of another three-judge bench had been made disregarding the law? The bench comprising Justices Kurian Joseph, Madan Lokur and Deepak Gupta had to direct the secretary general of the Supreme Court to urgently tell all High Courts not to deal with cases relating to that section of the act in question till they had decided whether the matter would be sent to a larger bench, and it had to request all other benches of the Supreme Court itself not to deal further with pending cases in this regard till the question of reference to the larger bench was decided. 'Be very clear,' Justice Kurian Joseph said, 'this is a matter of judicial properiety and consistency ... The system exists but if you start tinkering with it then it won't stop. This institution will go forever. There has to be wisdom and a proper method has to be followed ... It is [my] painful concern that if this institution is to remain as one, it should be one and you have to make it one. You have to have proper judicial discipline for that.'[24]

---

24 *State of Haryana v. G.D. Goenka Tourism Corporation Ltd.*, Order of 21 February 2018; *Bar and Bench*, 22 February 2018, and *The Indian Express*, 22 February 2018.

Apart from the chaos such instances would cause in litigation, there are other, and I would think graver, consequences. Such instances make the law uncertain. Worse, they breed cynicism—'The outcome does not depend so much on the law or the facts,' litigants come to conclude, 'but on who you get as your lawyer, and the bench before which your case gets listed.'

13

Circumstances, consequences, meta-consequences

As we rush to the courts to remedy wrongs farther and farther afield, the courts must assess the consequences that the law they will lay down shall have—and naturally, the consequences will extend beyond the immediate issue that they are addressing in the judgment. For this reason, I would urge a closer acquaintance with the world that we have to face, and what we must do to face it. Others are not going to slow down because we have not solved our problems: for a moment, consider the time it takes to obtain judgments in a case involving the impact of a project on the environment and contrast this with the pace at which China is building infrastructure in Tibet for troop movements. Similarly, consider the consequences that judgments on reservations—with half the service recruited and promoted by birth rather than competence—will have for our capacity to deal with a world changing at lightning speed. Yes, it is a world of opportunities but it is also a heartless world: there is no place for a second-rate individual, a second-rate firm, or a second-rate country. And yet when we look at the cumulative effect of *Thomas,*[1] *Indira Sawhney,*[2] *Nagaraj,*[3] there can be no

1 *State of Kerala v. N.M. Thomas,* (1976) 2 SCC 310.

2 *Indra Sawhney v. Union of India,* (1992) Supp (3) SCC 217; and *Indra Sawhney v. Union of India,* (2000) 1 SCC 168.

3 *M. Nagaraj v. Union of India,* (2006) 8 SCC 212.

doubt that together they strike a mighty blow against excellence and performance. Even though, in each round, the Supreme Court tried to restrain the political class, it went along in the subsequent rounds when the politicians came back with amended articles of the Constitution. As a result, today vulgarity has become a right, mediocrity has become the norm, standards are derided as a conspiracy to keep the poor down, ignorance of facts becomes a ground for sticking to an unfounded opinion, intimidation has become argument and assault is proof. And we are going to compete in the world? Similarly, by extending the definition of the 'State' and 'other authorities' to encompass governmental enterprises, have the courts not enabled a perverse 'work culture' to spread in them; and thereby helped in sending them to their deaths?

I would, therefore, plead that judges make an extra effort to learn where the world is, where it is headed—in particular, where our competitors and adversaries are headed. Every so often journalists do not visit factories and project sites about which they write. Their reports can cause authorities to take unwarranted decisions. But judges visit factories and project sites even less. And the consequences of the opinions they form are infinitely more substantial than the writings of journalists. As I sat in the Faridabad court, I often asked myself: here are 700-odd individuals being prosecuted; many of them must be in the same position as us—they too may not have laid a brick; on the other hand, the real problem—illegal mining—is going on in broad daylight; why does the judge not leave his room for a day and just make a surprise inspection of the site?

Of course, every case is important. But given the importance of the State in our lives in India, cases involving public servants need special attention and dispatch. In cases where, for instance, a public servant—a minister, a legislator, a judge, an officer or a policeman—is accused of having amassed assets which he cannot account for by his known sources of income,

- Judges must not allow adjournments at all. What a travesty it is that years and years go by after conclusive evidence is found about the accumulations of political leaders—buildings, land, cash—cases languish in courts. And they continue to make and unmake governments.

- As the Commission on the Working of the Constitution urged, the rule of evidence must not be 'beyond reasonable doubt' but 'the preponderance of probability'.
- Judges must go by brute facts rather than let public servants get off via legalisms.
- Except where it is established that the witness was pressured to make the original statement, witnesses who resile must be punished severely for perjury.

Courts have the power to punish for perjury—as they do to refuse adjournments. Yet it remains one of the least used of powers, and its non-use is responsible for great mischief. Look at the way the prosecution has gone back and witnesses have somersaulted on what they solemnly swore in courts in regard to blasts that killed scores. Similarly, it does not take a Sherlock Holmes to see when the prosecution is diluting its case—the very fact that this coincides so often with a change of rulers should itself be enough to alert any judge to what is happening.

THE WIDER CONTEXT

And one must consider not just the specific problem which is being addressed in a particular case. One must consider the wider contexts in which what the court lays down will be applicable. I may be permitted to follow the example of the learned judge, and reproduce an example that I used while delivering the Justice P.D. Desai Memorial Lecture in Ahmedabad.[4] As we know, along with extending the ambit of Article 21, the Supreme Court has used Article 22 creatively to enlarge our liberties.[5] Even as we welcome these, we must bear in mind the consequences that the formulations

---

4 'Individual Liberty and National Security', in Arun Shourie, *We Must Have No Price, And everyone must know that we have no price,* The Express Group and Rupa, 2010, pp. 10–45.

5 Article 22 provides:

22. Protection against arrest and detention in certain cases:

(1) No person who is arrested shall be detained in custody without being informed, as soon as may be, of the grounds for such arrest nor shall he be denied the right to consult, and to be defended by, a legal practitioner of his choice.

by the courts have for persons operating in the field. Consider the Supreme Court's prescriptions vis-à-vis the procedures that must be adhered to in regard to those who are suspected to have broken

---

(2) Every person who is arrested and detained in custody shall be produced before the nearest magistrate within a period of twenty-four hours of such arrest excluding the time necessary for the journey from the place of arrest to the court of the magistrate and no such person shall be detained in custody beyond the said period without the authority of a magistrate.

(3) Nothing in clauses (1) and (2) shall apply-

(a) to any person who for the time being is an enemy alien; or

(b) to any person who is arrested or detained under any law providing for preventive detention.

(4) No law providing for preventive detention shall authorise the detention of a person for a longer period than three months unless-

(a) an Advisory Board consisting of persons who are, or have been, or are qualified to be appointed as, Judges of a High Court has reported before the expiration of the said period of three months that there is in its opinion sufficient cause for such detention:

Provided that nothing in this sub-clause shall authorise the detention of any person beyond the maximum period prescribed by any law made by Parliament under sub-clause (b) of clause (7); or

(b) such person is detained in accordance with the provisions of any law made by Parliament under sub-clauses (a) and (b) of clause (7).

(5) When any person is detained in pursuance of an order made under any law providing for preventive detention, the authority making the order shall, as soon as may be, communicate to such person the grounds on which the order has been made and shall afford him the earliest opportunity of making a representation against the order.

(6) Nothing in clause (5) shall require the authority making any such order as is referred to in that clause to disclose facts which such authority considers to be against the public interest to disclose.

(7) Parliament may by law prescribe-

(a) the circumstances under which, and the class or classes of cases in which, a person may be detained for a period longer than three months under any law providing for preventive detention without obtaining the opinion of an Advisory Board in accordance with the provisions of sub-clause (a) of clause (4);

(b) the maximum period for which any person may in any class or classes of cases be detained under any law providing for preventive detention; and

(c) the procedure to be followed by an Advisory Board in an inquiry under sub-clause (a) of clause (4).

the law. The courts have repeatedly invoked the adage, 'The history of liberty is the history of procedural safeguards.' True, but now consider the consequences of the extent to which the safeguards have been stretched. You will recall the anguish of the Supreme Court at custodial deaths—everyone would share it. The court deliberated over the relevant case for *ten years*: that is one aspect of the matter—even when the court feels outraged at something, even when it feels that the impugned conduct is 'uncivilized', that it is 'the worst form of violence', the court takes ten years to come to a conclusion. But for the moment, I am not on that aspect. For the present what concerns us are the directions that the Supreme Court laid down to prevent this abuse.

From the moment the person is to be arrested, this is how the Supreme Court would have the personnel of the security forces conduct themselves:

1. The police personnel carrying out the arrest and handling the interrogation of the person who has been arrested should bear accurate, visible and clear identification and name tags with their designations. The particulars of all such police personnel who handle interrogation of the person arrested must be recorded in a register.
2. The police officer carrying out the arrest shall prepare a memo of arrest at the time of arrest and such memo shall be attested by at least one witness who may either be a member of the family of the arrestee or a respectable person of the locality from where the arrest is made. It shall also be countersigned by the arrestee and shall contain the time and date of arrest.
3. A person who has been arrested or detained and is being held in custody in a police station or interrogation centre or other lock-up shall be entitled to have one friend or relative or other person known to him or having an interest in his welfare being informed, as soon as practicable, that the attesting witness of the memo or arrest is himself such a friend or a relative of the arrestee.
4. Within eight to twelve hours of the arrest, the time, the place of arrest and the venue of custody of an arrestee must be notified by the police to his relatives. Where the friend or relative of the arrestee lives outside the district or town, this must be done

telegraphically through the legal aid organization in the district and the police station of the area concerned.

5. The person arrested must be made aware of this right to have someone informed of his arrest or detention as soon as he is put under arrest or is detained.
6. An entry must be made in the diary at the place of detention regarding the arrest of the person which shall also disclose the name of the relative or friend of the person who has been informed of the arrest and the names and particulars of the police officials in whose custody the arrestee is.
7. The arrestee should, where he so requests, be also examined at the time of his arrest, and if there are any major and minor injuries, these must be recorded at that time. The 'inspection memo' must be signed both by the arrestee and the police officer making the arrest and its copy must be provided to the arrestee.
8. The arrestee should be subjected to medical examination by a trained doctor every forty-eight hours during his detention in custody, the doctor being from the panel of approved doctors appointed by the director, health services, of the state or Union Territory concerned. The director, health services, should prepare such a panel for all tehsils and districts as well.
9. Copies of all the documents, including the memo of arrest referred to above, should be sent to the Illaqa magistrate for his record.
10. The arrestee may be permitted to meet his lawyer during interrogation, though the lawyer need not be present throughout the interrogation.
11. A police control room should be set up at all district and state headquarters. Information regarding the arrest and the place of custody of the arrestee shall be communicated to the control room by the officer causing the arrest, within twelve hours of effecting the arrest and, at the police control room, it should be displayed on a conspicuous notice board.[6]

---

6 *D.K. Basu v. State of West Bengal*, (1997) 1 SCC 416, at 435–36. See also, *D.K. Basu v. State of West Bengal*, (1998) 9 SCC 437; and for the course that the case took in the Supreme Court, Arvind Datar, *Constitution of India*, Volume I, Wadhwa and Company, Nagpur, Second edition, 2007, p. 246.

Now, imagine you are from one of our security forces. Transport yourself to the Kashmir Valley. An encounter is taking place. Some of your colleagues have been gunned down by the Pakistan-trained, local terrorists. Two of them have been killed. Two have been taken alive. Proceed step by step in accordance with the directions of the Supreme Court:

- Make sure that, as you approach the terrorists to arrest them, you are wearing your identification tags that bear your name and designation accurately and clearly. Make sure that these tags are clearly visible for all bystanders, among whom may be persons associated with the terrorists, to note down.
- Make sure that your particulars are recorded in a register at the local police station from which, as you know, getting to know your identity and the whereabouts of your family will be the easiest thing in the world for the sponsors and coordinators of the terrorists.
- Prepare a memo recording that you have arrested each of the terrorists. Have either a member of his family or a person who is respected in the locality witness the arrest. Have him or her sign the memo. Request the person you are arresting to countersign the memo. Unless the person who has signed as a witness is himself a friend or relative of the terrorist, be certain that you inform a friend or relative of the terrorist at the earliest possible.
- If the friend or relative resides elsewhere, inform him by telegraph through the legal aid organization of the district and the local police station.
- Make certain that the person you have arrested is informed that it is your duty to inform his friend or relative, and that you have carried out your duty.
- Write down all this—names, place, the times at which the steps have been taken and all—in the diary.
- Have the person examined for injuries. Record these. Request him to sign the record of the examination. Sign it yourself. Furnish a copy to the terrorist.

- Have a trained doctor from a panel approved by the director of health services in Srinagar examine him every forty-eight hours.
- Each time you and your colleagues interrogate him, ensure that all the foregoing steps are taken—for instance, that your name and designation tags are clearly visible to the person.
- Send copies of all documents—several of which will include your name and designation as well as those of other police officials and the doctor—to the magistrate of the locality.
- If he so wants, enable the terrorist to meet his lawyer periodically during the time you are interrogating him.
- Ensure that the police control room at the district headquarters and in Srinagar are informed of the arrest and that both display the information on a conspicuous notice board.

The court might as well have added a final guideline: 'And await the reprisals that will surely come down on you and your family'!

Is all this just miasma? Is it so because Article 22(3) expressly states that the protections under its first two clauses do not apply to alien enemies—but we assumed in our example that the terrorists were locals; nor to persons who are detained under a law that provides for preventive detention, and the laws on terrorism do provide for such detention? Please read *D.K. Basu* and see if, as a beleaguered security official, you will take the risk of proceeding on the assumption that the directions apply only to persons who are entitled to the protections of Article 22 and, hence, not to the persons you are apprehending.

But even though Article 22 does not apply to 'alien enemies' and those who are being arraigned under laws permitting preventive detention, Article 21 certainly applies to them also. May the court not hold that treating a suspect and detenu in accordance with these guidelines follows directly from Article 21 and the numerous judgments that have been given on it? That care for his physical and mental safety is an obvious part of the person's right to life and liberty, both being taken to include all the elements that the Supreme Court has held fall under them? After all, by the grace of the judgments, each suspect and detenu is entitled not just to 'animal existence' but to life with dignity. And here, by the *D.K. Basu* guidelines, we are ensuring just his physical survival.[7]

When I inquire from them, lawyers tell me that these guidelines technically remain binding. They have not been overruled, nor has their ambit been circumscribed by any subsequent judgment. The point is not that custodial deaths ought to be condoned. The point is about the consequence that the remedy which the courts formulate for meeting one ill—that is, of trampling upon the life and liberty of an individual—has for thwarting the incomparably greater evil—that of dismembering the country. And how it is necessary for the courts to bear that latter consequence also in mind. When this is not done, one of two consequences is unavoidable. Either the hands of the security forces will get so firmly tied that the fight against

7 An ambiguity in *D.K. Basu* leads to a typically unwarranted inference. This became clear when a senior judge of the Gujarat High Court came up to the podium after I had delivered the Justice P.D. Desai Memorial Lecture and sought to 'correct the record' as far as the Supreme Court's judgment in this case is concerned. He said that in *D.K. Basu* itself the Supreme Court had clearly stated that the guidelines would not apply to terrorists. He was emphatic, saying that he had himself studied the judgment and, in fact, had based his judgment in *Lok Adhikar Sangh v. State of Gujarat* [1998 (1) G.L.H. 768] in part on the distinction that the Supreme Court had made in this regard. He cited paragraph 32 of *D.K. Basu* for this purpose. He must have meant paragraph 33, as paragraph 32 consists of a passage from the judgment of the U.S. Supreme Court in *Miranda v. State of Arizona* to the opposite effect. In paragraph 33 of *D.K. Basu*, the Supreme Court does affirm that the freedom of the individual must yield to the security of the state; and also that 'in the very nature of things there would be a qualitative difference in the method of interrogation of such a person as compared to an ordinary criminal'. But, in the very same paragraph, the court is equally emphatic that the methods of interrogation adopted for even such a person shall have to be in strict conformity with the requirements of Article 21. More important, when it sets out the guidelines—in fact, it refers to them as *'requirements'*, and it italicizes the word for emphasis—the Supreme Court, in paragraphs 34 and 35, makes them mandatory for 'all cases of arrest and detention'—no distinction is drawn between terrorists, their accomplices and instigators on the one hand and ordinary criminals on the other. C.f., *D.K. Basu*, (1997) ISCC 416, paras 32–35.

enemies of the state will be hampered. Or the security forces will be compelled to disregard the guidelines in practice. In either case, respect for the law and the courts will be called into question.

How well I remember the day when I got a call from Mr K.P.S. Gill. He said that he wanted to come over to see me. No, no, sir, I had said spontaneously. You just tell me where I should come, *I* will come over. No, he said, there will be some officers with me: it will be easier for us to come over and meet your father and you both.

Punjab had fallen under the sway of Pakistan-instigated-armed-financed terrorists. Administration had evaporated. The police had evaporated. The magistracy had evaporated—terrorists and their sympathizers used to, in open court, direct the magistrate to issue the orders they wanted. It was in such circumstances that Mr Julio Ribeiro and Mr K.P.S. Gill were charged with the task of retrieving Punjab. When they took up the task, the police was not a force. Individual officers took up the challenge—almost as individuals. By the strategies he devised, by the leadership he gave, by his personal bravery, Mr K.P.S. Gill saved Punjab for our country.

As the terrorists were pushed back, their sympathizers began going around the state and exhorting people to file cases against specific officers—the very officers who had done the most to retrieve Punjab. The politicians who had assumed power once peace was restored would never have gained office but for what Mr K.P.S. Gill and his men had accomplished. But such was the opportunism and pusillanimity of these politicians that they went along, instituted 'inquiries' and the cases were indeed filed. Several of the officers were arrested, and thrown into the very jails where the terrorists were lodged. Some of them were thrashed by the terrorists, and had to be rescued. One of the bravest of them, Ajit Singh Sandhu, had committed suicide. And to top it all, Mr Gill was finding it difficult to get lawyers who would stand up for the brave officers.

The opportunism and cowardice of the rulers were matched by another feature: the exact sequence which had been enacted during and after the Emergency was repeated now. Courts which had abdicated their function suddenly became so punctilious about liberty and 'procedure prescribed by law'. After all, the officers were thrown into jails with the judges' concurrence. It took the greatest effort to get the rulers to see reason.

Hence, one must see the circumstances in which others have to function. One must see beyond the case in hand, one must visualize the situations in which the formulations that are being delivered may be used.

But I would urge more: one must see not just the consequences of one's judgments, one must see the meta-consequences. Once again, I will follow the example of the learned judge and draw attention to a sequence that I have dealt with at greater length elsewhere.

The activist's commitment

Over the years, as I have got know, work with and support activists, I have noticed one unexpected feature: often those who are striving to right one wrong are dismissive of the work of others who are devoting themselves to some other issue with as much commitment and zeal. This seems to be almost an inevitable result of their determination to right that particular wrong, it seems to be almost an accompaniment of the sacrifices that they are making for the cause they have taken up. A person sacrifices his career, his family, for preventing further denudation of the Himalayas. Another person sacrifices his career, his family, he risks his life to stop the killing of persons in false 'encounters'. When you mention the work of the person in the Himalayas, the one striving to put an end to killings in false 'encounters' exclaims, 'Of course, of course, he is doing good work, but he is not focusing on the *real* issue.' And vice versa. This is not because of any mean-heartedness. It is because sacrifice of the order that these persons are making requires almost exclusive devotion to, it requires almost an obsession for the particular issue. All other issues, important though they be, seem not to be the *real* issue.

I fear this happens to judges also once they are seized of a particular wrong: they come to focus on that particular issue so intensely that they become oblivious of the consequences that their rulings on this issue will have on other, equally important matters. After they have delivered some judgments advancing that particular cause—say, expanding the ambit of Article 21—they come to be known for their work in, say, enlarging the meaning of 'life' and the corresponding duties of the state to provide one thing after another. This reputation congeals into a self-image as the champion of, say, the right of every person to a life with dignity. And in subsequent rounds this self-image gives a further push to rulings in the same direction. This sequence can be traced without much effort in the rulings of judges who came to be viewed as 'progressive'—especially in the rulings they handed down after the Emergency. It almost seemed that the Supreme Court was compensating for its record during the Emergency.

In *Falling Over Backwards*,[8] I have documented the trajectory that the Supreme Court has followed in regard to reservations, and how these judgments have brought us to a precipice—not just in regard to competitiveness and fairness, but also in regard to the one dyke that the Supreme Court itself constructed, a dyke that has saved us from the excesses of authoritarian leaders, the doctrine of the Basic Structure.

If I may once again follow the sterling example of the eloquent judge, and cite two/three passages from that earlier study, we see the court advancing on three fronts.

First, with each round, Directive Principles were vaulted higher and higher above Fundamental Rights. First it was said that the two had to be *read harmoniously*. Then that the two cannot be read except as *complementing and supplementing each other*. Then that Fundamental Rights *must be read in the light of* Directive Principles. Then that the Directive Principles *must be read into* Fundamental Rights. Then that Fundamental Rights are *the means for achieving the goals set out in* the Directive Principles. Then that no distinction can be made between the Directive Principles and Fundamental Rights. Then that, when courts can adopt one 'principle of interpretation' or an alternative for excavating the import of an article of the Constitution or the validity of a law, they should choose the one that furthers a Directive Principle. The Directive Principles thus became touchstones for assessing

---

8 *Falling Over Backwards: An Essay against Reservations and against Judicial Populism*, HarperCollins, 2012. Original publication in 2006.

laws and amendments to the Constitution: any restriction imposed with the objective of—that should read 'with *the stated objective* of'—implementing a Directive Principle has to be presumed to be in the public interest, the courts held, and the law must be deemed to be valid even if it impairs a notion like equality guaranteed by Article 14.

Second, from holding that there must be *equality of opportunity*, the judges began ruling that there must be *equality of outcomes*. And in decisions like *Glanrock*,[9] equality of outcomes became the '*egalitarian equality of outcomes*'.

Third, the touchstone on which laws and even amendments were to be judged came to be transmogrified:

- The touchstone used to be the violation of a Fundamental Right—a law or an amendment of the Constitution would not pass muster if it violated a Fundamental Right.
- That became the violation not of the Fundamental Right but of '*the essence of the right*'.
- That in turn became not the violation of that 'essence of the right' but the *obliteration* of the essence of the right.
- That in a further turn became not the obliteration of the essence of one right but the violation of '*the overarching principles*' underlying different provisions of the Constitution.
- By *Indian Medical Association*,[10] it became not even the obliteration of the 'overarching principles'. The touchstone became the *obliteration* of the 'essence of the overarching principles'.
- That became the *obliteration* of the 'essence of the overarching principles' to such an extent that we got *in effect a new Constitution*.

In *Indian Medical Association*, a division bench of the Supreme Court enlarged what had come to be known as 'the degree test'—that one must assess not just whether, say, a Fundamental Right has been violated but the *degree to which it has been violated*—to

9 *Glanrock Estate Pvt. Ltd. v. State of Tamil Nadu,* (2010) 10 SCC 96.
10 *Indian Medical Association v. Union of India,* (2011) 7 SCC 179.

assessing a law or amendment by the Ship of Theseus test, so to say. As a plank of the ship got damaged or rotted, it would be replaced. The question was: at what stage does the ship become other than the ship it has been? I had argued that by this test, the infamous 39th Amendment that had been brought in to nullify the Allahabad High Court judgment holding Mrs Indira Gandhi guilty of corrupt electoral practices—and which put the elections of the president, vice president, speaker and prime minister beyond legal challenge—and even the 42nd Amendment would stand vindicated.

By the former, after all, the elections of only four out of thousands of officers of state had been put beyond legal scrutiny. By the latter, the overwhelming bulk of the Constitution had remained untouched. Even the successive mutilations of the 1973 Constitution of Pakistan by dictators like Zia-ul-Haq would have been held to have left that Constitution as akin to the original as the successive replacements of planks left the Ship of Theseus to be what it had been.[11]

In short, while delivering judgments, especially while penning grandiloquent passages and crafting enlargements of settled principles, judges must visualize consequences for the case at hand, of course. They must in addition visualize the manifold circumstances in which their prose and enlargements might be used. But not just that. They must visualize the consequences that their prose and enlargements are liable to have for the constitutional structure itself.

While such are the lessons for judges, there are lessons for the rest of us also.

Lessons for lawyers and us laymen

Professions have developed many self-serving 'principles'—these are nothing but rationalizations for going along. The civil servant says, 'But he is the elected representative of the people. My duty is to implement his decisions,' and thereby, instead of being a civil servant—a servant of civil society—he becomes a very civil *servant*

11 On this sequence, *Falling Over Backwards*, op. cit., in particular, pp. 369–490.

of whoever happens to be in office at the time. The journalist says that he has to be 'impartial' and thus gives equal space to the arsonist and the firefighter. Instead of being a judge-of-the-first-resort, instead of being an officer of the court, the lawyer says, 'But my duty is to defend whoever asks me to represent him. My task is not to judge—that is the task of the judge. My task is to defend the interests of my client to the best of my ability.' Thereby, the bigger the crook, the craftier the lawyer he is able to field.

Apart from the fact that justice is ill-served by this rationalization, there is in addition a personal cost to lawyers. My friend, K.G. Kannabiran, one of the most dogged defenders of freedom, educated me on what he called 'the lawyer's disease'. Over the years we defend so many criminals, he said, we defend them with any and every device and prevarication, and worse that we can, that we lose the sense of right and wrong. We become like the criminals we defend.

And then there is complicity. After all, if we complain of a judge who goes on giving adjournments to a well-heeled accused, it is the man's lawyer who argues for those adjournments. And can a judge be bribed without the knowledge, if not the active connivance, of a lawyer?

That is the price that the rationalization extracts.

Laypeople like us, and especially those who are in the media, too have lessons to learn from the kinds of sequences that we have encountered above. We must keep a hawk's eye on what is happening in courts. Even the simple act of publishing a monthly calendar of when the case was registered, of the number of times it has been adjourned, of the witnesses who have resiled, of the months that have passed since the hearings finished and the judgment has yet to be announced—even this simple act will have a salutary effect on the functioning of the courts.

Second, as we gleaned from Anita's case, while we must of course keep an eye on proceedings and judgments of the Supreme Court and the High Courts, we should from time to time send reporters to the local courts—and report what is happening there. Simple eyewitness descriptions of what transpired in the court during the day will open people's eyes to the real state of affairs, and, I believe, become a potent force for improvement.

Third, and here a more organized effort is required, we should keep tabs on senior magistrates and High Court judges—they are the ones who are liable to be promoted to the next rung. When an American nominated for a High Court comes up for confirmation before the Senate, a wealth of material is available on her or his record. That is because organizations devoted to, say, civil liberties, to race relations, etc., scholars in law colleges, keep tabs on judgments and the working of judges in the lower courts. The contrast couldn't be greater when a person is picked up from even a High Court in India for our Supreme Court. Next to nothing is available on the work she or he has been doing. Of course, the media can play a role in this regard. Members of law faculties can make a much larger, and a much more informed, contribution.

The sovereign device for ensuring better judgments, indeed for ensuring judicial accountability, however, is the simplest. We should analyse judgments, and we should publicize the results. The basic reason that judgments of the kind we have encountered above continue to be handed down is that the judges are confident that few will read them, and, the few that do, will keep silent—most of this tiny number will be lawyers, and each of them will know that he will have to appear before the same judges tomorrow.

Each of us can break this protective cover. Judgments are not as difficult to fathom as they are made out to be. Each of us can take up one theme, study the judgments that are handed down on that subject, and publish the results of our scrutiny. Even if we cannot publish them in the mass media, we can use the new media—the Internet—to broadcast our findings. Indeed, I am certain that even if we made just a few copies of our findings and sent them just to the judges and influential lawyers of the concerned court, we would be affecting perceptible improvement.

Table of cases

Abhay Nath v. University of Delhi, (2009) 17 SCC 205.
All India Judges' Association v. Union of India, (1992) 1 SCC 119.
All India Judges' Association v. Union of India, (2002) 4 SCC 247.
Anbazhagan K. v. State of Karnataka, (2015) 6 SCC 158.
Anbazhagan K. v. Superintendent of Police, (2004) 3 SCC 767.
Anbazhagan K. v. State of Karnataka, Writ Appeal No. 260 of 2015, decided on 11 February 2015 (KAR).
Arrive Safe Society of Chandigarh v. The Union Territory of Chandigarh, Special Leave Petition (Civil) Number 10243 of 2017, decided on 11 July 2017.
Ashok Kumar Mittal v. Ram Kumar Gupta, (2009) 2 SCC 656.

Basu D.K. v. State of West Bengal, (1997) 1 SCC 416, at 435-36.
Basu D.K. v. State of West Bengal, (1998) 9 SCC 437.
Bommai, S.R. v. Union of India, (1994) 3 SCC 1.
Brij Mohan Lal v. Union of India, (2012) 6 SCC 502.
Buddhi Prakash Sharma v. Union of India, (2005) 13 SCC 61.
Bunty alias Sandip v. State of Rajasthan, Writ 71/2016, High Court of Rajasthan.

Centre for Enquiry into Health and Allied Themes (CEHAT) and Ors. v. Union of India and Ors., (2001) 5 SCC 577.
Center for Enquiry into Health and Allied Themes (CEHAT) and Ors. v. Union of India and Ors., (2003) 8 SCC 398.
Central Bureau of Investigation v. Amitbhai Anil Chandra Shah with *Central Bureau of Investigation v. Dahyaji Gobarji Vanzara*, (2012) 10 SCC 545.
Chairman, Teachers Recruitment Board, College Road, Chennai, 600006 v. K. Veeramani, W.A. No. 1040 of 2017 and C.M.P. No. 14776 of 2017, decided on 12.10.2017.
Chaudri, Saurabh v. Union of India, (2004) 5 SCC 618.
Chouksey, Shyam Narayan v. Union of India, MANU/MP/0292/2003.
Chouksey, Shyam Narayan v. Union Of India, Writ Petition (Civil)

No. 855/2016, decided on 30 November 2016.

Chouksey, Shyam Narayan v. Union of India, I.A. No. 11/2017 in W.P. (C) No. 855/2016, Order of 23 October 2017.

Chouksey, Shyam Narayan v. Union of India, Writ Petition (Civil) No. 855 of 2016, Judgment of 9 January 2018.

Coelho, I.R., v. State of Tamil Nadu, (1999) 7 SCC 580.

Common Cause v. Union of India, (2015) 7 SCC 1, and the review Order (2016) 13 SCC.

Dattatraya Dr. v. State of Maharashtra and Taluka Adhikari @ The Medical Superintendent Class-I, 2014 ALLMR(Cri) 3977.

Dinesh Kumar v. Motilal Nehru Medical College, (1985) 3 SCC 22.

Dinesh Kumar v. Motilal Nehru Medical College, (1986) 3 SCC 727.

Gupta S.P. v. Union of India, (1981) Supp SCC 87.

Hussainara Khatoon v. Home Secretary, State of Bihar, AIR 1979 SC 1369.

Imtiyaz Ahmed v. State of Uttar Pradesh, Decided on 2nd January 2017 in Criminal Appeal Nos. 254–262 of 2012

Inamdar, P.A. v. State of Maharashtra, (2006) 13 SCC 293.

Indian Medical Association v. Union of India, (2011) 7 SCC 179.

Indore Development Authority v. Shailendra (deceased) through LR, (2018) SCC Online SC 100.

Indra Sawhney v. Union of India, (1992) Supp (3) SCC 217; and *Indra Sawhney v. Union of India,* (2000) 1 SCC 168.

Indra Sawhney v. Union of India, AIR 2000 SC 498.

Islamic Academy of Education v. State of Karnataka, (2003) 6 SCC 697.

J. Jayalalithaa v. State of Karnataka, (2014) 2 SCC 401.

J. Jayalalitha v. Union of India, (1999) 5 SCC 138.

Jago Janata Society v. State of Rajasthan, Civil Writ Number 15585/2010. Decided on 31 May 2015.

Jain, Pradeep v. Union of India, (1984) 3 SCC 654.

Kalpana, Pundlik Jamdade, Kalpana Pundlik v. State of Maharashtra, 2015 ALLMR (Cri) 17.

Kapur, B.R. v. State of Tamil Nadu, (2001) 7 SCC 231.

Karan Johar v. Union of India, Decided on 19 April 2004, MANU/SC/0535/2004, (2004) 5 SCC 127.

Kennedy, Dr A. v. State of Tamil Nadu represented by Inspector of Police, Ambur town Police Station, Vellore District, Cr. no. 396 of 2017.

Kesavananda Bharati v. Union of India, (1973) 4 SCC 225.

Krishnanand Agnihotri v. State of MP, (1977) 1 SCC 816.

Lily Thomas v. Union of India, (2013) 7 SCC 653.

Lok Adhikar Sangh v. State of Gujarat, (1998) 1 G.L.H. 768.

Luthra R.P. v. Union of India, decided on 27 October 2017, (2017) SCC Online 1254.

Mahendran, S. v. The Secretary, Travancore Devaswom Board, Decided on 5 April 1991: AIR 1993 Ker 42.

Minerva Mills v. Union of India, (1980) 3 SCC 625.

Minerva Mills v. Union of India, (1986) 4 SCC 222.

Minerva Mills v. Union of India, (1988) 4 SCC 130.

Majagvai, Ajit Savant v. State of Karnataka, (1997) 7 SCC 110.

Mohammed Salim v. State of Uttarakhand, 2017 (2) RCR (Civil) 636 (PIL) No. 126 of 2014, decided on 20.03.2017.

Mumbai Grahak Panchayat v. State of Maharashtra, PIL 156 of 2001, Civil Appeal 155 of 2015, Civil Appeal 157 of 2015, and several others, decided on 5 May 2017 by division bench of the Bombay High Court.

Nagaraj, M. v. Union of India, (2006) 8 SCC 212.

Nirmala, Dr. Sau. v. State of Maharashtra, through its Secretary and Appropriate Authority & Medical Superintendent through Dr. S.A. Sable, Beed, 2016 ALLMR(Cri) 1034.

Nirula, Manoj v. Union of India, (2014) 9 SCC 1.

Pai, T.M.A. Foundation v. State of Karnataka, (2002) 8 SCC 481.

Prakash Singh v. Union of India, Writ Petition (Civil) 310 of 1996; decided on 22 September 2006; (2006) 8 SCC 1.

Pune Municipal Corporation v. Harakchand Misirimal Solanki (2014) 3 SCC 183.

Radhakrishna v. State of Maharashtra, 2016 ALLMR(Cri) 1556.

Ramrameshwari Devi v. Nirmala Devi, (2011) 8 SCC 249.

Ramlila Maidan Incident, in Re, Suo Moto Writ Petition (Crl.) No. 122 of 2011, decided on June 20, 2011, (2012) 5 SCC 125.

Ravindra, Dr. and Dr. Sudarshana v. State of Maharashtra, through Dr. B.R. Sonwane, 2016 ALLMR(Cri) 1876.

Salem Advocate Bar Association v. Union of India, (2005) 6 SCC 344.

Sanjeev Kumar Jain v. Raghuvir Saran Charitable Trust, (2012) 1 SCC 455.

Sharma, Pawan Kumar v. Sarla Sood and Ors., CR No. 184 of 2011, Decided on December 5, 2016, 2016 SCC Online HP 2699.

Shyam Narayan v. Union of India, MCC No. 591 of 2003, Order of 28 July 2003, MANU/MP/1044/2003.

Sita Ram v. Balbir@Bali, Conmt. Pet. © No. 374/2014 in Crl. A. No. 1834/2013, Orders dated 3 October 2017 and 1 December 2017.

Sonowal, Sarbananda v. Union of India, (2007) 1 SCC 174.

Srivastava, Priyanka and Ors. v. State of UP, (2015) 6 SCC 287.

St. Stephen's College v. University of Delhi, (1992) SCC 558.

State of HP v. Narrottam Singh and Ors, decided on 20 May 2016:

State of Haryana v. Anita Shourie, FIR Case No. 363/09

State of Haryana v. G.D. Goenka Tourism Corporation Ltd., Order of 21 February 2018.

State of Karnataka v. Selvi J. Jayalalithaa, (2017) 6 SCC 263.

State of Kerala v. N.M. Thomas, (1976) 2 SCC 310.

State of Punjab v. Surjit Singh, AIR 1967 SC 1214.

State of Tamil Nadu v. K. Balu, (2017) 2 SCC 281.

Subramanian Swamy v. Union of India and Ors., (2016) 7 SCC 221.

Superintendent of Police v. J. Jayalalithaa and Ors., Spl. C.C. 208 of 2004, decided on 27 September 2014 http://164.100.138.228/casest/generatenew.php?path=data/judgment/2016/&fname= CRCR.R201742015.pdf&smflag=N

Supreme Court Advocates-on-Record Association, (2016) 5 SCC 1.

Veeramani K. v. Chairman, Teachers' Recruitment Board, College Road, Chennai-6, decided on 25 July 2017.

Veeraswami K. v. Union of India, 1991 (3) SCC 655.

Vinayak v. State of Maharashtra, 2014 ALLMR(Cri) 3393.

Vineet Narain v. Union of India, AIR 1998 SC 889.

Vinod Seth v. Devinder Bajaj, (2010) 8 SCC.

Voluntary Health Association of Punjab v. Union of India and Ors., (2016) 10 SCC 265.

Voluntary Health Association of Punjab v. Union of India, (2013) 4 SCC 1.

Yadav, Mrs. Nirmal v. Central Bureau of Investigation, Criminal Misc. Number M-14289 of 2011.

Zaheda v. State of Maharashtra, 2016 ALLMR(Cri) 2049.

Index